André Bazin and Italian Neorealism

André Bazin (1918–1958).

André Bazin and Italian Neorealism

Edited by Bert Cardullo

continuum

Continuum International Publishing Group
80 Maiden Lane, New York, NY 10038
The Tower Building, 11 York Road, London SE1 7NX

www.continuumbooks.com

© 2011 Bert Cardullo

All rights reserved. No part of this book may be reproduced, stored in a retrieval system, or transmitted, in any form or by any means, electronic, mechanical, photocopying, recording, or otherwise, without the permission of the publishers.

Library of Congress Cataloging-in-Publication Data
Bazin, André, 1918-1958.
 André Bazin and Italian neorealism / edited by Bert Cardullo.
   p. cm.
 Includes bibliographical references and index.
 ISBN-13: 978-1-4411-7752-0 (hardcover : alk. paper)
 ISBN-10: 1-4411-7752-3 (hardcover : alk. paper)
 ISBN-13: 978-1-4411-7075-0 (pbk. : alk. paper)
 ISBN-10: 1-4411-7075-8 (pbk. : alk. paper) 1. Motion pictures--Italy. 2. Realism in motion pictures. I. Cardullo, Bert. II. Title.

 PN1993.5.I88B3314 2011
 791.430945--dc22
                         2011004814

ISBN: 978-1-4411-7752-0 (hardcover)
       978-1-4411-7075-0 (paperback)

Typeset by Fakenham Prepress Solutions, Fakenham, Norfolk NR21 8NN
Printed and bound in the United States of America

Contents

1. Defining the Real: The Film Theory and Criticism of André Bazin   1
2. What Is Neorealism?   18
3. "Cinematic Realism and the Italian School of the Liberation"   29
4. "*La Terra Trema*"   51
5. "*Germany, Year Zero*"   57
6. "*Bicycle Thieves*"   61
7. "Vittorio De Sica: *Metteur en Scène*"   74
8. "A Saint Becomes a Saint Only After the Fact: *Heaven over the Marshes*"   89
9. "Neorealism, Opera, and Propaganda" (*Forbidden Christ*)   94
10. "*The Road to Hope*"   103
11. "*Two Cents' Worth of Hope*"   106
12. "*Umberto D.*: A Great Work"   111
13. "In Italy"   117
14. "Is the Italian Cinema Going to Disown Itself?"   142
15. "*La Strada*"   148

16.	"Cruel Naples" (*Gold of Naples*)	155
17.	"In Defense of Rossellini"	163
18.	"De Sica and Rossellini"	172
19.	"*Senso*"	176
20.	"*Il Bidone*, or the Road to Salvation Reconsidered"	180
21.	"*The Roof*"	184
22.	"Neorealism Returns: *Love in the City*"	187
23.	"The Profound Originality of *I Vitelloni*"	192
24.	"*Cabiria*: The Voyage to the End of Neorealism"	195
	Chronology and Credits of the Films of Italian Neorealism (including precursors and successors)	204
	Select Bibliography of Italian Neorealism	237
	A Bazin Bibliography	243
	Index	246

Chapter One

Defining the Real: The Film Theory and Criticism of André Bazin

BY BERT CARDULLO

"A modest fellow, sickly, slowly and prematurely dying, he it was who gave the patent of royalty to the cinema just as the poets of the past had crowned their kings." So wrote Jean Renoir of the great French critic and theorist André Bazin, nine years after he had succumbed to leukemia a few months past his fortieth birthday. The occasion was the 1967 publication of volume one of *What Is Cinema?*, the first selection of his articles and reviews to be translated into English (volume two followed in 1971), and Renoir added the following in his preface: "There is no doubt about the influence that Bazin will have in the years to come."

This prophecy was amply fulfilled, though (as is often the case with prophecies) not quite in the way Renoir had imagined. It's no exaggeration to say that Bazin is the single thinker most responsible for bestowing on the cinema the prestige both of an object of knowledge and of an art form—what has become *the* art form of our visual age in that it incorporates all others and in that, more and more, via DVDs and the Internet, it is the most widely available one. While scattered attempts had been made before to define the "essence" of cinema (most notably in the works of Rudolf Arnheim and Siegfried Kracauer), Bazin's ideas were to prove the decisive ones in establishing its credentials as a separate and legitimate field of intellectual inquiry, and one that has become even more legitimate now that so many of us satisfy so much of our intellectual curiosity, let alone our aesthetic craving, through visual rather than print media. In one of his essays from the 1940s Bazin himself projected that distant day when film studies would enter the university curriculum—and it was Bazin more than anyone else who played the role of midwife.

André Bazin was born on April 18, 1918, in the city of Angers in northwest France, but moved with his family to the western seaport of La Rochelle when he was five years old. Since he had wanted from an early age to become a teacher, he studied first at the École normale of La Rochelle (1936) and the École normale of Versailles (1937–1938), then at the École normale supérieure of Saint-Cloud (1938–1941). Bazin graduated from Saint-Cloud with the highest honors (after he was called up for military service in 1939, then demobilized in mid-1940) but was disqualified from teaching in French schools because of a stutter. The failed teacher quickly turned into a missionary of the cinema, his passion for which was part of his general passion for culture, aesthetic truth, and moral or spiritual sensibility.

In 1942, during the German Occupation, Bazin became a member of an organization in Paris—the Maison des Lettres—that was founded to take care of young students whose regular scholastic routine had been interrupted by the war. There he founded a cinema club where he showed politically banned films in defiance of the Nazi authorities and the Vichy government. During World War II, in 1943, Bazin also worked at the Institut des hautes études cinématographiques (I.D.H.E.C.), the French film school; there he was appointed director of cultural services after the war; and there he first began to crystallize his ideas in oral presentations and debates.

Bazin came to film criticism by way of his collaboration with *Travail et Culture,* a semi-official body concerned with cultural activities among working-class people, for whom he organized innumerable screenings. After the Liberation, he was appointed film critic of a new daily newspaper, *Le Parisien libéré*—a large-circulation daily tabloid with lots of sports coverage and "human interest" stories but little politics. Thus began Bazin's formal or official life as a public critic and with it the development of a new type of movie reviewing—one of his singular achievements being the ability to make his insights understood by readers on all levels without any concessions to popularizing. Yet Bazin never entirely lost sight of his educational ambitions, evidenced in an heuristic style of argument that implies more than it states and forces readers to think for themselves.

Bazin's blend of the logical and the poetical (though never the political, despite the fact that he himself belonged to the left) drew the attention of Jean-Paul

Sartre, who commissioned him to write essays for the distinguished philosophical journal *Les temps modernes*. Thereafter his name became associated with a staggering array of popular and specialist magazines, the most notable being *L'Écran français, France-Observateur, Radio-Cinéma-Télévision, La Revue du cinéma, Critique, L'Education Nationale, Esprit*—and finally the historically momentous *Cahiers du cinéma*, which he founded with Lo Duca and Jacques Doniol-Valcroze in 1951. In all Bazin is said to have penned something approaching 1,500 pieces, including contributions to foreign magazines (mainly Italian) as well as French ones. (He needed to be prolific since by this time he had a family to support: his wife, Janine, and a small son, Florent.)

André Bazin.

The remainder of his life was an uneventful round of festivals, conferences, and association or editorial meetings, all of them progressively overshadowed by the illness with which he was diagnosed in 1954. Bazin died at Nogent-sur-Marne on November 11, 1958. At the time he was completing a book-length study of Jean Renoir (later edited for publication by his loyal disciple François Truffaut) and working on the script for *Les Églises romanes de Saintonge,* a short documentary about Romanesque churches that he planned to direct himself. Indeed, there was always something a little medieval and monkish about Bazin, who himself was a practicing Catholic. Renoir compared him to one of the saints pictured in the stained-glass windows at Chartres; Truffaut went so far as to call him a creature from the time before original sin. Nearly everyone acquainted with Bazin eulogized his wisdom together with his personal goodness—and couched both in terms drawn from religious asceticism.

While the merest rumor of the transcendent is enough to scandalize most film theorists, it helps to explain Bazin's enduring appeal among those at least open to the possibility of the divine. Reading Bazin, one never has the sense of a professional flogging his secular academic specialty in return for institutional preferment. Instead, one comes into contact with a person—or, more correctly, a soul—bound by a sacred charge to inquire after truth. The luminous quality of Bazin's writing can no doubt be attributed in part to his chronic frail health, for reality stands out in colors all the more radiant for being contemplated under the shadow of death. But, even though it comprises the biggest stumbling block even for critics otherwise congenial to Bazin, there is no denying the primary source of his inspiration: faith. I'd like to emphasize that in this introduction, because Bazin was an intellectual and a Christian—better, a Christian intellectual—when it was still possible publicly to be both and at the same time to be taken seriously. Obviously, I don't think this is true anymore—certainly not in the United States—and I lament that fact, for the sake of intellectuals as well as Christians.

At the heart of Bazin's strictures on cinematic realism lies the conviction that the movie camera, by the simple act of photographing the world, testifies to the miracle of God's creation. It is sanctioned to do so precisely—and paradoxically—because it is an invention of science. Throughout the ages, Bazin argues, mankind has dreamed of being able to see the surface of the world faithfully copied in art (see "The Ontology of the Photographic Image," 1945). He ascribes this wish to what he calls the "mummy complex"—an innate human need to halt the ceaseless flow of time by embalming it in an image. But it was not until the development of photography in the nineteenth century that this appetite for the real could be fully satisfied. For Bazin, a photograph holds an irrational power to persuade us of its truth because it results from a process of mechanical reproduction in which human agency plays no part. A painting, however lifelike, is still the obvious product of human craft and intention, whereas the photographic image is just what happens automatically when the light reflected from objects strikes a layer of sensitive chemical emulsion.

"Photography," Bazin writes, "affects like a phenomenon in nature, like a flower or a snowflake whose vegetable or earthly origins are an inseparable part of their supernal beauty." In Bazin's view, it's this objective quality of the photograph—the fact that it is first of all a sensory datum and only later perhaps a work of art—which gives the medium its privileged relationship with the real. It follows that both photography and its spawn, the motion picture, have a special obligation toward reality. Their principal responsibility is to document the world before attempting to interpret or criticize it. And for Bazin, this moral duty is ultimately a sacred one—the photographic media being, in effect, preordained to bear endless witness to the beauty of the cosmos.

Bazin's criticism is not remotely doctrinal in its Catholicism, however; it is fundamentally holistic, its source lying elsewhere than in aesthetic dissection. His true filmmaker attains power through "style," which is not a thing to be expressed but an inner orientation enabling an outward search or quest. Such spiritual sensitivity and its enablement through film are central to Bazin's view of film as obligated to God, to honor God's universe by using film to render the reality of the universe and, through its reality, it mystery-cum-musicality. This view led Bazin to certain specific espousals—of Italian neorealism, the technique of deep focus, and more—but these were all secondary consequences for him of the way that film could best bear witness to the miracle of the creation. Éric Rohmer, who became a filmmaker in the Bazinian tradition but who in the 1950s was a critical-editorial colleague of Bazin's, has said: "Without a doubt, the whole body of Bazin's work is based on one central idea, an affirmation of the objectivity of the cinema."

Since Bazin's general idea was to discover in the nature of the photographic image an objectively realistic feature, the concept of objective reality as a fundamental quality of the cinematic shot in fact became the key to his theoretical and critical work. For him, the photographic origin of film explains the novelty of and fascination with the cinema. The picture is a kind of double of the world, a reflection petrified in time but brought back to life by cinematic projection; in other words, everything that is filmed once *was* in reality. A rapt Bazin thus speaks of the ontological realism of the cinema, and, according to him, the camera is naturally the objective tool with which to achieve it.

He granted this camera a purifying power and a superhuman impassiveness that could restore the virgin object in all its purity to the attention and love of the viewer. And he saw almost perfect examples of this "brute representation" of the cinema in documentary as well as scientific films, in which the filmmaker interferes or tampers very little with nature. Bazin saw such brute representation additionally in the deep-focus *mise en scène* of William Wyler's films, which tended toward a neutrality or objectivity that was eminently moral and liberal, hence perfectly characteristic of American freedom and democracy. For him, only ontological realism of this type was capable of restoring to the object and its setting the spiritual density of their being.

Predictably, Bazin's thesis has been assailed for placing the metaphysical cart before the materialist horse. And, as if resolved to tweak the noses of his Marxist opponents, Bazin propounds the fanciful notion that technical change arises less as the outcome of economic and historical forces than from an ineffable "something" one can only call spiritual will (see "The Myth of Total Cinema," 1946). Photography and cinema, together with such innovations as color stock, sound recording, anamorphic lenses, and 3-D, are thus successive responses to an obscurely planted desire for an ever more perfect approximation of the real. Although Bazin is generally too discreet a writer to let his theological slip show, it's clear that here he conceives of such artistic and industrial gains as prompted by an esoteric design. His thought in this instance betrays its sizeable debt to the science-cum-mysticism of the radical Catholic visionary Pierre Teilhard de Chardin, who projected an evolutionary spiraling of human consciousness until it fuses with divine revelation. (In more secular terms, there's also a tinge of Sartrean existentialism in Bazin's emphasis on a cinema of "being" in the act or process of "becoming.")

Still, Bazin sets a hypothetical limit to his "myth of total cinema." If the cinema ever could succeed in becoming the exact double of reality, it would also fail—since it would then cease to exist as cinema. Like a mathematical asymptote, filmic representation is always doomed to fall a little short of its goal. But if cinema never quite merges with life, that's what allows it to be an art form whose mission is to reveal life. Bazin concedes that there is no art without artifice and that one must therefore surrender a measure of reality in the process of translating it onto celluloid. The cinematic staging or rendering of the real can be carried out in untold ways, however, so it would be more suitable to speak of filmic "realisms" than of a single, definitive realist mode. And in this respect Bazin comes closer to endorsing the postmodern shibboleth of pluralism than his adversaries tend to realize—though he happily foregoes postmodernism's nihilism.

Yet his pristine vision of an aesthetic reality remains, strictly speaking, the inaccessible alpha and omega of the movie medium, since it is inevitably contaminated by human subjectivity. Individual films and filmmakers all carve up the unbroken plenitude of the real, imposing on it style and meaning. But the crucial distinction for Bazin is (in an oft-quoted phrase from "The Evolution of the Language of Cinema," 1950–1955) between "those directors who put their faith in the image and those who put their faith in reality." He took a notoriously dim view, for example, of Robert Wiene's *The Cabinet of Dr. Caligari* (1920) and other films made in the German expressionist style, because he judged their elaborate manipulations of lighting and décor to be a willful attempt to bend reality out of shape and force it to reflect perverse states of mind. What Bazin objected to in the work of Sergei Eisenstein was precisely how the Soviet director splintered reality into a series of isolated shots, which he then reassembled through the art of *montage*.

Indeed, Bazin's basic position cannot be understood except as a strong reaction against principles of filmmaking that had prevailed before then: of subjectivity, of an arrangement and interpretation of the world—what might be called Eisenstein-Pudovkin principles (different though those two men were) in editing. Bazin was opposed to such an approach as "self-willed" and "manipulative," as the imposition of opinion where the filmmaker should try, in effect, to stand aside and reveal reality. By contrast, the first line of Pudovkin's *Film Technique* (1929) is: "The foundation of film art is *editing*." Bazin upheld *mise en scène* against editing or *montage* because, to him, the former represented "true continuity" and reproduced situations more realistically, leaving the interpretation of a particular scene to the viewer rather than to the director's viewpoint through cutting. Consistent with this view, he argued in support of both the shot-in-depth and the long or uninterrupted take, and commended the switch from silent to talking pictures as one step toward the attainment of total realism on film.

The Russians themselves had derived their methods from American movies, especially those of D. W. Griffith, and American cinema had continued in the "editing" vein. In Hollywood pictures and, through their example, in most pictures everywhere, the guiding rule was to edit the film to conform to the flow of the viewer's attention, to anticipate and control that attention. The director and editor or cutter chose the fraction of space that they thought the viewer would most want to see each fraction of a second: the hero's face when he declares his love, then the heroine's reaction, then the door when someone else enters, and so on, bit by bit. Now the Russians' use of *montage* had much more complex aims, aesthetic and ideological, than presumed audience gratification of the Hollywood kind, but technically it, too, was a mosaic or discontinuous approach to reality.

Bazin disagreed strongly and, one can legitimately say, religiously. He distrusted *montage* on the ground that its dynamic juxtaposition of images hurtles the viewer along a predetermined path of attention, the aim being to construct a synthetic reality in support of a propagandist or partial (in both senses of the word) message. To Bazin this was a minor heresy, since it arrogated the power of God, who alone is entitled to confer meaning on the universe. But inasmuch as God absents himself from the world and leaves it up to us to detect the signs of his grace, Bazin valued those film artists who respected the mystery embedded in creation.

One such director was the Italian neorealist Vittorio De Sica, who in films such as *Bicycle Thieves* (1948) and *Umberto D.* (1952) humbly renounced the hubristic display of authorial personality and thus enabled his audience to intuit the numinous significance of people, things, and places. "The *mise en scène* seems to take shape after the fashion of a natural form in living matter," Bazin wrote in 1951 in "De Sica: *Metteur en scène.*" He recognized that film art always condenses, shapes, and orders the reality it records, but what he looked for in filmmakers was what he found in De Sica's work: a kind of spiritual disposition toward reality, an intention to serve it by a scrupulous effacement of means and a corresponding unwillingness to do violence to it through ideological abstraction or self-aggrandizing technique.

The best director, then—Orson Welles, Roberto Rossellini, Renoir, and F. W. Murnau also rank high for Bazin—is the one who mediates least, the one who exercises selectivity just sufficiently to put us in much the same relation of regard and choice toward the narrative as we are toward reality in life: a director who thus imitates (not arrogates), within his scale, the divine disposition toward man. Other than such an anomalous director as Miklós Jancsó, to whom one reel equals one shot, most modern movie directors, of course, use the reality of the held, "plumbed" shot as well as the mega-reality of *montage*. One need look no further than the work of Bazin's venerator Truffaut for an example of this. And such a balance between *montage* and *mise en scène* in film practice doesn't smugly patronize Bazin, since no one before him had spoken up so fully and influentially for his side of the question.

Given Bazin's passionate advocacy of this cinema of "transparency," it may seem puzzling that he is likewise remembered in film history as an architect of the celebrated *politique des auteurs*. Under his tutelage, the younger journalists at *Cahiers* championed such previously patronized talents as Alfred Hitchcock, Howard Hawks, and Douglas Sirk, thereby shifting the critical goalposts forever. (Since many of Bazin's reviewing colleagues, Truffaut, Jean-Luc Godard, Rohmer, Claude Chabrol, and Jacques Rivette among them, went on to direct their own films—and thus become the first generation of cineastes whose work was thoroughly grounded in film history and theory—he is also often regarded as the spiritual father of the *nouvelle vague*.) If Bazin's criticism constitutes a cine-theology, it might almost be said that his ideal *auteur* fulfills the role of saint—an inspired intercessor in or with reality.

Bazin's stake in the *politique* can probably be traced back to his involvement in the 1930s Christian existential movement known as personalism, which posited the creative individual who takes risks, makes choices, and exercises his or her God-given faculty of free will. It should be added, however, that Bazin eventually distanced himself from the priestly cult of the director-author because he felt it ignored the commercial context in which most movies were produced—a context where the work of art is not necessarily stamped with the personality of its creator, in which the director may not be the one above all who gives a film its distinctive quality. A keen observer of Hollywood cinema (whose "classical" adaptability he was among the first to appreciate), he nonetheless set its gifted practitioners on a lower rung than those masters who answered to his chaste and simple ideals: Renoir, Charlie Chaplin, De Sica, Rossellini, Carl Dreyer, and Robert Bresson.

Despite differences in stylistic approach, these film artists converge on the same enigmatic reality like the radii of a mandala. If anything joins them more specifically, it's a concern to find the technical means for a concrete rendering of space and time. And this is another charge that Bazin brought against *montage:* its sacrifice of the dimensional integrity of the photographed event. Though we live in duration and extension, *montage* can only cheat on our experience since it is an art of ellipsis. In the name of a higher realism, then, Bazin celebrated the long, uninterrupted take for its capacity to simulate the most elemental aspect of nature—its continuousness. Though Bazin knew, of course, that the camera must restrict itself to slicing out a tiny portion of space, he thought a tactful deployment of the *mise en scène* could sustain the illusion of life spilling over the borders of the frame.

His great hero in this regard was Renoir, who, significantly for Bazin, combined long takes with the technique of deep-focus cinematography. Bazin considered this not just one aesthetic option among others but in fact the very essence of modern cinematic realism. For him, the incalculable virtue of deep focus is its ambiguity: since everything in the film frame can be seen with equal clarity, the audience has to decide for itself what is meaningful or interesting. While a director such as Welles or Wyler (to whose 1941 film *The Little Foxes* Bazin would return again and again) may provide accents or directions in the composition of the image, each nonetheless opens up the possibility that the viewer can, so to speak, do the editing in his or her own head. In short, deep-focus cinematography invites an awareness of both personal freedom and ethical responsibility; in cinema as in life, we must be free to choose our own salvation.

Possibly the best example of Bazin's advocacy of the long take, photographed in depth, occurs in his essay "The Technique of *Citizen Kane*" (1947), in particular his analysis of the famous scene depicting Susan Alexander Kane's attempted suicide and its immediate aftermath—a scene that takes place entirely in one shot, in deep focus. Traditional editing, the five or six shots into which this scene could be divided, would give us, according to Bazin, "the illusion of being at real events unraveling before us in everyday reality. But this illusion conceals an essential bit of deceit because reality exists in continuous space and the screen presents us, by contrast, with a succession of fragments called "shots."" Instead, Welles presents the experience whole, in order to give us the same privileges and responsibilities of choice that life itself affords. In "The Evolution of the Language of Cinema," Bazin says further that "*Citizen Kane* is unthinkable shot in any other way than in depth. The uncertainty in which we find ourselves as to the spiritual key or the thematic interpretation we should put on the film is thus built into the very design of the image."

On his death, an obituary notice in *Esprit* cited Bazin as predicting that "the year 2000 will salute the advent of a cinema free of the artificialities of *montage,* renouncing the role of an 'art of reality' so that it may climb to its final level on which it will become once and for all 'reality made art.'" But in this as in so much else, Bazin the jubilant millenarian has been proved exactly wrong. At no other period in its history, in fact, has the cinema been so enslaved by escapist fantasy—and never have we been less certain of the status of the real. Now the digitalization of the image threatens to cut the umbilical cord between photograph and referent on which Bazin founded his entire theory.

Moreover, the particular forms of "transparency" that he admired have themselves grown opaque in just a few decades. Italian neorealism increasingly yields up its melodrama and fakery to all those who would look beneath its surface, while the mannered and rigid *mise en scène* of deep focus betrays the theatricality of its proscenium-like full shot. In the end, every living realism petrifies, to become a relic in the museum of obsolete artistic styles. Yet, as Bazin might have said (of himself above all), the certainty of failure doesn't rule out the necessity for each artist to strive to honor reality according to his or her own lights and those of the time. All it requires is a leap of faith.

Realist or not, unlike all the other authors of major film theories, Bazin was a working or practical critic who wrote regularly about individual films. He never left a systematic book of theory, instead preferring to have implicit theoretical dialogues with filmmakers and other critics through his critical writing in a number of journals. Indeed, it has been suggested that the best of his criticism has been lost because it occurred in the form of oral presentations and debates at such places as I.D.H.E.C. That may be the case; however, the most important of his essays—some sixty of them culled from the many pieces he wrote for various magazines—were collected in the posthumously published *Qu'est-ce que le cinéma?* (1958–1962). Then there are Bazin's books on Renoir, Welles, and Chaplin, all published after his death, like the four volumes of *Qu'est-ce que le cinéma?*.

Bazin based his criticism on the films actually made rather than on any preconceived aesthetic or sociological principles; and film theory for the first time became, with him, a matter not of pronouncement and prescription, but of description, analysis, and deduction. He tried to answer the question, not "Is the movie worth the money?" but rather, "If a film is worth seeing, why is it worth seeing as a *film?*" And while the fragmentary method of Bazin's writing may have prevented him from organizing a fully elaborated system like Kracauer's in *Theory of Film* (1960), it gives to his criticism a density of thought, as well as a constructive dependence on examples, that is absent from Kracauer's work.

Bazin's usual procedure was to watch a film closely—more than once, if possible—appreciating its special values and noting its difficulties or contradictions. Then he would imagine the kind of film it was or was trying to be, placing it within a genre or fabricating a new genre for it. He would then formulate the laws of this genre, constantly reverting to examples from this picture and others like it. Finally, these "laws" would be seen in the context of an entire theory of cinema. Thus Bazin begins with the most particular facts available in the individual movie before his eyes, and, through a process of logical yet imaginative reflection, he arrives at a general theory of film art.

In this he showed himself to be a college graduate accustomed to the rigors of scientific analysis, bringing to the study of motion pictures a mind of unremitting objectivity and going about his work very much in the manner of a geologist or zoologist in front of his microscope. Without forgetting the special quality of cinema as an art form, moreover, he never lost sight of film as a social document that reflects its times—not like a mere carbon copy, but more like an X-ray, penetrating the surface of reality so as to bring out the pattern that lies underneath.

Using only fair or mediocre works as a starting point—*The Battle of Stalingrad* (1949–1950) and *The Man in the Gray Flannel Suit* (1956), for example—Bazin could write exemplary criticism about the insights they provided into the less familiar aspects of the Soviet and American ways of thinking. His long essay "The Myth of Stalin," which appeared in *Esprit* in the summer of 1950, acquired a prophetic note in the light of Nikita Khrushchev's famous secret report; and Darryl F. Zanuck's lengthy, tedious super-production of Sloan Wilson's novel provided the occasion for a devastating analysis of the modern American obsession with success at any price.

Every movie, then, even a bad one, is an opportunity for Bazin to develop an historical or sociological hypothesis, or to postulate about the manner of artistic creation. Bazin founds his critical method on the fecundity of paradox—dialectically speaking, something true that seems false and is all the truer for seeming so. Starting from a film's most paradoxical aspect, he demonstrates its utter artistic necessity. Bresson's *Diary of a Country Priest* (1951) and Jean Cocteau's *Les Parents terribles* (1948), for instance, are all the more cinematic for the former's scrupulous faithfulness to its novelistic source and the latter's strict adherence to its dramatic antecedent; thus for Bazin they are instances of "impure" or "mixed" cinema. A special effect, for him, is most effectively fantastic when it is also the most realistic; films are most sacred when they mostly work against the medium's affinity for religious iconography; and a picture like Federico Fellini's *I vitelloni* (1953), Bazin argues, reveals most about the souls of its characters as it focuses most exclusively on appearances. He even anticipates deconstructive analysis by justifying the shortcomings or anomalies of so-called masterpieces, maintaining that they are as necessary to the success of these works as their aesthetic virtues.

Above all, one principle lies at the basis of every piece Bazin ever penned. It can be called "the tactful principle," and this for two reasons. First, he had a way of criticizing films that he did not like which was firm and without concessions, but which was also devoid of any bitterness or meanness. This made him appear to be the kind of man "you would love to be criticized by," to paraphrase an expression applied to Bazin by no less than Erich von Stroheim. Second, this principle of tact in fact characterizes a method of subtle analysis and differentiation applied to the complex and varied living organisms that were films to Bazin—organisms whose delicate mechanisms he tried to discern without losing sight of or even obscuring their general movement. His development of a critical argument, his caution and reservations, the frequent "granted," "to be sure," "you will object," "and yet"—none of these betray any negative spirit or mediocre taste, but instead a nuanced attitude bent on discovering purer and purer qualities and distinctions.

There is in Bazin's thought and writing no Byzantine attitude, no ornamental preciosity, no tendency to "split hair," for which some of his critical opponents reproached him (or if he did so, it was horizontally). There was only an artistic, even clinical inclination to deconstruct complex constructions, to join together separate lines here and there, or to disassociate those lines only in order to reassemble them some place else. Henri Bergson's influence is implicit here and explicit in Bazin's famous essay on the ontology of the photographic image, as well as in his excellent article on Henri-Georges Clouzot's 1956 film *The Picasso Mystery* (a piece actually titled "A Bergsonian Film"). This influence is equally present everywhere in Bazin's work, it must be said, as when he contemplates the notions of time and memory or confronts the forces of change and flux.

If most of Bazin's articles—the long theoretical essays together with the short analytical ones—relentlessly pose the question "What is cinema?" it is not because motion pictures were for him the objects of a mechanical, secondary application of some pre-existing theory, but because he had first designed and refined a rigorous *method* consisting of a series of questions to put to the cinema, even if this meant that a picture forced him to change his initial hypothesis on account of its aesthetic novelty (as happened in the case of Renoir's American films). In an article from *Cahiers du cinéma* titled "The Sum of André Bazin," Éric Rohmer aptly noted the partial provenance of Bazin's method: the fields of geology, botany, zoology, physics, and chemistry, on which he leaned heavily for a series of splendid metaphors that recur throughout his writing.

That is to say, precisely the fields where the most powerful and transforming movement of time is the most obvious: slow, invisible ripenings that change the landscape or sudden, instantaneous transmutations that alter this or that state (like the crystallization of an oversaturated solution in response to a minor shock or jolt). The cinema is the field *par excellence* of such unstable balances, of fragile or even fatal symbioses. And Bazin waited with a simultaneously vexed and excited attention—almost a morbid anxiety—for the appearance of catalysts that could alter "the purity of filmic purity" at any particular moment or gradually, over the course of a movie's length.

And do I need to recall here Bazin's unfailing ability to detect, analyze, and of course admire new things? He supported Welles in his time against the resistance of puzzled technicians and the conservatism of his timorous fellow filmmakers; he supported neorealism, in its ideal form, against the advocates of "classical" moviemaking style; he supported Rossellini against those who, as of *Europe '51* (1952), were ready to burn him at the stake; he supported the ever resilient will of Chaplin against those who wanted to bury him with the character of the Tramp; and he supported Renoir's seemingly confused changes of direction against those who wanted merely to see *Toni* (1935) over and over again.

But Bazin also supported the marginal forms of cinema (scientific or geographical, touristic or travel, amateur or nonprofessional) against the harsh defenders of standard filmic formats; he supported the advent both of

CinemaScope and of television; finally, shortly before his death, he supported the emergence of filmmakers who were bringing with them a new artistic freedom (Astruc, Marker, Resnais, Rouch, Vadim, Varda, Chabrol, and Truffaut). To renew Bazin's legacy today, then, is not simply to write the umpteenth essay on this or that film, theory, or critic, but to apply some of his strength, sharpness, and humor to the chaos of composite, "impure" pictures that come out everywhere, every day. It is to distinguish original cinematic experiment from falsely inventive sham, in the way that Bazin did—could not help but do—with every fiber of his being.

Truly mourned by many—among them filmmakers such as Renoir, Truffaut, Visconti, and Bresson—André Bazin died just ahead of the movement that placed cinema in college classrooms. He did his teaching in film clubs, at conferences, and in published articles. Yet while many people now make their livings teaching film (and far better livings than Bazin ever enjoyed), some teachers look back with longing to that era when reflection about the movies took place in a natural arena rather than in the hothouse atmosphere common to universities. Film theory as well as criticism is for the most part now an acquired discipline, not a spontaneous activity, and the cinema is seen as a field of "research" rather than as an aesthetic activity—indeed, a human reality. Current film scholars, including those hostile to his views, look in wonder to Bazin, who in 1958 was in command of a complete, coherent, and thoroughly humanistic view of the cinema.

Though he didn't live to see the first flowering of academic film theory in the late 1960s, the pedagogic side of Bazin would doubtless have been gratified that cinema was no longer a trivial pursuit but henceforth would be a serious discipline calling for the most concentrated attention and rigor on the part of its adherents. Yet the poet in him—the fecund wielder of figure and metaphor, who drew on the fathomless well of his own imaginative intuition—would just as surely have experienced a sense of loss. For the scholarly discourse of cinema soon developed a pomp and rigidity that increasingly excluded those dazzling imaginative leaps that were at the heart of Bazin's prose style.

It was his good fortune, then, to write in the period just before film studies congealed into an institution. As a working critic, contributing irregularly and—so he thought—ephemerally to the pages of *Cahiers du cinéma*, Bazin could allow his mind free play in an atmosphere as yet unhampered by Jesuital nit-picking. He enjoyed the privilege of being a critic able to cut to the quick of an argument with no other justification than his own unerring instinct. In consequence, Bazin's thought is infinitely more concrete, nimble, and flexible than the lucubrations of those obliged to flag each theoretical moved with a sheaf of footnotes.

Yet it was for his very virtues that Bazin came under attack by the budding generation of film pedants—and, ironically, almost at the same moment as he was being canonized as a classic. Bazin, it was claimed, refused to follow due process. His vaunted theory of realism amounted to little more than a loose patchwork of ideas that never coalesced into a stringent system, but instead remained dangerously impressionistic and often flatly contradictory. Professional intellectuals who jumped on Bazin's alleged incoherence, however, also underrated the profoundly dialectical nature of his thinking. To put it another way, they were stone-blind to Bazin's poetic genius—his ability to hold contrary terms in a state of paradoxical suspension that transcends mere theory and approaches mystical comprehension.

But there was worse to come. For Bazin, a rhapsodist of the cinema and a true believer in its perfectibility, had replied to his own sweeping question "What is cinema?" with a resoundingly affirmative answer—whereas the new breed of theorists responded to the same question increasingly in the negative. In the wake of the 1960s counterculture, film-studies departments across Europe as well as the United States were transformed into hubs of self-styled revolutionary activity. Fueled by the absolutist views of the French structuralist and Marxist Louis Althusser (who proclaimed the function of the mass media to be an endless endorsement of ruling-class values), radical academics came not to praise cinema but to bury it. And deconstructionists, structuralists, semioticians, Marxists, and other such fellow travelers of the left reductively reviled Bazin with lethal epithets like "bourgeois idealist," "mystical humanist," and "reactionary Catholic."

Perhaps it was impossible to avoid a head-on collision between Bazin's meditative humanism and a knee-jerk dogmatism that saw popular cinema as an ideological apparatus—an efficient mechanism for turning out docile citizens of oppressive nations. As the most eminent critic of the preceding decade of the 1950s in France, Bazin became a figurehead for the establishment, and the militant new regime at *Cahiers* hammered him for his supposed political complicity (an Oedipal rebellion if ever there was one). Crossing over to Great Britain by way of the influential theoretical journal *Screen*, the sport of Bazin-bashing proliferated throughout the 1970s and 1980s. How could anyone be fool enough to suppose that the cinema was capable of recording reality directly, when the reciprocal insights of semiotics and Lacanian psychoanalysis had demonstrated that human perception is always mediated by language? It might almost be said that the whole Byzantine edifice of contemporary theory sprang out of an irresistible desire to prove Bazin wrong.

Nowadays, of course, it is a truth universally acknowledged that reality is a construction, and Bazin's reputed innocence on this score no longer raises sectarian hackles—more like a condescending smile instead. Admittedly, his earnest belief in the intrinsically realist vocation of film puts him on the far side of postmodern relativism and doubt. Yet insofar as a compulsive skepticism and a jaded cynicism have become the orthodoxies of our age, this may be the moment to start rehabilitating reality—and André Bazin. All the more so because Bazin's formalist and spiritualist enterprise may have aimed, finally, less at discovering a conservative synthesis, communion, or unity in art as in life, than at freeing aesthetic pleasure from dramaturgical exigency alone, at implicating the viewer in an active relationship with the screen, and at freeing cinematic space and time from slavery to the anecdotal. As such, Bazin was, as if anything, a species of transcendentalist, a kind of cinematic Hegel, who proposed to discover the nature of filmic reality as much by investigating the process of critical thought as by examining the artistic objects of sensory experiences themselves, among which he would have welcomed digital film and web-movies, even as he welcomed the advent of television in the 1950s (in addition to writing about this then-new medium in his final years).

Despite Bazin's tragically premature death of leukemia in 1958, he left much material behind—in his four-volume *Qu'est-ce que le cinéma?* as well as in such magazines as *Esprit*, *L'Écran français*, and *France-Observateur*—some of the best of which I gathered in *Bazin at Work: Major Essays and Reviews from the '40s and '50s* (Routledge, 1997). To this earlier work my *André Bazin and Italian Cinema* may be considered a complement. This new book contains, for the first time in English, all of Bazin's writing about neorealism (writing that he himself never collected in French), a movement that had a profound global impact on the evolution of cinematic style and subject matter during the post-World War II period. For this reason, *André Bazin and Italian Neorealism* performs a scholarly, consolidating service of great benefit to students and teachers of film.

This new collection addresses such prominent directors as Vittorio De Sica, Roberto Rossellini, Luchino Visconti, Michelangelo Antonioni, and Pietro Germi; lesser known but important films such as *The Roof*, *Forbidden Christ*, and *Love in the City*, as well as major works like *Umberto D.* and *Senso*; and vital topics like realism versus reality, film censorship, neorealism's eclipse amid postwar Italy's economic prosperity, and the relationship between neorealism and comedy, on the one hand, and neorealism and propaganda, on the other. *André Bazin and Italian Neorealism* also features a sizable scholarly apparatus: including an extensive index, a contextual introduction to Bazin's life and work, a Bazin bibliography in French and English, a bibliography of critical writings on Italian neorealism, and complete credits for the films of Italian neorealism (including precursors and successors). This volume thus represents a major contribution to the still growing academic discipline of cinema studies.

Yet *André Bazin and Italian Neorealism* is aimed, as Bazin would want, not only at scholars, teachers, and critics of film, but also at educated or cultivated moviegoers and students of the cinema at all levels. In his modesty and simplicity André Bazin considered himself such a student, such an "interested" filmgoer, and it is to the spirit of his humility before the god of cinema, as well as to the steadfastness of his courage in life, that this book is dedicated.

Izmir University of Economics, Turkey

Chapter Two

What Is Neorealism?

BY BERT CARDULLO

Rome, Open City, dir. Roberto Rossellini, 1945.

What Is Neorealism?

The term "neorealism" was first applied by the critic Antonio Pietrangeli to Luchino Visconti's *Ossessione* (1942), and the style came to fruition in the mid-to-late forties in such films of Roberto Rossellini, Visconti, and Vittorio De Sica as *Rome, Open City* (1945), *Shoeshine* (1946), *Paisan* (1946), *Bicycle Thieves* (1948), and *The Earth Trembles* (1948). These pictures reacted not only against the banality that had long been the dominant mode of Italian cinema, but also against prevailing socioeconomic conditions in Italy. With minimal resources, the neorealist filmmakers worked in real locations using local people as well as professional actors; they improvised their scripts, as need be, on site; and their films conveyed a powerful sense of the plight of ordinary individuals oppressed by political circumstances beyond their control. Thus Italian neorealism was the first postwar cinema to liberate filmmaking from the artificial confines of the studio and, by extension, from the Hollywood-originated studio system. But neorealism was the expression of an entire moral or ethical philosophy, as well, and not simply just another new cinematic style.

Still, the post-World War II birth or creation of neorealism was anything but a collective theoretical enterprise—the origins of Italian neorealist cinema were far more complex than that. Generally stated, its roots were political,

The Earth Trembles, dir. Luchino Visconti, 1948.

in that neorealism reacted ideologically to the control and censorship of the prewar cinema; aesthetic, for the intuitive, imaginative response of neorealist directors coincided with the rise or resurgence of realism in Italian literature, particularly the novels of Italo Calvino, Alberto Moravia, Cesare Pavese, Elio Vittorini, and Vasco Pratolini (a realism that can be traced to the veristic style first cultivated in the Italian cinema between 1913 and 1916, when films inspired by the writings of Giovanni Verga and others dealt with human problems as well as social themes in natural settings); and economic, in that this new realism posed basic solutions to the lack of production funds, of functioning studios, and of working equipment.

Indeed, what is sometimes overlooked in the growth of the neorealist movement in Italy is the fact that some of its most admired aspects sprang from the dictates of postwar adversity: a shortage of money made shooting in real locations an imperative choice over the use of expensive studio sets; and against such locations any introduction of the phony or the fake would appear glaringly obvious, whether in the appearance of the actors or the style of the acting. It must have been paradoxically exhilarating for neorealist filmmakers to be able to stare unflinchingly at the tragic spectacle of a society in shambles, its values utterly shattered, after years of making nice little movies approved by the powers that were within the walls of Cinecittà.

Obsession, dir. Luchino Visconti, 1942.

In fact, it was the Fascists who, in 1937, opened Cinecittà, the largest and best-equipped movie studio in all of Europe. Like the German Nazis and the Russian Communists, the Italian Fascists realized the power of cinema as a medium of propaganda, and when they came to power, they took over the film industry. Although this meant that those who opposed Fascism could not make movies and that foreign pictures were censored, the Fascists helped to establish the essential requirements for a flourishing postwar film industry. They even founded (in 1935) a film school, the Centro Sperimentale in Rome, which was headed by Luigi Chiarini and taught all aspects of movie production. Many important neorealist directors attended this school, including Rossellini, Michelangelo Antonioni, Luigi Zampa, Pietro Germi, and Giuseppe De Santis (but not De Sica); it also produced cameramen, editors, and technicians. Moreover, Chiarini was allowed to publish *Bianco e Nero* (*Black and White*), the film journal that later became the official voice of neorealism. Once Mussolini fell from power, then, the stage was set for the development of a strong left-wing cinema.

The Axis defeat happened to transform the Italian film industry into a close approximation of the ideal market of classical economists: a multitude of small producers engaged in fierce competition. There were no clearly dominant firms among Italian movie producers, and in fact the Italian film industry as a whole exhibited considerable weakness. The very atomization and weakness of a privately-owned and profit-oriented motion-picture industry, however, led to a *de facto* tolerance toward the left-wing ideology of neorealism. In addition, the political climate of postwar Italy was favorable to the rise of cinematic neorealism, since this artistic movement was initially a product of the spirit of resistance fostered by the Partisan movement. The presence of Nenni Socialists (Pietro Nenni was Minister of Foreign Affairs) and Communists in the Italian government from 1945 to 1947 contributed to the governmental tolerance of neorealism's left-wing ideology, as did the absence of censorship during the period from 1945 to 1949.

Rossellini's *Rome, Open City* became the landmark film in the promulgation of neorealist ideology. It so completely reflected the moral and psychological atmosphere of its historical moment that this picture alerted both the public and the critics—on the international level (including the United States) as well as the national one—to a new direction in Italian cinema. Furthermore, the conditions of this picture's production (relatively little shooting in the studio, film stock bought on the black market and developed without the typical viewing of daily rushes, post-synchronization of sound to avoid laboratory costs, limited financial backing) did much to create many of the myths surrounding neorealism. With a daring combination of styles and tones—from the use of documentary footage to the deployment of the most blatant melodrama, from the deployment of comic relief to the depiction of the most tragic human events—Rossellini almost effortlessly captured forever the tension and drama of the Italian experience during the German Occupation and the Partisan struggle against the Nazi invasion.

Rome, Open City, dir. Roberto Rossellini, 1945.

If, practically speaking, Rossellini at once introduced Italian cinematic neorealism to the world, De Sica's collaborator Cesare Zavattini—with whom he forged one of the most fruitful writer-director partnerships in the history of cinema—eventually became the theoretical spokesman for the neorealists. By his definition, neorealism does not concern itself with superficial themes and synthetic forms; in his famous manifesto "Some Ideas on the Cinema" (1952), Zavattini declared that the camera has a "hunger for reality," and that the invention of plots to make reality palatable or spectacular is a flight from the historical richness as well as the political importance of actual, everyday life.

Although inconsistently or irregularly observed, the basic tenets of this new realism were threefold: to portray real or everyday people (using nonprofessional actors) in actual settings; to examine socially significant themes (the genuine problems of living); and to promote, not the arbitrary manipulation of events, but instead the organic development of situations (i.e., the real flow of life, in which complications are seldom resolved by coincidence, contrivance, or miracle). These tenets were clearly opposed to the prewar cinematic style that used polished actors on studio sets, conventional and even fatuous themes, and artificial, gratuitously resolved plots—the very style, of course, that De Sica himself had employed in the first four pictures he made, from 1940 to 1942 (*Red Roses* [1940], *Maddalena, Zero for Conduct* [1941], *Teresa Venerdì* [1941], and *A Garibaldian in the Convent* [1942]).

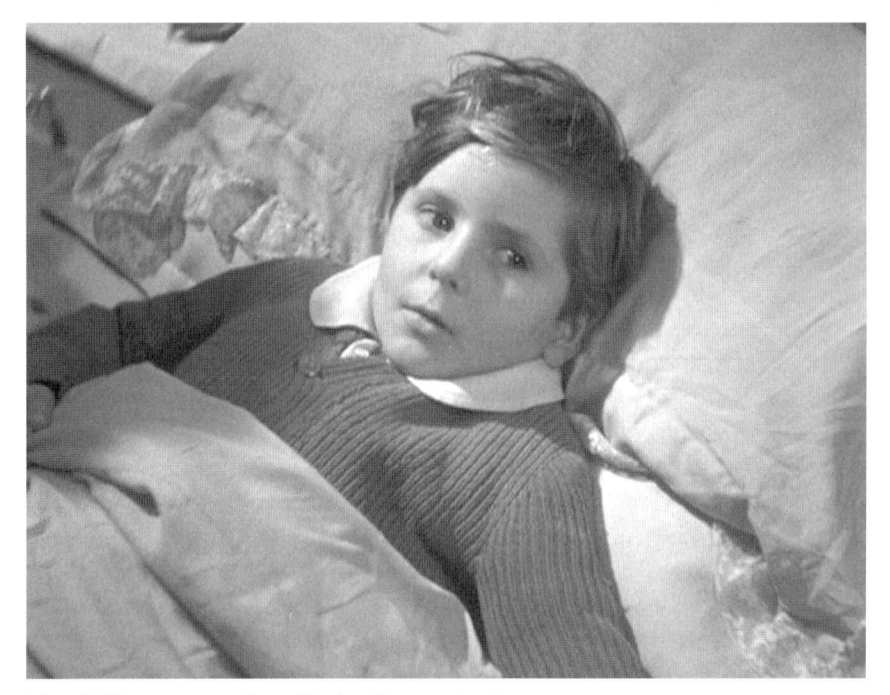

The Children Are Watching Us, dir. Vittorio De Sica, 1943.

Unfortunately, this was the cinematic style that the Italian public continued to demand after the war, despite the fact that during it such precursors of neorealism as Visconti's *Ossessione* and De Sica's own fifth film, *The Children Are Watching Us* (1943), had offered a serious alternative. Indeed, it was as early as 1942, when *Ossessione* and *The Children Are Watching Us* were either being made or released, that the idea of the cinema was being transformed in Italy. Around the same time, Gianni Franciolini's *Headlights in the Fog* (1941) was portraying infidelity among truck drivers and seamstresses, while Alessandro Blasetti's *Four Steps in the Clouds* (1942) was being praised for its return to realism in a warm-hearted story of peasant life shot in natural settings.

Obsession, dir. Luchino Visconti, 1942.

Influenced by French cinematic realism as well as by prevailing Italian literary trends, *Ossessione,* for its part, was shot on location in the region of Romagna; its atmosphere and plot (based on James M. Cain's novel *The Postman Always Rings Twice* [1934]), moreover, were seamy in addition to steamy, and did not adhere to the polished, resolved structures of conventional Italian movies. Visconti's film was previewed in the spring of 1943 and quickly censored, not to be appreciated until after the war.

In its thematic attempt to reveal the underside of Italy's moral life, shared with *Ossessione, The Children Are Watching Us* itself was indicative of a rising new vision in Italian cinema. In exhibiting semi-documentary qualities by being shot partially on location at the beaches of Alassio and by using nonprofessional actors in some roles, *The Children Are Watching Us* was, again along with *Ossessione* as well as the aforementioned pictures by Blasetti and Franciolini, a precursor of the neorealism that would issue forth after the liberation of occupied Rome.

De Sica's film was not a financial success, however, and its negative reception was in part engineered by those who saw it as an impudent criticism of Italian morality. The unfavorable reaction to *The Children Are Watching Us* was also influenced, of course, by the strictures of the past: during the era of Mussolini's regime and "white telephone" movies (the term applied to trivial romantic comedies set in blatantly artificial studio surroundings symbolized by the ever-present white telephone), an insidious censorship had made it almost impossible for artists to deal with—and for audiences to appreciate—the moral, social, political, and spiritual components of actual, everyday life.

The Children Are Watching Us, dir. Vittorio De Sica, 1943.

After the Second World War, a different kind of "censorship" obtained: that of the *lira*. For, in 1946, viewers wanted to spend their hard-earned *lire* on Hollywood movies through which they could escape their everyday lives, not on films that realistically depicted the effects of war—effects that they already knew only too well through direct experience.

Italian audiences, it seems, were reluctant to respond without prompting to an indigenous neorealist cinema intent on exploring the postwar themes of rampant unemployment, inadequate housing, and neglected children, in alternately open-ended and tragic dramatic structures populated by mundane nonprofessional actors instead of glamorous stars. (Indeed, one reason for neorealism's ultimate decline was that its aesthetic principle of using nonprofessional actors conflicted with the economic interests of the various organizations of professional Italian actors.) It was the unexceptional, not the extraordinary, man in which neorealism was interested—above all in the socioeconomic interaction of that man with his environment, not the exploration of his psychological problems or complexities. And to pursue that interest, neorealist cinema had to place such a man in his own straitened circumstances. Hence no famous monument or other tourist attraction shows that the action of De Sica's *Bicycle Thieves* or *Shoeshine*, for example, takes place in Rome; furthermore, instead of the city's ancient ruins, we get contemporary ones: drab, run-down city streets, ugly, dilapidated houses, and dusty, deserted embankments that look out on a sluggish, dirty river Tiber.

Shoeshine, dir. Vittorio De Sica, 1946.

As for the Italian government's own response to the settings, characters, and plots of neorealist films, in January 1952, Giulio Andreotti, State Undersecretary and head of the Direzione Generale dello Spettacolo (a powerful position that had direct influence on government grants as well as censorship, and that led ultimately to the right-wing Andreotti's own corruption, exposure, and disgrace), published an open letter in *Libertas* (a Christian-Democratic weekly) bitterly deploring the neorealist trend in the Italian cinema and its negative image of the country—a letter that was quickly reprinted in other journals. Andreotti took direct aim at De Sica, who was castigated for exhibiting a subversively "pessimistic vision" and exhorted to be more "constructively optimistic." (De Sica later stated that if he had had to do *Umberto D.* [1952], for one, over again, he would have changed nothing except to remove the "uplifting" final shots of children playing—precisely the kind of "positive" conclusion Andreotti seemed to be calling for.)

It was this atmosphere of interventionist government criticism that hampered the exportation of neorealist films during the 1950s; the "Andreotti

Law" of 1949 had established wide government control over the financing and censorship of films, including a right to ban the export of any Italian movie that Andreotti himself judged "might give an erroneous view of the true nature of our country." In November 1955 the "Manifesto of Italian Cinema" was published in response to Andreotti's *Libertas* letter by the French journal *Positif*—a manifesto that spoke out against movie censorship and was signed by the leaders of Italian neorealism, with the names of De Sica and Zavattini prominent among the signatures. By this time, however, postwar neorealism was rapidly waning as the burning social and political causes that had stimulated the movement were to some extent alleviated or glossed over by increasing prosperity. In a society becoming ever more economically as well as politically conservative, nobody wanted to throw away his capital on yet another tale of hardship and heartbreak on the side streets of Rome.

Although neorealism was gradually phased out of the Italian cinema in the early 1950s as economic conditions improved and film producers succumbed to the growing demand for escapist entertainment, the movement's effects have been far-reaching. One can trace neorealism's influence back to the entire postwar tradition of films about children, from Luis Buñuel's *Los Olvidados* (1950), René Clément's *Forbidden Games* (1952), and Kjell Grede's *Hugo and Josephine* (1967) to Kobei Oguri's *Muddy River* (1981), Hector Babenco's *Pixote* (1981), and Mira Nair's *Salaam Bombay!* (1988); one can also trace neorealism's influence beyond the twentieth century into the twenty-first, in such children's films as Mahamat-Saleh Haroun's *Abouna* (2002), Hirokazu Kore-eda's *Nobody Knows* (2004), and Andrei Kravchuk's *The Italian* (2005). It could even be argued that François Truffaut's *The Four Hundred Blows* (1959) owes as much to De Sica's *Shoeshine* as to the following films of his fellow Frenchmen: Jean Vigo's *Zero for Conduct* (1933), Jean Benoît-Lévy's *La Maternelle* (1932), Julien Duvivier's *Poil de carotte* (1932), and Louis Daquin's *Portrait of Innocence* (1941).

Most recently, the Iranian cinema has confirmed the neorealist legacy in such pictures (some of them also concerned with the lives of children) as Kianoush Ayari's *The Abadanis* (1993), a virtual reworking of *Bicycle Thieves* in contemporary Tehran; Abbas Kiarostami's Koker trilogy (1987–1994) presenting a documentary-style look at mountain life in northern Iran before and after the terrible earthquake of 1990, particularly the first of these three films, titled *Where Is the Friend's House?*; Jafar Panahi's *The White Balloon* (1995); Majid Majidi's *The Children of Heaven* (1997); and Samira Makhmalbaf's *The Apple* (1998).

Neorealism's influence on French New Wave directors like Truffaut is a matter of record, but its impact on the American cinema has generally been ignored. For, in the postwar work of American moviemakers as diverse as

Nicholas Ray (*They Live by Night*, 1948), Elia Kazan (*Boomerang!*, 1947), Jules Dassin (*The Naked City*, 1948), Joseph Losey (*The Lawless*, 1950), Robert Rossen (*Body and Soul*, 1947), and Edward Dymytryk (*Crossfire*, 1947), stylistic elements of neorealism can be found together with neorealism's thematic concern with social and political problems. The Italian movement has even had a profound impact on filmmakers in countries that once lacked strong national cinemas of their own, such as India, where Satyajit Ray adopted a typically neorealist stance in his Apu trilogy, outstanding among whose three films is *Pather Panchali* (1955).

In Italy itself, neorealist principles were perpetuated first by Federico Fellini and Michelangelo Antonioni. De Sica himself exerted a profound influence on both of these directors: to wit, with its grotesque processions of fancily as well as raggedly dressed extras against an almost abstract horizon, *Miracle in Milan* (1951) is "Fellinian" two or more years before Fellini became so; and without De Sica's unembellished portrait of modern-day alienation in *Umberto D.*— his astringent detachment and strict avoidance of sentimentalism—a later portrait of alienation such as Antonioni's *La notte* (1960) seems almost inconceivable.

Neorealist principles were perpetuated not only by Fellini and Antonioni but also by the first as well as the second generation of filmmakers to succeed them. Among members of the first generation we may count Ermanno Olmi, with his compassionate studies of working-class life like *Il posto* (1961), and Francesco Rosi, with his vigorous attacks on the abuse of power such as *Salvatore Giuliano* (1961). These two directors are joined, among others, by Pier Paolo Pasolini (*Accattone*, 1961), Vittorio De Seta (*Bandits of Orgosolo*, 1961), Marco Bellocchio (*Fist in His Pocket*, 1965), and the Taviani brothers, Vittorio and Paolo (*Padre Padrone*, 1977). And these filmmakers themselves have been followed by Gianni Amelio (*Stolen Children*, 1990), Nanni Moretti (*The Mass Is Ended*, 1988), Giuseppe Tornatore (*Cinema Paradiso*, 1988), and Maurizio Nichetti (*The Icicle Thief*, 1989), to name only the most prominent beneficiaries of neorealism's influence.

What happened to neorealism, then, after the disappearance of the forces that produced it—World War II, the resistance, and the liberation, followed by the postwar reconstruction of a once morally, politically, and economically devastated society? Instead of itself disappearing, neorealism changed its form (depending on the filmmaker and the film) but not its profoundly humanistic concerns. Indeed, I think we can confidently say by now that neorealism is eternally, as well as universally, "neo" or new.

Chapter Three

"Cinematic Realism and the Italian School of the Liberation"

"Le réalisme cinématographique et l'école italienne de la liberation," from *L'Esprit* (January 1948), in *Qu'est-ce que le cinéma?* Vol. 4 (Éditions du Cerf, 1962), pp. 9–37; in *Qu'est-ce que le cinéma?* (Cerf, 1975 [single-volume version]), pp. 257–281; translated into English by Hugh Gray in *What Is Cinema?* Vol. 2 (Univ. of California Press, 1971), pp. 16–40, and edited below by Bert Cardullo.

The historical importance of Rossellini's film *Paisà* (1946) has been rightly compared with that of a number of classical screen masterpieces. Georges Sadoul has not hesitated to mention it alongside Murnau's *Nosferatu* (1922), Lang's *Die Nibelungen* (1924), or von Stroheim's *Greed* (1924). I subscribe wholeheartedly to this high praise as long as the allusion to German expressionism is understood to refer to the level of greatness of the film but not to the profound nature of the aesthetics involved. A better comparison might be with the appearance in 1925 of Eisenstein's *Battleship Potemkin*. For the rest, the realism of the current Italian films has been frequently contrasted with the aestheticism of American and, in part, of French productions. Was it not from the outset their search for realism that characterized the Russian films of Eisenstein, Pudovkin, and Dovzhenko as revolutionary both in art and politics, in contrast to the expressionist aestheticism of the German films and Hollywood's mawkish star worship? *Paisà*, *Sciuscià* (1946) and *Roma, città aperta* (1945), like *Potemkin*, mark a new stage in the long-standing opposition between realism and aestheticism on the screen. But history does not repeat itself; we have to get clear the particular form this aesthetic quarrel assumes today, the new solutions to which Italian neorealism owed its triumph in 1947.

Rome, Open City, dir. Roberto Rossellini, 1945.

THE PRECURSORS

Confronted with the originality of the Italian output, and in the enthusiasm engendered by the surprise that this has caused, we have perhaps neglected to go deeply into the origins of this renaissance, preferring to see it rather as something spontaneously generated, issuing like a swarm of bees from the decaying corpses of fascism and the war. There is no question that the Liberation and the social, moral, and economic forms that it assumed in Italy have played a decisive role in film production. We shall return to this later. It was simply a lack of information about the Italian cinema that trapped us into believing in a sudden miracle.

It could well be that, today, Italy is the country where the understanding of film is at its highest, to judge by the importance and the quality of the film output. The Centro Sperimentale at Rome [founded 1935] came into existence before our own Institut des Hautes Etudes Cinématographiques [founded 1943]; above all, intellectual speculation in Italy is not, as it is in France, without its impact on filmmaking. Radical separation between criticism and direction no more exists in the Italian cinema than it does in France in the world of literature.

Furthermore, fascism which, unlike Nazism, allowed for the existence of artistic pluralism, was particularly concerned with cinema. One may have reservations about the connection between the Venice Film Festival and the political interests of the Duce but one cannot deny that the idea of an international festival has subsequently made good, and one can measure its prestige today by the fact that five or six European countries are vying for the spoils. The capitalists and the Fascist authorities at least provided Italy with modern studios. If they turned out films which were ridiculously melodramatic and overly spectacular, that did not prevent a handful of right men, smart enough to shoot films on current themes without making any concessions to the regime, from making high-quality films that foreshadowed their current work. If during the war we had not been, albeit justifiably, so prejudiced, films like *S.O.S. 103* (1941) or *La nave bianca* (1941) of Rossellini might have caught our attention more. In addition, even when capitalist or political stupidity controlled commercial production completely, intelligence, culture, and experimental research took refuge in publications, in film archive congresses, and in making short films. In 1941, Lattuada, the director of *Il bandito* (1946) and, at the time, the head of the Milan archive, barely escaped jail for showing the complete version of *La grande illusion* (1937). (The influence of Jean Renoir on the Italian cinema is paramount and definitive. Only that of René Clair in any way approaches it.)

Beyond that, the history of the Italian cinema is little known. We stop short at Giovanni Pastrone's *Cabiria* (1914) and Enrico Guazzoni's *Quo Vadis* (1912), finding in the recent and memorable *La corona di ferro* (1941) all the proof we need that the supposed characteristics of films made beyond the Alps remain unchanged: a taste, and a poor taste at that, for sets, idealization of the principal actors, childish emphasis on acting, atrophy of *mise en scène*, the dragging in of the traditional paraphernalia of *bel canto* and opera, conventional scripts influenced by the theater, the romantic melodrama and the *chanson de geste* reduced to an adventure story. Undoubtedly too many Italian films do their best to justify such a caricature and too many directors, including some of the best, sacrificed themselves, sometimes with self-irony, to commercial necessity. The great spectacles like Carmine Gallone's *Scipio Africanus* (1937) were, of course, the primary export. There was another artistic vein, however, almost exclusively reserved for the home market. Today, when the thunder of the charging elephants of Scipio is only a distant rumble, we can the better lend an ear to the discreet but delightful sounds made by *Quattro passi fra le nuvole* (1942).

The reader, at least one who has seen this latter film, will undoubtedly be as surprised as we were to learn that this comedy with its unfettered sensibility, brimming over with poetry, the lightly handled social realism of which is directly related to the recent Italian cinema, was shot in 1942, two years after the famous *La corona di ferro* and by the same director: Alessandro Blasetti, to whom, about the same time, we owe *Un'avventura di Salvator Rosa* (1939) and most recently *Un giorno nella vita* (1946). Directors like Vittorio De Sica, who made the admirable *Sciuscià*, were always concerned to turn out human and sensitive comedies full of realism, among them, in 1943, *I bambini ci guardano*. Since 1932, Mario Camerini has made *Gli uomini, che mascalzoni!* (1932), the action of which, like *Roma, città aperta*, is laid in the streets of the capital, and Mario Soldati has filmed *Piccolo mondo antico* (1940), no less typically Italian.

As a matter of fact, there are not so many new names among the directors in Italy today. The youngest, like Rossellini, started to make films at the beginning of the war. Older directors, like Blasetti and Mario Soldati, were already known in the early days of the talkies. But let us not go from one extreme to the other and conclude that there is no such thing as a new Italian school. The realist trend, the domestic, satirical, and social descriptions of everyday life, the sensitive and poetic verism, were, before the war, minor qualities, modest violets flowering at the feet of the giant sequoias of production. It appears that from the beginning of the war, a light began to be shed on the papier-mâché forests. In *La corona di ferro* the style seems to parody itself. Rossellini, Lattuada, and Blasetti were striving toward a realism of international importance. Nevertheless, it is the Liberation that set these aesthetic trends so completely free as to allow them to develop under new conditions that were destined to have their share in inducing a noticeable change in direction and meaning.

THE LIBERATION: RUPTURE AND RENAISSANCE

Some components of the new Italian school existed before the Liberation: personnel, techniques, aesthetic trends. But it was their historical, social, and economic combination that suddenly created a synthesis in which new elements also made themselves manifest. Over the past two years, Resistance and Liberation have furnished the principal themes, but unlike the French, and indeed one might say unlike the European cinema as a whole, Italian films have not been limited to themes of the Resistance. In France, the Resistance immediately became legendary. Recent as it was, on the day of the actual Liberation it already belonged to the realm of history. The Germans having departed, life began again.

By contrast, in Italy the Liberation did not signify a return to the old and recent freedom; it meant political revolution, Allied occupation, economic and social upheaval. The Liberation came slowly through endless months. It had a profound effect on the economic, social, and moral life of the country. Thus, in Italy, Resistance and Liberation, unlike the Paris uprising, are in no sense just words with an historical connotation. When Rossellini made *Paisà*, his script was concerned with things actually happening at the time. *Il bandito* showed how prostitution and the black market developed on the heels of the advancing army, how disillusion and lack of employment turned a liberated prisoner into a gangster. Except for unmistakable Resistance films like *Vivere in pace* (1946) or *Il sole sorge ancora* (1947), the Italian cinema was noted for its concern with actual day-to-day events.

The French critics had not failed to emphasize (whether in praise or blame but always with solemn surprise) the few specific allusions to the postwar period that Carné deliberately introduced into his last film. If the director and his writer took so much trouble to make us understand this, it is because nineteen out of twenty French films cannot be dated within a decade. On the other hand, even when the central scene of the script is not concerned with an actual occurrence, Italian films are first and foremost reconstituted reportage. The action could not unfold in just any social context, historically neutral, partly abstract like the setting of a tragedy, as so frequently happens to varying degrees with the American, French, or English cinema. As a result, the Italian films have an exceptionally documentary quality that could not be removed from the script without thereby eliminating the whole social setting into which its roots are so deeply sunk.

This perfect and natural adherence to actuality is explained and justified from within by a spiritual attachment to the period. Undoubtedly, the tide of recent Italian history cannot be reversed. Thus, the war is felt to be not an interlude but the end of an era. In one sense Italy is only three years old. But other effects could have resulted from the same cause. What is a ceaseless source of wonder, ensuring the Italian cinema a wide moral audience among the Western nations, is the significance it gives to the portrayal of actuality. In a world already once again obsessed by terror and hate, in which reality is scarcely any longer favored for its own sake but rather is rejected or excluded as a political symbol, the Italian cinema is certainly the only one which preserves, in the midst of the period it depicts, a revolutionary humanism.

LOVE AND REJECTION OF REALITY

The recent Italian films are at least prerevolutionary. They all reject implicitly or explicitly, with humor, satire, or poetry, the reality they are using, but they know better, no matter how clear the stand taken, than to treat this reality as a medium or a means to an end. To condemn it does not of necessity mean to be in bad faith. They never forget that the world *is,* quite simply, before it is something to be condemned. It is silly and perhaps as naïve as Beaumarchais's praise of the tears induced by melodrama. But does one not, when coming out of an Italian film, feel better, an urge to change the order of things, preferably by persuading people, at least those who can be persuaded, whom only blindness, prejudice, or ill-fortune had led to harm their fellow men?

That is why, when one reads résumés of them, the scenarios of many Italian films are open to ridicule. Reduced to their plots, they are often just moralizing melodramas, but on the screen everybody in the film is overwhelmingly real. Nobody is reduced to the condition of an object or a symbol that would allow one to hate them in comfort without having first to leap the hurdle of their humanity. I am prepared to see the fundamental humanism of the current Italian films as their chief merit. They offer an opportunity to savor, before the time finally runs out on us, a revolutionary flavor in which terror has yet no part.

That said, I do not hide from myself the astute political role more or less consciously concealed under this communicative generosity. It could happen that tomorrow the priest in *Roma, città aperta* and the Communist former member of the Resistance might not get on so well. It could happen that the Italian cinema might soon become political and partisan. There might be a few half-lies hidden somewhere in all this. The cleverly pro-American *Paisà* was shot by Christian Democrats and Communists. But it is not being a dupe, it is simply being sensible to accept in a work what is in it. At the moment the Italian cinema is more sociological than political. By that I mean that such concrete social realities as poverty, the black market, the administration, prostitution, and unemployment do not seem to have given place in the public conscience to the *a priori* values of politics. Italian films rarely tell us the political party of the director or whom he is intending to flatter. This state of affairs derives doubtless from ethnic temperament, but it also derives from the political situation in Italy and what is customary in the Communist party on that peninsula.

Political associations apart, this revolutionary humanism has its source likewise in a certain consideration for the individual; the masses are but rarely considered to be a positive social force. When they are mentioned it is usually in order to demonstrate their destructive and negative character *vis-à-vis* the heroes: the theme of the man in the crowd. From this point of view the two latest important Italian films, *Caccia tragica* (1947) and *Il sole sorge ancora,* are significant exceptions, indicating perhaps a new trend. The director De Santis, who worked very closely with Vergano as his assistant on *Il sole sorge ancora,* is the only one ever to take a group of men, a collective, as the protagonist of a drama.

AN AMALGAM OF PLAYERS

What naturally first struck the public was the high quality of the acting. *Roma, città aperta* enriched the world's screen with a performer of the first order, Anna Magnani the unforgettable pregnant young woman, Fabrizi the priest, Pagliero a member of the Resistance, and others whose performances rival in retrospect the most stirring of film characterizations in the past. Reports and news items in the public press naturally made a point of letting us know that *Sciuscà* was filled with genuine street urchins, that Rossellini shot crowds taken at random at the scene of the action, that the heroine of the first story of *Paisà* was an illiterate girl discovered on the dockside. As for Anna Magnani, admittedly she was a professional but from the world of the *café-concert*. Maria Michi, well, she was just a little girl who worked in a movie house.

Although this type of casting is unusual in films, it is not new. On the contrary, its continual use, by various realistic schools ever since the days of Lumière, shows it to be a true law of the cinema, which the Italian school simply confirms and allows us to formulate with conviction. In the old days of the Russian cinema, too, we admired its preference for nonprofessional actors who played on the screen the roles of their daily lives. Actually, a legend has grown up around the Russian films. The theater had a strong influence on certain Soviet schools and although the early films of Eisenstein had no professional actors, as realistic a film as Nikolai Ekk's *The Road to Life* (1931) was in fact played by professionals from the theater, and ever since then the actors in Soviet films have continued to be professionals, just as they have in other countries.

No major cinematographic school between 1925 and the present Italian cinema can boast of the absence of actors, but from time to time a film outside the ordinary run will remind us of the advantage of not using them. Such a film will always be only slightly removed from a social document. Take two examples: *L'Espoir* (1945) and *La dernière chance* (1945). Around them, too, a legend has grown up. The heroes in the André Malraux film are not all part-time actors called on for the moment to play their day-to-day selves. It is true that some of them are, but not the principal characters. The peasant, for example, was a well-known Madrid comic actor. As regards Leopold Lindtberg's *La dernière chance,* the Allied soldiers were actually airmen shot down over Switzerland, but the Jewish woman was a stage actress. Only productions like F. W. Murnau's *Tabu* (1931) are entirely without professional actors, but here, as in children's films, we are dealing with a special genre in which a professional actor would be almost unthinkable.

More recently, Georges Rouquier in *Farrebique* (1946) set out to play the game to the hilt. While noting his success, let us also note that it is practically unique and that the problems presented by a peasant film, so far as the acting is concerned, are no different from those of an exotic film. So far from being an example to be followed, *Farrebique* is a special case in no way invalidating the law that I propose to call the law of the amalgam. It is not the absence of professional actors that is, historically, the hallmark of social realism or of the Italian film. Rather, it is specifically the rejection of the star concept and the casual mixing of professionals and of those who just act occasionally. It is important to avoid casting the professional in the role for which he is known. The public should not be burdened with any preconceptions. It is significant that the peasant in *L'Espoir* was a theater comedian, Anna Magnani a singer of popular songs, and Fabrizi a music-hall clown.

That someone is an actor thus does not mean he must not be used. Quite the opposite. But his professionalism should be called into service only insofar as it allows him to be more flexible in his response to the requirements of the *mise en scène,* and to have a better grasp of the character. The nonprofessionals are naturally chosen for their suitability for the part, either because they fit it physically or because there is some parallel between the role and their lives. When the amalgamation comes off—but experience shows that it will not unless some "moral" requirements are met in the script—the result is precisely that extraordinary feeling of truth that one gets from the current Italian films. Their faithfulness to a script which stirs them deeply and which calls for the minimum of theatrical pretense sets up a kind of osmosis among the cast. The technical inexperience of the amateur is helped out by the experience of the professionals, while the professionals themselves benefit from the general atmosphere of authenticity.

However, if a method so beneficent to the art of the cinema has only been employed here and there, it is because unfortunately it contains within itself the seeds of its own destruction. The chemical balance of the amalgam is of necessity unstable, and nothing can prevent it from evolving to the point at which it reintroduces the aesthetic dilemma it originally solved—that between the enslavement of the star and the documentary without actors.

This disintegration can be observed most clearly and quickly in children's films or films using native peoples. Little Rari of *Tabu,* they say, ended up as a prostitute in Poland, and we all know what happens to children raised to stardom by their first film. At best they turn out to be infant actor prodigies, but that is something else again. Indispensable as are the factors of inexperience and naïveté, obviously they cannot survive repetition. One cannot envisage the Farrebique family appearing in half a dozen films and finally being signed up by Hollywood.

As for the professionals who are not stars, the process of disintegration operates a little differently. The public is to blame. While an accepted star is received everywhere as himself, the success of a film is apt to identify the ordinary actor with the role he plays in it. Producers are only too glad to repeat a success by catering to the well-known public fondness for seeing their favorite actors in their established roles. And even if an actor has sense enough to avoid being confined to a single role, it is still a fact that his face and some recurring mannerisms in his acting having become familiar will prevent the amalgam with nonprofessionals from taking place.

AESTHETICISM, REALISM, AND REALITY

Faithfulness to everyday life in the scenario, truth to his part in an actor, however, are simply the basic materials of the aesthetic of the Italian film. One must beware of contrasting aesthetic refinement and a certain crudeness, a certain instant effectiveness of a realism which is satisfied just to present reality. In my view, one merit of the Italian film will be that it has demonstrated that every realism in art was first profoundly aesthetic. One always felt it was so, but in the reverberations of the accusations of witchcraft that some people today are making against actors suspected of a pact with the demon of art for art's sake, one has tended to forget it. The real like the imaginary in art is the concern of the artist alone. The flesh and blood of reality are no easier to capture in the net of literature or cinema than are gratuitous flights of the imagination. Or to put it another way, even when inventions and complexity of forms are no longer being applied to the actual content of the work, they do not cease thereby to have an influence on the effectiveness of the means.

Because the Soviet cinema was too forgetful of this, it slipped in twenty years from first to last place among the great film-producing nations. *Potemkin* turned the cinema world upside down not just because of its political message, not even because it replaced the studio plaster sets with real settings and the star with an anonymous crowd, but because Eisenstein was the greatest montage theoretician of his day, because he worked with Tisse, the finest cameraman of his day, and because Russia was the focal point of cinematographic thought—in short, because the "realist" films Russia turned out secreted more aesthetic know-how than all the sets and performances and lighting and artistic interpretation of the artiest works of German expressionism. It is the same today with the Italian cinema. There is nothing aesthetically retrogressive about its neorealism; on the contrary, there is progress in expression, a triumphant evolution of the language of cinema, an extension of its stylistics.

Let us first take a good look at the cinema to see where it stands today. Since the expressionist heresy came to an end, particularly after the arrival of sound, one may take it that the general trend of cinema has been toward realism. Let us agree, by and large, that film sought to give the spectator as perfect an illusion of reality as possible within the limits of the logical demands of cinematographic narrative and of the current limits of technique. Thus the cinema stands in contrast to poetry, painting, and theater, and comes ever closer to the novel. It is not my intention here to justify this basic aesthetic trend of modem cinema, be it on technical, psychological, or economic grounds. I simply state it for this once without thereby pre-judging either the intrinsic validity of such an evolution or the extent to which it is final. But, realism in art can only be achieved in one way—through artifice.

Every form of aesthetic must necessarily choose between what is worth preserving and what should be discarded, and what should not even be considered. But when this aesthetic aims in essence at creating the illusion of reality, as does the cinema, this choice sets up a fundamental contradiction which is at once unacceptable and necessary: necessary because art can only exist when such a choice is made. Without it, supposing total cinema was here and now technically possible, we would go back purely to reality. Unacceptable because it would be done definitely at the expense of that reality which the cinema proposes to restore integrally. That is why it would be absurd to resist every new technical development aiming to add to the realism of cinema, namely sound, color, and stereoscopy.

Actually the "art" of cinema lives off this contradiction. It gets the most out of the potential for abstraction and symbolism provided by the present limits of the screen, but this utilization of the residue of conventions abandoned by technique can work either to the advantage or to the detriment of realism. It can magnify or neutralize the effectiveness of the elements of reality that the camera captures. One might group, if not classify in order of importance, the various styles of cinematography in terms of the added measure of reality. We would define as "realist," then, all narrative means tending to bring an added measure of reality to the screen. Reality is not to be taken quantitatively. The same event, the same object, can be represented in various ways. Each representation discards or retains various of the qualities that permit us to recognize the object on the screen. Each introduces, for didactic or aesthetic reasons, abstractions that operate more or less corrosively and thus do not permit the original to subsist in its entirety.

At the conclusion of this inevitable and necessary "chemical" action, for the initial reality there has been substituted an illusion of reality composed of a complex of abstraction (black and white, plane surface), of conventions (the rules of montage, for example), and of authentic reality. It is a necessary illusion but it quickly induces a loss of awareness of the reality itself, which becomes identified in the mind of the spectator with its cinematographic representation. As for the filmmaker, the moment he has secured this unwitting complicity of the public, he is increasingly tempted to ignore reality. From habit and laziness he reaches the point when he himself is no longer able to tell where lies begin or end. There could never be any question of calling him a liar because his art consists in lying. He is just no longer in control of his art. He is its dupe, and hence he is held back from any further conquest of reality.

FROM *CITIZEN KANE* TO *FARREBIQUE*

Recent years have brought a noticeable evolution of the aesthetic of cinema in the direction of realism. The two most significant events in this evolution in the history of the cinema since 1940 are Orson Welles's *Citizen Kane* (1941) and *Paisà*. Both mark a decisive step forward in the direction of realism but by different paths. If I bring up the film of Orson Welles before I analyze the stylistics of the Italian film, it is because it will allow us to place the latter in its true perspective. Welles restored to cinematographic illusion a fundamental quality of reality—its continuity. Classical editing, deriving from Griffith, separated reality into successive shots which were just a series of either logical or subjective points of view of an event. A man locked in a cell is waiting for the arrival of his executioner. His anguished eyes are on the door. At the moment the executioner is about to enter we can be quite sure that the director will cut to a close shot of the door handle as it slowly turns. This close-up is justified psychologically by the victim's concentration on the symbol of his extreme distress. It is this ordering of the shots, this conventional analysis of the reality continuum, that truly goes to make up the cinematographic language of the period.

The construction thus introduces an obviously abstract element into reality. Because we are so used to such abstractions, we no longer sense them. Orson Welles started a revolution by systematically employing a depth of focus that had so far not been used. Whereas the camera lens, classically, had focused successively on different parts of the scene, the camera of Welles takes in with equal sharpness the whole field of vision contained simultaneously within the dramatic field. It is no longer the editing that selects what we see, thus giving it an *a priori* significance; it is the mind of the spectator which is forced to discern, as in a sort of parallelepiped or six-sided prism of reality with the screen as its cross-section, the dramatic spectrum proper to the scene. It is therefore to an intelligent use of a specific step forward that *Citizen Kane* owes its realism. Thanks to the depth of focus of the lens, Welles restored to reality its visible continuity.

We clearly see with what elements of reality the cinema has enriched itself. But from other points of view, it is also evident that it has moved away from reality or at least that it gets no nearer to it than does the classical aesthetic. In ruling out, because of the complexity of his techniques, all recourse to nature in the raw, natural settings, exteriors, sunlight, and nonprofessional actors, Orson Welles rejects those qualities of the authentic document for which there is no substitute and which, being likewise a part of reality, can themselves establish a form of realism.

Here, especially in urban settings, the Italians are at an undoubted advantage. The Italian city, ancient or modern, is prodigiously photogenic. From antiquity, Italian city planning has remained theatrical and decorative. City life is a spectacle, a *commedia dell'arte* that the Italians stage for their own pleasure. And even in the poorest quarters of the town, the coral-like groupings of the houses, thanks to the terraces and balconies, offer outstanding possibilities for spectacle. The courtyard is an Elizabethan set in which the show is seen from below, the spectators in the gallery being the actors in the comedy. A poetic documentary was shown at Venice consisting entirely of an assemblage of shots of courtyards. What more can you say when the theatrical façades of the palazzi combine their operatic effects with the stage-like architecture of the houses of the poor? Add to this the sunshine and the absence of clouds (chief enemy of shooting on exteriors) and you have explained why the urban exteriors of Italian films are superior to all others.

Let us contrast *Citizen Kane* and *Farrebique*—in the latter, a systematic determination to exclude everything that was not primarily natural material is precisely the reason why Rouquier failed in the area of technical perfection. Thus, the most realistic of the arts shares the common lot. It cannot make reality entirely its own because reality must inevitably elude it at some point. Undoubtedly an improved technique, skillfully applied, may narrow the holes of the net, but one is compelled to choose between one kind of reality and another. This sensitiveness resembles the sensitiveness of the retina. The nerve endings that register color and intensity of light are not at all the same, the density of one being ordinarily in inverse ratio to that of the other. Animals that have no difficulty in making out the shape of their quarry in the dark are almost color blind.

Between the contrasting but equally pure kinds of realism represented by *Farrebique* on the one hand and *Citizen Kane* on the other, there is a wide variety of possible combinations. For the rest, the margin of loss of the real, implicit in any realist choice, frequently allows the artist, through the use of any aesthetic convention he may introduce into the area thus left vacant, to increase the effectiveness of his chosen form of reality. Indeed, we have a remarkable example of this in the recent Italian cinema. In the absence of technical equipment, the Italian directors have been obliged to record the sound and dialogue after the actual filming. The net result is a loss of realism. However, left free to use the camera unfettered by the microphone, such directors have thereby profited by the occasion to enlarge the camera's field of action and its mobility with, consequently, an immediate raising of the reality coefficient.

Future technical improvements which will permit the conquest of the properties of the real (color and stereoscopy, for example) can only increase the distance between the two realist poles which today are situated in the area surrounding *Farrebique* and *Citizen Kane*. The quality of interior shots will in fact increasingly depend on a complex, delicate, and cumbersome apparatus. Some measure of reality must always be sacrificed in the effort of achieving it.

PAISÀ

How do you fit the Italian film into the realist spectrum? After trying to trace the geographical boundaries of this cinema, so penetrating in its portrayal of the social setting, so meticulous and perceptive in its choice of authentic and significant detail, it now remains for us to fathom its aesthetic geology.

We would clearly be deluding ourselves if we pretended to reduce recent Italian production to certain common, easily definable characteristics applicable to all directors. We will simply try to single out those characteristics with the widest application, reserving the right when the occasion arises to limit our concern to the most significant films. Since we must also make a choice, we will arrange, by implication, the major Italian films in concentric circles of decreasing interest around *Paisà*, since it is this film of Rossellini's that yields the most aesthetic secrets.

NARRATIVE TECHNIQUE

As in the novel, the aesthetic implicit in the cinema reveals itself in its narrative technique. A film is always presented as a succession of fragments of imaged reality on a rectangular surface of given proportions, the ordering of the images and their duration on the screen determining its import.

The objective nature of the modem novel, by reducing the strictly grammatical aspect of its stylistics to a minimum, has laid bare the secret essence of style. (In Camus's *L'Étranger* [1942], for example, Sartre has clearly demonstrated the link between the author's metaphysic and the repeated use of the *passé composé*, a tense of singular modal poverty.) Certain qualities of the language of Faulkner, Hemingway, or Malraux would certainly not come through in translation, but the essential quality of their styles would not suffer because their style is almost completely identical with their narrative technique—the ordering in time of fragments of reality. The style becomes the inner dynamic principle of the narrative, somewhat like the relation of energy to matter or the specific physics of the work, as it were. This it is which distributes the fragmented realities across the aesthetic spectrum of the narrative, which polarizes the filings of the facts without changing their chemical composition. A Faulkner, a Malraux, a Dos Passos, each has his personal universe which is defined by the nature of the facts reported, but also by the law of gravity which holds them suspended above chaos.

It will be useful, therefore, to arrive at a definition of the Italian style on the basis of the scenario, of its genesis, and of the forms of exposition that it follows. Nearly all the credits of an Italian film, incidentally, list under the heading "scenario" a good dozen names. This imposing evidence of collaboration need not be taken too seriously. It is intended to provide the producers with a naïvely political assurance. It usually consists of one Christian Democrat and one Communist (just as in the film there is a Marxist and a priest); the third screenwriter has a reputation for story construction; the fourth is a gag man; the fifth because he is a good dialogue writer; the sixth because he has a fine feeling for life. The result is no better or no worse than if there had been only one screen writer, but the Italian notion of a scenario fits in with their concept of a collective paternity according to which everyone contributes an idea without any obligation on the part of the director to use it. Rather than the assembly line of American screenwriters, this interdependence of improvisation is like that of *commedia dell'arte* or jazz.

Unfortunately, the demon of melodrama that Italian filmmakers seem incapable of exorcising takes over every so often, thus imposing a dramatic necessity on strictly foreseeable events. But that is another story. What matters is the creative surge, the special way in which the situations are brought to life. The necessity inherent in the narrative is biological rather than dramatic. It burgeons and grows with all the verisimilitude of life. One must not conclude that this method, on the face of it, is less aesthetic than a slow and meticulous preplanning. But the old prejudice that time, money, and resources have a value of their own is so rooted that people forget to relate them to the work and to the artist. Van Gogh repainted the same picture ten times, very quickly, while Cézanne would return to a painting time and again over the years. Certain genres call for speed, for work done in the heat of the moment, but surgery could not call for a greater sureness of touch, for greater precision.

It is only at this price that the Italian film has that air of documentary, a naturalness nearer to the spoken than to the written account, to the sketch rather than to the painting. It calls for the ease and sure eye of Rossellini, Lattuada, Vergano, and De Santis. In their hands the camera is endowed with well-defined cinematographic tact, wonderfully sensitive antennae which allow them with one stroke to get precisely what they are after. In *Il bandito*, for example, the prisoner, returning from Germany, finds his house in ruins. Where a solid building once stood there is now just a pile of stones surrounded by broken-down walls. The camera shows us the man's face. Then, following the movement of his eyes, it travels through a 360-degree turn which gives us the whole spectacle. This panning shot is doubly original. First, because at the outset, we stand off from the actor since we are looking at him by way of a camera trick, but during the traveling shot we become identified with him to the point of feeling surprised when, the 360-degree pan having been completed, we return to his face with its expression of utter horror. Second, because the speed of this subjective panning shot varies. It starts with a long slide, then it comes almost to a halt, slowly studying the burned and shattered walls with the same rhythm of the man's watching eye, as if directly impelled by his concentration.

I have had to dwell at some length on this minor example to avoid making a purely abstract affirmation concerning what I regard, in an almost psychological sense of the word, as cinematic "tact." A shot of this kind by virtue of its dynamism belongs with the movement of a hand drawing a sketch, leaving a space here, filling in there, here sketching round the subject, and there bringing it into relief. I am thinking of the slow motion in the documentary on Matisse which allows us to observe, beneath the continuous and uniform arabesques of the stroke, the varying hesitations of the artist's hand. In such a case the camera movement is important. The camera must be equally as ready to move as to remain still. Traveling and panning shots do not have the same god-like character that the Hollywood camera crane has bestowed on them.

Everything is shot from eye-level or from a concrete point of view, such as a rooftop or window.

Technically speaking, all the memorable poetry of the children's ride on the white horse in *Sciuscià*, for its part, can be attributed to a low-level camera angle which gives the riders on their mounts the appearance of an equestrian statue. In *Sortilège* (1945), Christian-Jaque went to a great deal more trouble over his phantom horse. But all that cinematic virtuosity did not prevent his animal from having the prosaic look of a broken-down cab horse. The Italian camera retains something of the human quality of the Bell and Howell newsreel camera, a projection of hand and eye, almost a living part of the operator, instantly in tune with his awareness. As for the photography itself, the lighting plays only a minor expressive role. First, because lighting calls for a studio, and the greater part of the filming is done on exteriors or in real-life settings. Second, because documentary camera work is identified in our minds with the gray tones of newsreels. It would be a contradiction to take any great pains with or to touch up excessively the plastic quality of the style.

As we have thus far attempted to describe it, the style of Italian films would appear to belong with a greater or lesser degree of skill and mastery of technique or feeling to the same family as quasi-literary journalism, to an ingenious art, pleasing, lively, and even moving, but basically a minor art. This is sometimes true even though one may actually rank the genre fairly high in the aesthetic hierarchy. It would be unjust and untrue to see such an assessment as the final measure of this particular technique. Just as, in literature, reportage with its ethic of objectivity (perhaps it would be more correct to say with its ethic of seeming objectivity) has simply provided a basis for a new aesthetic of the novel, so the technique of the Italian filmmakers results in the best films, especially in *Paisà* with its aesthetic of narrative that is both complex and original. (I will not at this point get into an historical argument over the origins or the foreshadowing of the "novel of reportage" in the nineteenth century. Besides, the novels of Stendhal or the naturalists were concerned with frankness, acuteness, and perspicacity of observation, rather than with objectivity properly so called. Facts for their own sake had not yet acquired that kind of ontological autonomy, which makes of them a succession of sealed off monads, strictly limited by their appearance.)

Paisà is unquestionably the first film to resemble closely a collection of short stories. Up to now we had only known the film composed of sketches—a bastard and phony type of film if ever there was one. Rossellini tells us, in succession, six stories of the Italian Liberation. This historical element is the only thing they have in common. Three of them, the first, the fourth, and the last, are taken from the Resistance. The others are droll or pathetic or tragic episodes occurring on the fringes of the Allied advance. Prostitution, the black market, and a Franciscan convent alike provide the story material. There is no progression other than a chronological ordering of the story beginning with the landing of an Allied force in Sicily. But their social, historical, and human foundation gives them a unity enough to constitute a collection perfectly homogeneous in its diversity.

Above all, the length of each story, its form, contents, and aesthetic duration, gives us for the first time precisely the impression of a short story. The Naples episode of the urchin—a black-market expert, selling the clothes of a drunk Negro soldier—is an excellent Saroyan story. Another makes us think of Hemingway, yet another (the first) of Faulkner. I am not merely referring to the tone or the subject, but in a profound way to the style. Unfortunately, one cannot put a film sequence in quotation marks like a paragraph, and hence any literary description of one must of necessity be incomplete. However, what follows is an episode from the final story which reminds me now of Hemingway, now of Faulkner.

Paisan, "Rome episode," dir. Roberto Rossellini, 1946.

1. A small group of Italian partisans and Allied soldiers have been given a supply of food by a family of fisher folk living in an isolated farmhouse in the heart of the marshlands of the Po delta. Having been handed a basket of eels, they take off. Some while later, a German patrol discovers this, and executes the inhabitants of the farm.
2. An American officer and a partisan are wandering at twilight in the marshes. There is a burst of gunfire in the distance. From a highly elliptical conversation we gather that the Germans have shot the fishermen.

3. The dead bodies of the men and women lie stretched out in front of the little farmhouse. In the twilight, a half-naked baby cries endlessly.

Even with such a succinct description, this fragment of the story reveals enormous ellipses—or rather, great holes. A complex train of action is reduced to three or four brief fragments, in themselves already elliptical enough in comparison with the reality they are unfolding. Let us pass over the first purely descriptive fragment. The second event is conveyed to us by something only the partisans can know—distant gunfire. The third is presented to us independently of the presence of the partisans. It is not even certain that there were any witnesses to the scene. A baby cries besides its dead parents. There is a fact. How did the Germans discover that the parents were guilty? How is it that the child is still alive? That is not the film's concern, and yet a whole train of connected events led to this particular outcome.

In any case, the filmmaker does not ordinarily show us everything. That is impossible—but the things he selects and the things he leaves out tend to form a logical pattern by way of which the mind passes easily from cause to effect. The technique of Rossellini undoubtedly maintains an intelligible succession of events, but these do not mesh like a chain with the sprockets of a wheel. The mind has to leap from one event to the other as one leaps from stone to stone in crossing a river. It may happen that one's foot hesitates between two rocks, or that one misses one's footing and slips. The mind does likewise. Actually it is not of the essence of a stone to allow people to cross rivers without wetting their feet any more than the divisions of a melon exist to allow the head of the family to divide it equally. Facts are facts and our imagination makes use of them, but they do not exist inherently for this purpose.

In the usual shooting script (according to a process resembling the form of the classical novel) the fact comes under the scrutiny of the camera, is divided up, analyzed, and put together again, undoubtedly without entirely losing its factual nature; but the latter, presumably, is enveloped in abstraction, as the clay of a brick is enveloped by the wall which is not as yet present but which will multiply its parallelipeds. For Rossellini, facts take on a meaning, but not like a tool whose function has predetermined its form. The facts follow one another, and the mind is forced to observe their resemblance; and thus, by recalling one another, they end up by meaning something which was inherent in each and which is, so to speak, the moral of the story—a moral the mind cannot fail to grasp since it was drawn from reality itself.

In the Florentine episode, a woman crosses the city while it is still occupied by a number of Germans and groups of Italian Fascists; she is on her way to meet her fiancé, a leader of the Italian underground, accompanied by a man who likewise is looking for his wife and child. The attention of the camera following them, step by step, though it will share all the difficulties they encounter, all their dangers, will however be impartially divided between the heroes of the adventure and the conditions they must encounter. Actually, everything that is happening in a Florence in the throes of the Liberation is of a similar importance. The personal adventures of the two individuals blend into the mass of other adventures, just as one attempts to elbow one's way into a crowd to recover something one has lost. In the course of making one's way one sees in the eyes of those who stand aside the reflections of other concerns, other passions, other dangers alongside which one's own may well be merely laughable. Ultimately and by chance, the woman learns, from a wounded partisan, that the man she is looking for is dead. But the statement from which she learned the news was not aimed straight at her—but hit her like a stray bullet.

The impeccable line followed by this summary owes nothing to classical forms that are standard for a story of this kind. Attention is never artificially focused on the heroine. The camera makes no pretense at being psychologically subjective. We share all the more fully in the feelings of the protagonists because it is easy for us to sense what they are feeling; and also because the pathetic aspect of the episode does not derive from the fact that a woman has lost the man she loves but from the special place this drama holds among a thousand others, apart from and yet also part of the complete drama of the Liberation of Florence. The camera, as if making an impartial report, confines itself to following a woman searching for a man, leaving to us the task of being alone with her, of understanding her, and of sharing her suffering.

In the admirable final episode of the partisans surrounded in the marshlands, the muddy waters of the Po delta, the reeds stretching away to the horizon, just sufficiently tall to hide the man crouching down in the little flat-bottomed boat, the lapping of the waves against the wood, all occupy a place of equal importance with the men. This dramatic role played by the marsh is due in great measure to deliberately intended qualities in the photography. This is why the horizon is always at the same height. Maintaining the same proportions between water and sky in every shot brings out one of the basic characteristics of this landscape. It is the exact equivalent, under conditions imposed by the screen, of the inner feeling men experience who are living between the sky and the water and whose lives are at the mercy of an infinitesimal shift of angle in relation to the horizon. This shows how much subtlety of expression can be got on exteriors from a camera in the hands of the man who photographed *Paisà*.

The unit of cinematic narrative in *Paisà* is not the "shot," an abstract view of a reality which is being analyzed, but the "fact." A fragment of concrete reality in itself multiple and full of ambiguity, whose meaning emerges only after the fact, thanks to other imposed facts between which the mind establishes certain relationships. Unquestionably, the director chose these "facts" carefully while at the same time respecting their factual integrity. The close-up of the doorknob referred to earlier was less a fact than a sign brought into arbitrary relief by the camera, and no more independent semantically than a preposition in a sentence. The opposite is true of the marsh or the death of the peasants.

But the nature of the "image facts" is not only to maintain with the other image facts the relationships invented by the mind. These are in a sense the centrifugal properties of the images—those which make the narrative possible. Each image being on its own just a fragment of reality existing before any meanings, the entire surface of the scene should manifest an equally concrete density. Once again we have here the opposite of the "doorknob" type of scene, in which the color of the enamel, the dirt marks at the level of the hand, the shine of the metal, the worn-away look are just so many useless facts, concrete parasites of an abstraction fittingly dispensed with.

In *Paisà* (and I repeat that I imply by this, in varying degrees, all Italian films) the close-up of the doorknob would be replaced, without any loss of that peculiar quality of which it is part, by the "image fact" of a door whose concrete characteristics would be equally visible. For the same reason the actors will take care never to dissociate their performance from the décor or from the performance of their fellow actors. Man himself is just one fact among others, to whom no pride of place should be given *a priori*. That is why the Italian filmmakers alone know how to shoot successful scenes in buses, trucks, or trains, namely because these scenes combine to create a special density within the framework of which they know how to portray an action without separating it from its material context, and without loss of that uniquely human quality of which it is an integral part. The subtlety and suppleness of movement within these cluttered spaces, the naturalness of the behavior of everyone in the shooting area, make of these scenes supreme bravura moments of the Italian cinema.

THE REALISM OF THE ITALIAN CINEMA AND THE TECHNIQUE OF THE AMERICAN NOVEL

The absence of any film documentation may have operated against a clear understanding of what I have so far written. I have arrived at the point of characterizing as similar the styles of Rossellini in *Paisà* and of Orson Welles in *Citizen Kane*. By diametrically opposite technical routes, each arrives at a scenario with roughly the same approach to reality—the depth of focus of Welles and the predisposition toward reality of Rossellini. In both we find the same dependence of the actor relative to the setting, the same realistic acting demanded of everyone in the scene whatever their dramatic importance. Better still, although the styles are so different, the narrative follows basically the same pattern in *Citizen Kane* and in *Paisà*. In short, although they use independent techniques, without the least possibility of a direct influence one on the other, and possessed of temperaments that could hardly be less compatible, Rossellini and Welles have, to all intents and purposes, the same basic aesthetic objective, the same aesthetic concept of realism.

I had leisure enough as I watched the film to compare the narrative of *Paisà* with that of some modern novelists and short-story writers. Besides, the resemblances between the technique of Orson Welles and that of the American novel, notably Dos Passos, are sufficiently obvious to allow me now to expound my thesis. The aesthetic of the Italian cinema, at least in its most elaborate manifestations and in the work of a director as conscious of his medium as Rossellini, is simply the equivalent on film of the American novel. Let us clearly understand that we are concerned here with something quite other than banal adaptation.

Hollywood, in fact, never stops adapting American novels for the screen. We are familiar with what Sam Wood did to *For Whom the Bell Tolls* (1943). Basically all he wanted was to retell a plot. Even if he had been faithful to the original, sentence by sentence, he would not, properly speaking, have transferred anything from the book to the screen. The films that have managed to translate something of the style of novels into images can be counted on the fingers of one hand, by which I mean the very fabric of the narrative, the law of gravity that governs the ordering of the facts. The cinema nevertheless has come close to these truths on several occasions, in the case of Louis Feuillade for example, or of Erich von Stroheim. More recently, André Malraux has clearly understood the parallel between a certain style of novel and film narrative. Finally, instinctively and by virtue of his genius, Jean Renoir had already applied in *La Règle du jeu* (1939) the essentials of the principles of depth of focus and the simultaneous presentation of all the actors in a scene. We had to wait for Orson Welles to show what the cinema of the American novel would be.

So then, while Hollywood adapts bestseller after bestseller at the same time moving further away from the spirit of this literature, it is in Italy, naturally and with an ease that excludes any notion of deliberate and willful imitation, that the cinema of American literature has become a reality. Unquestionably we must not underestimate the popularity of the American novelists in Italy, where their works were translated and assimilated long before they were in France, and the influence for example of Saroyan on Vittorini is common knowledge.

I would sooner cite, in preference to these dubious cause-and-effect relations, the exceptional affinity of the two civilizations as revealed by the Allied occupation. The G.I. felt himself at home at once in Italy, and the *paisan* was at once on familiar terms with the G.I., black or white. The widespread black market and the presence everywhere of prostitution, wherever the American army went, is by no means the least convincing example of the symbiosis of two civilizations. It is not for nothing that American soldiers are important characters in most recent Italian films; and that they are much at home there speaks volumes.

Although some paths have been opened by literature and the occupation, the phenomenon cannot be explained on this level alone. American films are being made in Italy today but never has the Italian film been at the same time more typically Italian. The body of references I have adopted has excluded similarities even less disputable, for example the Italian "tale," the *commedia dell'arte,* and the technique of the fresco. Rather than an influence one on the other, it is an accord between cinema and literature, based on the same profound aesthetic data, on the same concept of the relation between art and reality. It is a long while since the modern novel created its realist revolution, since it combined behaviorism, a reporter's technique, and the ethic of violence. Far from the cinema's having the slightest effect on this evolution, as is commonly held today, a film like *Paisà* proves that the cinema was twenty years behind the contemporary novel. It is not the least of the merits of the Italian cinema that it has been able to find the truly cinematic equivalent for the most important literary revolution of our time.

Chapter Four

"La Terra Trema"

"*La terra trema*," from *L'Esprit* (December 1948), in *Qu'est-ce que le cinéma?* Vol. 4 (Éditions du Cerf, 1962), pp. 38–44; in *Qu'est-ce que le cinéma?* (Cerf, 1975 [single-volume version]), pp. 287–293; translated into English by Hugh Gray in *What Is Cinema?* Vol. 2 (Univ. of California Press, 1971), pp. 41–46, and edited below by Bert Cardullo.

The subject matter of *La terra trema* (1948), owes nothing to the war: it deals with an attempted revolt by the fishermen of a small Sicilian village against the economic stranglehold exerted by the local fleet-owning fish merchants. I might define the film as a kind of super-*Farrebique* about fishermen. The parallels with Georges Rouquier's 1946 film are many: first, its quasi-documentary realism; then (if one may so put it) the exoticism intrinsic to the subject matter; and, too, the underlying "human geography" (for the Sicilian family, the hope of freeing themselves from the merchants amounts to the same thing as the installation of electricity for the Farrebique family).

Although in *La terra trema,* a Communist film, the whole village is involved, the story is told in terms of a single family, ranging from grandfather to grandchildren. This family was as much out of its element in the sumptuous reception Universalia gave in its honor at the Excelsior in Venice as the Farrebique family had been at its press party in Paris. Visconti, like Rouquier, did not want to use professional actors, not even Rossellini's kind of "amalgam." His fishermen are fishermen in real life. He recruited them at the scene of his story's action—if that is the proper term, for here (as in *Farrebique*) the action deliberately resists the seductions of "drama"; the story unfolds—without regard for the rules of suspense, its only resource a concern with things themselves, as in life. But with these "negative" rather than "positive" aspects of the story the resemblances to *Farrebique* end; *La terra trema* is as remote as could be in style from *Farrebique*.

Visconti, like Rouquier, aimed at and unquestionably achieved a paradoxical synthesis of realism and aestheticism, but the poetry of *Farrebique* is due, in essence, to montage—for example, the winter and spring sequences. To obtain this synthesis in his film, Visconti has not had recourse to the effects one can produce from the juxtaposition of images. Each image here contains a meaning of its own, which it expresses fully. This is the reason why it is difficult to see more than a tenuous relation between *La terra trema* and the Soviet cinema of the second half of the twenties, to which montage was essential. We may add now that it is not by means of symbolism in the imagery, either, that meaning manifests itself here—I mean, the symbolism to which Eisenstein and Rouquier resort. The aesthetic peculiar to the image in this film is always plastic; it avoids any inclination to the epic. As staggeringly beautiful as the fishing fleet may be when it leaves the harbor, it is still just the village fleet, not, as in *The Battleship Potemkin* (1925), the Enthusiasm and the Support of the people of Odessa who send out the fishing boats loaded with food for the rebels.

The Earth Trembles, dir. Luchino Visconti, 1948.

But, one may ask, where is art to take refuge if the realism one is proposing is so ascetic? Everywhere else: in the quality of the photography, especially. Our compatriot Aldo, who before his work on this film did nothing of real note and was known only as a studio cameraman, has here created a profoundly original style of image, unequaled anywhere (as far as I know) but in the short films which are being made in Sweden by Arne Sucksdorff.

To keep the discussion brief, I will only note that, in an article on Italian film of 1946, titled "Cinematic Realism and the Italian School of the Liberation" (*Esprit*, January 1948), I had examined some aspects of the kind of film realism then current, and that I was led to see *Farrebique* and Orson Welles's *Citizen Kane* (1941) as the two poles of realistic technique. The realism of *Farrebique* derives from the object itself, of *Citizen Kane* from the way it structures what it represents. In *Farrebique* everything is real. In *Citizen Kane* everything has been reconstructed in a studio—but only because such depth of field and such rigorously composed images could not be obtained on location. *Paisà* (1946) stands somewhere between the two but closer to *Farrebique* for its images, while the realistic aesthetic works its way into the film between the component blocs of reality through its peculiar conception of narrative.

The images of *La terra trema* achieve what is at once a paradox and a *tour de force* in integrating the aesthetic realism of *Citizen Kane* with the documentary realism of *Farrebique*. If this is not, strictly speaking, the first time depth of focus has been used outside the studio, it is at least the first time it has been used as consciously and as systematically as it is here out of doors, in the rain and even in the dead of night, as well as indoors in the real-life settings of the fishermen's homes. I cannot linger over the technical *tour de force* which this represents, but I would like to emphasize that depth of focus has naturally led Visconti (as it led Welles) not only to reject montage but, in some literal sense, to invent a new kind of shooting script.

His "shots" (if one is justified in retaining the term) are unusually long—some lasting three or four minutes. In each, as one might expect, several actions are going on simultaneously. Visconti also seems to have wanted, in some systematic sense, to base the construction of his image on the event itself. If a fisherman rolls a cigarette, he spares us nothing: we see the whole operation; it will not be reduced to its dramatic or symbolic meaning, as is usual with montage. The shots are often fixed-frame, so that people and things may enter the frame and take up position; but Visconti is also in the habit of using a special kind of panning shot which moves very slowly over an extremely wide arc: this is the only camera movement that he allows himself, for he excludes all tracking shots and, of course, every unusual camera angle.

The unlikely sobriety of this structure is possible only because of the remarkable plastic balance maintained—a balance which only a photograph could render absolutely. But above and beyond the merits of its purely formal properties, the image reveals an intimate knowledge of the subject matter on the part of the filmmakers. This is especially remarkable in the interiors, which hitherto have eluded film. The difficulties attendant on lighting and shooting make it almost impossible to use real interiors as settings. It has been done occasionally, but the results from an aesthetic point of view have been far inferior to what can be achieved on exteriors. Here, for the first time throughout an entire film, there was no variation in quality between interior and exterior as to the style of the shooting script, the performance of the actors, and the results of the photography. Visconti is worthy of the novelty of his triumph. Despite the poverty—or even because of the simple "ordinariness"—of this household of fishermen, an extraordinary kind of poetry, at once intimate and social, emanates from it.

The masterly way in which Visconti has handled his actors deserves the highest praise. This is by no means the first time in the history of film that nonprofessional actors have been used, but never before (except perhaps in "exotic" films, where the problem is somewhat specialized) have the actors been so skillfully integrated with the most specifically aesthetic elements of the film. Rouquier never knew how to handle his family without our being conscious of a camera. The embarrassment, the repressed laughter, the awkwardness are skillfully covered up by the editing, which always cuts just in the nick of time. In *La terra trema,* the actor, sometimes on camera for several minutes at a time, speaks, moves, and acts with complete naturalness—one might even say, with unimaginable grace. Visconti is from the theater, so he has known how to communicate to the nonprofessionals of *La terra trema* something more than naturalness: namely that stylization of gesture which is the crowning achievement of an actor's profession. If festival juries were not what they are, the Venice Film Festival prize for best acting should have gone to the fishermen of *La terra trema.*

Visconti lets us sees that the Italian neorealism of 1946 has been left far behind on more than one score. Hierarchies in art are fairly pointless, but cinema is too young an art still, too involved in its own evolution, to be able to indulge in repeating itself for any length of time. Five years in cinema is the equivalent of an entire literary generation. It is the merit of Visconti to have managed a dialectical integration of the achievements of recent Italian film with a larger, richer aesthetic for which the term "realism" no longer has much meaning. I am not saying that *La terra trema* is superior to *Paisà* or to *Caccia tragica* (1947) but only that it does, at least, have the merit of having left them behind from an historical standpoint.

Seeing the best Italian films of 1948, I had the impression that Italian cinema was doomed to repeat itself to its utter exhaustion. *La terra trema* is the only original way out of the aesthetic impasse, and in that sense, one might suppose, it bears the burden of our hopes. Does this mean that those hopes will be fulfilled? No, unhappily, it is not certain, for *La terra trema* runs counter, still, to some cinematic principles with which Visconti will have to deal in future films somewhat more convincingly than he does here. In particular, his disinclination to sacrifice anything to drama has one obvious and serious consequence: *La terra trema* bores the public. A film with a limited action, it lasts longer than three hours. If you add that the language used in the film is a dialectal Sicilian (which, given the photographic style of the image, it is impossible to subtitle), and that not even mainland Italians understand it, you can see that this is somewhat austere "entertainment" and faces no more than a restricted commercial future.

I am sincere when I say that I hope Universalia will play the role of [the Roman patron] Maecenas sufficiently to enable Visconti, while himself sharing the cost from his large personal fortune, to finish the trilogy he projects of which *La terra trema* is only the first part. We will then, at best, have some filmic monster, whose highly social and political preoccupations will nonetheless remain inaccessible to the general public. In the world of cinema, it is not necessary that everyone approve every film, provided that what prompts the public's incomprehension can be compensated for by the other things. In other words, the aesthetic of *La terra trema* must be applicable to dramatic ends if it is to be of service in the evolution of cinema. One also has to take into account—and this is even more disturbing, in view of what one has the right to expect from Visconti himself—a dangerous inclination to aestheticism.

This great aristocrat, an artist to the tips of his fingers, is a Communist, too—dare I say a synthetic one? *La terra trema* in the end lacks inner fire, by which I mean inner commitment. One is reminded of the great Renaissance painters who, without having to do violence to themselves, were able to paint such fine religious frescoes in spite of their deep indifference to Christianity. I am not passing judgment on the sincerity of Visconti's communism. But what is sincerity? Obviously, at issue is not some paternalistic feeling for the proletariat. Paternalism is a bourgeois phenomenon, and Visconti is an aristocrat. What is at issue, maybe, is an aesthetic participation in history. Whatever it be, though, we are a long way off from the telling conviction of Eisenstein's *Battleship Potemkin* or Pudovkin's *The End of Saint Petersburg* (1927) or even (the theme is the same) Erwin Piscator's film *The Revolt of the Fishermen* (1934).

There is no doubt that *La terra trema* does have propaganda value, but this value is purely objective: there is no moving eloquence to bolster its documentary vigor. This is how Visconti intended it to be, a decision that is not in itself unattractive. But it involves him in a fairly risky bet, which he may not necessarily be able to cover, at least in terms of film. Let us hope that Visconti's future work will show us that he can. As it stands, however, he won't succeed unless he can avoid falling in the direction in which his cinema is already perilously leaning.

Chapter Five

"Germany, Year Zero"

"*Allemagne année zero*," from *L'Esprit* (1949), in *Qu'est-ce que le cinéma?* Vol. 3 (Éditions du Cerf, 1961), pp. 29–32; in *Qu'est-ce que le cinéma?* (Cerf, 1975 [single-volume version]), pp. 203–206; translated into English by Bert Cardullo.

A child's face elicits from us conflicting responses. We marvel at it because of its already unique yet specifically childlike characteristics—hence Mickey Rooney's success and the proliferation of freckles on the faces of young American stars. The days of Shirley Temple, who unduly prolonged her own private theatrical, lite6rary, and visual aesthetic, are now over; children in the cinema no longer look like china dolls or Renaissance representations of the infant Jesus. But mystery continues to frighten us, and we want to be reassured against it by the faces of children; we thoughtlessly ask of these faces that they reflect feelings we know very well because they are our own. We demand of them signs of complicity, and the audience quickly becomes enraptured and teary when children show feelings that are usually associated with grown-ups. We are thus seeking to contemplate ourselves in them: ourselves, plus the innocence, awkwardness, and naïveté we have lost. This kind of cinema moves us, but aren't we in fact just feeling sorry for ourselves?

With very few exceptions (like Vigo's *Zero for Conduct* [1933], which is pervaded with irony), children's films fully play on the ambiguity of our interest in these miniature human beings. Come to think of it, these films treat childhood precisely as if it were open to our understanding and empathy; they are made in the name of anthropomorphism. *It Happened in Europe* (1947) is no exception to this rule. Quite the contrary: Géza Radványi, the Hungarian director, manipulates that anthropomorphism with diabolical skill. I won't reproach him for his demagogy to the extent that I accept the world he creates.

Germany, Year Zero, dir. Roberto Rossellini, 1947.

But even though I get a tear in my eye like everybody else, I can't help seeing that the death of the ten-year-old boy, who is shot down while playing the "Marseillaise" on his harmonica, is so moving only because it confirms our adult conception of heroism. By contrast, the atrocious strangling of the truck driver with a slipknot of iron wire contains, because of the pathetic reason behind it (to get a piece of bread and a strip of bacon for ten famished boys), something inexplicable and unforeseen that has its origin in the irreducible mystery of childhood. All in all, however, this film relies much more on our sympathy for children who manifest feelings that are comprehensible to us.

Roberto Rossellini's profound originality in *Germany, Year Zero* (1947) lies in his deliberate refusal to resort to any such sentimental sympathy, to make any concession to anthropomorphism. His kid is eleven or twelve years old, and it would be easy, even normal, most of the time for the script and the acting to introduce us into the innermost recesses of his conscience. If we do know some things about this boy's thoughts and feelings, however, it is never because of signs that can be read directly on his face, nor even because of his behavior, for we get to understand it only by inference and conjecture. Of course, the speech of the Nazi schoolmaster is the immediate source of the boy's murder of his sickly and "useless" father ("the weak must perish so that the strong may live"), but when he pours the poison into the cup of tea, we look in vain on his face for anything other than concentration and calculation. We cannot see on it any sign of indifference, or cruelty, or possible sorrow. A schoolmaster has pronounced some words in front of him, and these have made their way through to his mind and caused him to make this decision: but how, and at the cost of how much inner conflict? This is not the filmmaker's concern; it is only the child's. Rossellini could have given us an interpretation of the murder only through a piece of trickery, by projecting his own explanation onto the boy and having him reflect it for us.

Rossellini's aesthetic clearly triumphs in the final fifteen minutes of the film, during the boy's long quest for some sign of confirmation or approval, ending with his suicide in response to being betrayed by the world. First, the schoolmaster refuses to assume any responsibility for the incriminating gesture of his disciple. Driven into the street, the boy walks and walks, searching here and there among the ruins; but, one after the other, people and things abandon him. He finds his girlfriend playing with his pals, but they pick up their ball when he tries to approach them. The close-ups that punctuate this endless quest never show us anything other than a worried, pensive, perhaps frightened face, but frightened of what? Of making some transaction on the black market? Of swapping a knife for two cigarettes? Of the thrashing he's going to get when he returns home? Only the final scene will give us a retrospective clue to the answer. The fact is, simply, that the signs of play and the signs of death may be the same on a child's face, at least for those of us who cannot penetrate its mystery.

The boy hops on one leg along the edge of a broken-up sidewalk. He picks up among the masses of stone and twisted steel a piece of rusty metal that he handles as if it were a gun. He aims through a hole in the ruins at an imaginary target: bang, bang, bang. ... Then, with exactly the same playful spontaneity he puts the imaginary gun to his temple. Finally, the suicide: the

Germany, Year Zero, dir. Roberto Rossellini, 1947.

kid climbs to the top floor of the bombed-out building facing his own house; he looks down and sees a hearse pick up a coffin and take it away, leaving the family behind; an iron beam sticks out sideways through the devastated floor, like a toboggan; he slides down it on his behind and leaps into the void. His little corpse lies on the ground now behind a pile of stones at the edge of the sidewalk. A woman puts down her shopping bag and kneels beside him. A streetcar passes by with a rattling noise. The woman leans back against the pile of stones, her arms hanging about her in the eternal pose of a *Pietà*.

One can clearly see how Rossellini was led to treat his main character in this way. Such psychological objectivity was within the logic of his style. Rossellini's "realism" has nothing in common with all that the cinema has given to us up to now in the name of realism (with the exception of Jean Renoir's films). His realism lies not in the subject matter but in the style. Rossellini is perhaps the only filmmaker in the world who knows how to get us interested in an action while leaving it in its objective context. Our emotion is thus rid of all sentimentality, for it has been filtered by force through our intelligence. We are moved not by the actor or the event, but by the meaning we are forced to extract from the action. In this *mise en scène*, the moral or dramatic significance is never visible on the surface of reality; yet we can't fail to sense what that significance is if we pay attention. Isn't this, then, a sound definition of realism in art: to force the mind to draw its own conclusions about people and events, instead of manipulating it into accepting someone else's interpretation?

Chapter Six

"Bicycle Thieves"

"*Voleur de bicyclette*," from *L'Esprit*, 18.161 (November 1949), pp. 820–832; in *Qu'est-ce que le cinéma?* Vol. 4 (Éditions du Cerf, 1962), pp. 45–59; in *Qu'est-ce que le cinéma?* (Cerf, 1975 [single-volume version]), pp. 295–309; translated into English by Hugh Gray in *What Is Cinema?* Vol. 2 (Univ. of California Press, 1971), pp. 47–60, and edited below by Bert Cardullo.

What seems to me most astonishing about the Italian cinema is that it appears to feel it should escape from the aesthetic impasse to which neorealism is said to have led. The dazzling effects of 1946 and 1947 having faded away, one could reasonably fear that this useful and intelligent reaction against the Italian aesthetic of the super-spectacle and, for that matter, more generally, against the technical aestheticism from which cinema suffered all over the world, would never get beyond an interest in a kind of super-documentary, or romanticized reportage. One began to realize that the success of *Roma, città aperta* (1945), *Paisà* (1946), or *Sciuscià* (1946) was inseparable from a special conjunction of historical circumstances that took its meaning from the Liberation, and that the technique of the films was in some way magnified by the revolutionary value of the subject. Just as some books by Malraux or Hemingway find in a crystallization of journalistic style the best narrative form for a tragedy of current events, so the films of Rossellini or De Sica owed the fact that they were major works, masterpieces, simply to a fortuitous combination of form and subject matter.

But when the novelty and above all the flavor of their technical crudity have exhausted their surprise effect, what remains of Italian neorealism when by force of circumstances it must revert to traditional subjects: crime stories, psychological dramas, social customs? The camera in the street we can still accept, but doesn't that admirable nonprofessional acting stand self-condemned in proportion as its discoveries swell the ranks of international stars? And, by way of generalizing about this aesthetic pessimism: realism can only occupy in art a dialectical position—it is more a reaction than a truth. It remains then to make it part of the aesthetic it came into existence to verify. In any case, the Italians were not the last to downgrade their neorealism. I think there is not a single Italian director, including the most neorealist, who does not insist that he must get away from it.

French critics, too, feel themselves a prey to scruples—especially since this vaunted neorealism early showed signs of running out of steam. Comedies, agreeable enough in themselves, appeared on the scene to exploit with visible ease the formula of *Quattro passi fra le nuvole* (1942) or *Vivere in pace* (1946). But worst of all was the emergence of a neorealist super-spectacle in which the search for real settings, action taken from everyday life, portrayals of lower-class milieux, "social" backgrounds, became an academic stereotype far more detestable than the elephants of Carmine Gallone's *Scipio Africanus* (1937). For a neorealist film may have every defect except that of being academic. Thus at Venice *Il patto col diavolo* (1949), by Luigi Chiarini, a somber melodrama of rural love, took visible pains to find a contemporary "alibi" in a story of conflict between shepherds and woodsmen. Although well done on some accounts, Pietro Germi's *In nome della legge* (1949), which the Italians tried to push to the fore at Knokke-le-Zoute, cannot escape similar criticisms. One will notice incidentally, from these two examples, that neorealism is now preoccupied with rural problems, perhaps prudently in view of the fate of urban neorealism. The closed-in countryside has replaced the open city.

However that may be, the hopes that we placed in the new Italian school had started to turn into uneasiness, or even skepticism, all the more since the aesthetic of neorealism forbids it to repeat itself or plagiarize itself in the way that is possible and even normal in some traditional genres (the crime film, the western, the atmospheric film, and so on). Already we were beginning to look toward England, whose recent cinematic rebirth is likewise, in part, the fruit of realism: that of the school of documentarians who, before and during the war, had gone deeply into the resources offered by social and technical realities. A film like David Lean's *Brief Encounter* (1945) would probably have been impossible without the ten years of preparation by John Grierson, Alberto Cavalcanti, or Paul Rotha. But the English, instead of breaking with the technique and the history of European and American cinema, have succeeded in combining a highly refined aestheticism with the advances of a certain realism. Nothing could be more tightly structured, more carefully prepared, than *Brief Encounter*—nothing less conceivable without the most up-to-date studio resources, without clever and established actors; yet can we imagine a more realistic portrait of English manners and psychology? Certainly, Lean has gained nothing by making over, this year, a kind of second *Brief Encounter*: *The Passionate Friends* (1949), presented at the Cannes Film Festival. But it is against repetition of the subject matter that one can reasonably protest, not against the repetition of the techniques, which could be used over and over indefinitely.

Have I played devil's advocate long enough? For let me now make a confession: my doubts about the Italian cinema have never gone so far, but all the arguments I have invoked have been used by intelligent men—especially in Italy—nor are they unfortunately without some semblance of validity. They have also often troubled me, and I subscribe to some of them. On the other hand there is a film called *Ladri di biciclette* (1948) and two other films that I hope we will soon get to know in France. With *Ladri di biciclette* De Sica has managed to escape from the impasse, to reaffirm anew the entire aesthetic of neorealism.

Ladri di biciclette certainly *is* neorealist, by all the principles one can deduce from the best Italian films since 1946. The story is from the lower classes, almost populist: an incident in the daily life of a worker. But the film

Bicycle Thieves, dir. Vittorio De Sica, 1948.

shows no extraordinary events such as those which befall the fated workers in Jean Gabin films. There are no crimes of passion, none of those grandiose coincidences common in detective stories which simply transfer to a realm of proletarian exoticism the great tragic debates once reserved for the dwellers on Olympus. Truly an insignificant, even a banal incident: a workman spends a whole day looking in vain in the streets of Rome for the bicycle someone has stolen from him. This bicycle has been the tool of his trade, and if he doesn't find it he will again be unemployed. Late in the day, after hours of fruitless wandering, he too tries to steal a bicycle. Apprehended and then released, he is as poor as ever, but now he feels the shame of having sunk to the level of the thief.

Plainly there is not enough material here even for a news item: the whole story would not deserve two lines in a stray-dog column. One must take care not to confuse it with realist tragedy in the Jacques Prévert or James M. Cain manner, where the initial news item is a diabolic trap placed by the gods amid the cobble stones of the street. In itself the event contains no proper dramatic valence. It takes on meaning only because of the social (and not psychological or aesthetic) position of the victim. Without the haunting specter of unemployment, which places the event in the Italian society of 1948, it would be an utterly banal misadventure. Likewise, the choice of a bicycle as the key object in the drama is characteristic both of Italian urban life and of a period when mechanical means of transportation were still rare and expensive. There is no need to insist on the hundreds of other meaningful details that multiply the vital links between the scenario and actuality, situating the event in political and social history, in a given place at a given time.

The techniques employed in the *mise en scène* likewise meet the most exacting specifications of Italian neorealism. Not one scene shot in a studio. Everything was filmed in the streets. As for the actors, none had the slightest experience in theater or film. The workman came from the Breda factory, the child was found hanging around in the street, the wife was a journalist. These then are the facts of the case. It is clear that they do not appear to recall in any sense the neorealism of *Quattro passi fra le nuvole*, *Vivere in pace*, or *Sciuscià*. On the face of it, then, one should have special reasons for being wary. The sordid side of the tale tends toward that most debatable aspect of Italian stories: indulgence in the wretched, a systematic search for squalid detail.

If *Ladri di biciclette* is a true masterpiece, comparable in rigor to *Paisà*, it is for certain precise reasons, none of which emerge either from a simple outline of the scenario or from a superficial disquisition on the technique of the *mise en scène*. The scenario is diabolically clever in its construction; beginning with the alibi of a current event, it makes good use of a number of systems of dramatic coordinates radiating in all directions. *Ladri di biciclette* is certainly the only valid Communist film of the whole past decade precisely because it still has meaning even when you have abstracted its social significance. Its social message is not detached; it remains immanent in the event, but it is so clear that nobody can overlook it, still less take exception to it, since it is never made explicitly a message. The thesis implied is wondrously and outrageously simple: in the world where this workman lives, the poor must steal from each other in order to survive.

But this thesis is never stated as such; it is just that events are so linked together that they have the appearance of a formal truth while retaining an anecdotal quality. Basically, the workman might have found his bicycle in the middle of the film; only then there would have been no film. (Sorry to have bothered you, the director might say; we really did think he would never find it, but since he has, all is well, good for him, the performance is over, you can turn up the lights.) In other words, a propaganda film would try to prove that the workman could not find his bicycle, and that he is inevitably trapped in the vicious circle of poverty. De Sica limits himself to showing that the workman cannot find his bicycle and that as a result he doubtless will be unemployed again. No one can fail to see that it is the accidental nature of the script that gives the thesis its quality of necessity; the slightest doubt cast on the necessity of the events in the scenario of a propaganda film renders the argument hypothetical.

Although on the basis of the workman's misfortune we have no alternative but to condemn a certain kind of relation between a man and his work, the film never makes the events or the people part of an economic or political Manichaeism. It takes care not to cheat on reality, not only by contriving to give the succession of events the appearance of an accidental and as it were anecdotal chronology, but in treating each of them according to its phenomenological integrity. In the middle of the chase the little boy suddenly needs to piss. So he does. A downpour forces the father and son to shelter in a carriageway, so like them we have to forego the chase and wait till the storm is over. The events are not necessarily signs of something, of a truth of which we are to be convinced; they all carry their own weight, their complete uniqueness, that ambiguity which characterizes any fact. So, if you do not have the eyes to see, you are free to attribute what happens to bad luck or to chance.

The same applies to the people in the film. The worker is just as deprived and isolated among his fellow trade unionists as he is walking along the street or even in that ineffable scene of the Catholic "Quakers" into whose company he will shortly stray, because the trade union does not exist to find lost bikes but to transform a world in which losing his bike condemns a man to poverty.

Nor does the worker come to lodge a complaint with the trade union but to find comrades who will be able to help him discover the stolen object. So here you have a collection of proletarian members of a union who behave no differently from a group of paternalistic bourgeois toward an unfortunate workman. In his private misfortune, the poster hanger is just as alone in his union as in church (buddies apart, that is—but then who your buddies are is your own affair).

Bicycle Thieves, dir. Vittorio De Sica, 1948.

 This parallel is extremely useful, however, because it points up a striking contrast. The indifference of the trade union is normal and justified because a trade union is striving for justice, not for charity. But the cumbersome paternalism of the Catholic "Quakers" is unbearable, because their eyes are closed to his personal tragedy while they in fact actually do nothing to change the world that is the cause of it. On this score the most successful scene is that in the storm under the porch when a flock of Austrian seminarians crowd around the worker and his son. We have no valid reason to blame them for chattering so much and still less for talking German. But it would be difficult to create a more objectively anticlerical scene.

 Clearly, and I could find twenty more examples: events and people are never introduced in support of a social thesis—but the thesis emerges fully armed and all the more irrefutable because it is presented to us as something thrown in into the bargain. It is our intelligence that discerns and shapes it, not the film. De Sica wins every play on the board without ever having made a bet. This technique is not entirely new in Italian films and we have elsewhere stressed its value at length both apropos of *Paisà* and of *Germania, anno zero* (1947), but these two films were based on themes from either the Resistance or the war. *Ladri di biciclette* is the first decisive example of the possibility of the conversion of this kind of objectivity to other, similar subjects. De Sica and Zavattini have transferred neorealism from the Resistance to the Revolution.

Thus the thesis of the film is hidden behind an objective social reality which in turn moves into the background of the moral and psychological drama that could of itself justify the film. The idea of the boy is a stroke of genius, and one does not know definitely whether it came from the script or in the process of directing, so little does this distinction mean here anymore. It is the child who gives to the workman's adventure its ethical dimension and fashions, from an individual moral standpoint, a drama that might well have been only social. Remove the boy, and the story remains much the same. The proof: a summary of it would not differ in detail. In fact, the boy's part is confined to trotting along beside his father. But he is the intimate witness of the tragedy, its private chorus.

It is supremely clever to have virtually eliminated the role of the wife in order to give flesh and blood to the private character of the tragedy in the person of the child. The complicity between father and son is so subtle that it reaches down to the foundations of the moral life. It is the admiration the child feels for his father and the father's awareness of it which gives its tragic stature to the ending. The public shame of the worker, exposed and clouted in the open street, is of little account compared with the fact that his son witnessed it. When he feels tempted to steal the bike, the silent presence of the little child, who guesses what his father is thinking, is cruel to the verge of obscenity. Trying to get rid of him by sending him to take the streetcar is like telling a child in some cramped apartment to go and wait on the landing outside for an hour. Only in the best Chaplin films are there situations of an equally overwhelming conciseness.

In this connection, the final gesture of the little boy in giving his hand to his father has been frequently misinterpreted. It would be unworthy of the film to see here a concession to the feelings of the audience. If De Sica gives them this satisfaction it is because it is a logical part of the drama. This experience marks henceforth a definite stage in the relations between father and son, rather like reaching puberty. Up to that moment the man has been like a god to his son; their relations come under the heading of admiration. By his action the father has now compromised them. The tears they shed as they walk side by side, arms swinging, signify their despair over a paradise lost. But the son returns to a father who has fallen from grace. He will love him henceforth as a human being, shame and all. The hand that slips into his is neither a symbol of forgiveness nor of a childish act of consolation. It is rather the most solemn gesture that could ever mark the relations between a father and his son: one that makes them equals.

It would take too long to enumerate the multiple secondary functions of the boy in the film, both as to the story structure and as to the *mise en scène* itself. However, one should at least pay attention to the change of tone (almost in the musical sense of the term) that his presence introduces into the middle of the film. As we slowly wander back and forth between the little boy and the workman we are taken from the social and economic plane to that of their private lives, and the supposed death by drowning of the child, in making the father suddenly realize the relative insignificance of his misfortune, creates a dramatic oasis (the restaurant scene) at the heart of the story. It is, however, an illusory one, because the reality of this intimate happiness in the long run depends on the precious bike. Thus the child provides a dramatic reserve which, as the occasion arises, serves as a counterpoint, as an accompaniment, or moves on the contrary into the foreground of the melodic structure.

This function in the story is, furthermore, clearly observable in the orchestration of the steps of the child and of the grown-up. Before choosing this particular child, De Sica did not ask him to perform, just to walk. He wanted to play off the striding gait of the man against the short trotting steps of the child, the harmony of this discord being for him of capital importance for the understanding of the film as a whole. It would be no exaggeration to say that *Ladri di biciclette* is the story of a walk through Rome by a father and his son. Whether the child is ahead, behind, alongside—or when, sulking after having had his ears boxed, he is dawdling behind in a gesture of revenge—what he is doing is never without meaning. On the contrary, it is the phenomenology of the script.

It is difficult, after the success of this pairing of a workman and his son, to imagine De Sica having recourse to established actors. The absence of professional actors is nothing new. But here again *Ladri di biciclette* goes further than previous films. Henceforth the cinematic purity of the actors does not derive from skill, luck, or a happy combination of a subject, a period, and a people. Probably too much importance has been attached to the ethnic factor. Admittedly the Italians, like the Russians, are the most naturally theatrical of people. In Italy any little street urchin is the equal of a Jackie Coogan and life is a perpetual *commedia dell'arte*. However, it seems to me unlikely that these acting talents are shared equally by the Milanese, the Neapolitans, the peasants of the Po, and the fishermen of Sicily. Racial difference apart, the contrasts in their history, language, and economic and social condition would suffice to cast doubt on a thesis that sought to attribute the natural acting ability of the Italian people simply to an ethnic quality.

It is inconceivable, then, that films as different as *Paisà, Ladri di biciclette, La terra trema* (1948), and even *Cielo sulla palude* (1949) could share in common such a superbly high level of acting. One could conceive that the urban Italian has a special gift for spontaneous histrionics, but the peasants in *Cielo sulla palude* are absolute cavemen beside the farmers of *Farrebique* (1946). Merely to recall Rouquier's film in connection with Genina's is enough at least in this respect to relegate the experiment of the French director to the level of a touchingly patronizing effort. Half the dialogue in *Farrebique* is spoken off-camera because Rouquier could never get the peasants not to laugh during a speech of any length.

Genina in *Cielo sulla palude*, Visconti in *La terra trema*, both handling peasants or fishermen by the dozen, gave them complicated roles and got them to recite long speeches in scenes in which the camera concentrated on their faces as pitilessly as in an American studio. It is an understatement to say that these temporary actors are good or even perfect. In these films the very concept of actor, performance, character no longer has any meaning. An actorless cinema? Undoubtedly. But the original meaning of the formula is now outdated, and we should talk today of a cinema without acting, of a cinema of which we no longer ask whether the character gives a good performance or not, since here man and the character he portrays are so completely one.

We have not strayed as far as it might seem from *Ladri di biciclette*. De Sica hunted for his cast for a long time and selected them for specific characteristics. Natural nobility, that purity of countenance and bearing that the common people have ... He hesitated for months between this person and that, took a hundred tests only to decide finally, in a flash and by intuition on the basis of a silhouette suddenly come upon at the bend of a road. But there is nothing miraculous about that. It is not the unique excellence of this workman and this child that guarantees the quality of their performance, but the whole aesthetic scheme into which they are fitted.

When De Sica was looking for a producer to finance his film, he finally found one, but on condition that the workman was played by Cary Grant.

The mere statement of the problem in these terms shows the absurdity of it. Actually, Cary Grant plays this kind of part extremely well, but it is obvious that the question here is not one of playing of a part but of getting away from the very notion of doing any such thing. The worker had to be at once as perfect and as anonymous and as objective as his bicycle. This concept of the actor is no less "artistic" than the other. The performance of this workman implies as many gifts of body and of mind and as much capacity to take direction as any established actor has at his command.

Hitherto films that have been made either totally or in part without actors, such as F. W. Murnau's *Tabu* (1931), Eisenstein's *Thunder over Mexico* (1933), and Pudovkin's *Mother* (1926), have seemingly been successes that are either out of the ordinary or limited to a certain genre. There is nothing, on the other hand, unless it be sound prudence, to prevent De Sica from making fifty films like *Ladri di biciclette*. From now on we know that the absence of professional actors in no way limits the choice of subject. The film without names has finally established its own aesthetic existence. This in no sense means that the cinema of the future will no longer use actors: De Sica, who is one of the world's finest actors, would be the first to deny this. All it means is that some subjects handled in a certain style can no longer be made with professional actors and that the Italian cinema has definitely imposed these working conditions, just as naturally as it imposed authentic settings. It is this transition from an admirable *tour de force,* precarious as this may be, into an exact and infallible technique, that marks a decisive stage in the growth of Italian neorealism.

With the disappearance of the concept of the actor into a transparency seemingly as natural as life itself, comes the disappearance of the set. Let us understand one another, however. De Sica's film took a long time to prepare, and everything was as minutely planned as for a studio super-production, which, as a matter of fact, allows for last-minute improvisations, but I cannot remember a single shot in which a dramatic effect is born of the shooting script properly so called, which seems as neutral as in a Chaplin film. All the same, the numbering and titling of shots does not noticeably distinguish *Ladri di biciclette* from any ordinary film. But their selection has been made with a view to raising the limpidity of the event to a maximum, while keeping the index of refraction from the style to a minimum.

This objectivity is rather different from Rossellini's in *Paisà* but it belongs to the same school of aesthetics. One may compare it to the objectivity found in the kind of prose fiction that, according to André Gide and Martin du Gard, necessarily tends in the direction of the most neutral kind of transparency. Just as the disappearance of the actor is the result of transcending a style of performance, the disappearance of the *mise en scène* is likewise the fruit of a dialectical progress in the style of the narrative. If the event is sufficient unto itself without the direction having to shed any further light on it by means of camera angles, purposely chosen camera positions, it is because it has reached that stage of perfect luminosity which makes it possible for an art to unmask a nature which in the end resembles it. That is why the impression made on us by *Ladri di biciclette* is unfailingly that of truth.

If this supreme naturalness, the sense of events observed haphazardly as the hours roll by, is the result of an ever-present although invisible system of aesthetics, it is definitely the prior conception of the scenario which allows this to happen. Disappearance of the actor, disappearance of *mise en scène*? Unquestionably, but because the very principle of *Ladri di biciclette* is the disappearance of a story. The term is equivocal. I know of course that there is a story but of a different kind from those we ordinarily see on the screen. This is even the reason why De Sica could not find a producer to back him.

When Roger Leenhardt in a prophetic critical statement asked years ago "if the cinema is a spectacle," he was contrasting the dramatic cinema with the novel-like structure of the cinematic narrative. The former borrows from the theater its hidden springs. Its plot, conceived as it may be specifically for the screen, is still the alibi for an action identical in essence with the action of the classical theater. On this score the film is a spectacle like a play. But on the other hand, because of its realism and the equal treatment it gives to man and to nature, the cinema is related, aesthetically speaking, to the novel.

Without going too far into a theory of the novel—a debatable subject—let us say that the narrative form of the novel or that which derives from it differs by and large from the theater in the primacy given to events over action, to succession over causality, to mind over will. The conjunction belonging to the theater is "therefore," the particle belonging to the novel is "then." This scandalously rough definition is correct to the extent that it characterizes the two different movements of the mind in thinking, namely that of the reader and that of the onlooker. Proust can lose us in a madeleine, but a playwright fails in his task if every reply does not link our interest to the reply that is to follow. That is why a novel may be laid down and then picked up again. A play cannot be cut into pieces. The total unity of a spectacle is of its essence.

To the extent that it can realize the physical requirements of a spectacle, the cinema cannot apparently escape the spectacle's psychological laws, but it has also at its disposal all the resources of the novel. For that reason, doubtless, the cinema is congenitally a hybrid. It conceals a contradiction. Besides, clearly, the progression of the cinema is toward increasing its novel-like potential. Not that we are against filmed theater, but if the screen can in some conditions develop and give a new dimension to the theater, it is of necessity at the expense of certain scenic values—the first of which is the physical presence of the actor. Contrariwise, the novel at least ideally need surrender nothing to the cinema. One may think of the film as a super-novel of which the written form is a feeble and provisional version.

This much briefly said, how much of it can be found in the present condition of the cinematographic spectacle? It is impossible to overlook the spectacular and theatrical needs demanded of the screen. What remains to be decided is how to reconcile the contradiction. The Italian cinema of today is the first anywhere in the world to have enough courage to cast aside the imperatives of the spectacular. *La terra trema* and *Cielo sulla palude* are films without "action," in the unfolding of which, somewhat after the style of the epic novel, no concession is made to dramatic tension. Things happen in them each at its appointed hour, one after the other, but each carries an equal weight. If some are fuller of meaning than others, it is only in retrospect. We are free to use either "therefore" or "then." *La terra trema*, especially, is a film destined to be virtually a commercial failure, unexploitable without cuts that would leave it unrecognizable.

That is the virtue of De Sica and Zavattini. Their *Ladri di biciclette* is solidly structured in the mold of a tragedy. There is not one frame that is not charged with an intense dramatic power, yet there is not one either which we cannot fail to find interesting, its dramatic continuity apart. The film unfolds on the level of pure accident: the rain, the seminarians, the Catholic Quakers, the restaurant—all these are seemingly interchangeable; no one seems to have arranged them in order on a dramatic spectrum. The scene in the thieves' quarter is significant. We are not sure that the man who was chased by the workman is actually the bicycle thief, and we shall never know if the epileptic fit was a pretense or genuine. As an "action" this episode would be meaningless had not its novel-like interest, its value as a fact, given it a dramatic meaning to boot.

It is in fact on its reverse side, and by parallels, that the action is assembled—less in terms of "tension" than of a "summation" of the events. Yes, it is a spectacle, and what a spectacle! *Ladri di biciclette*, however, does not depend on the mathematical elements of drama; the action does not exist beforehand as if it were an "essence." It follows from the preexistence of the narrative; it is the "integral" of reality. De Sica's supreme achievement, which others have so far only approached with a varying degree of success or failure, is to have succeeded in discovering the cinematographic dialectic capable of transcending the contradiction between the action of a "spectacle" and of an event. For this reason, *Ladri di biciclette* is one of the first examples of pure cinema. No more actors, no more story, no more sets, which is to say that in the perfect aesthetic illusion of reality there is no more cinema.

Chapter Seven

"Vittorio De Sica: Metteur en Scène"

"Vittorio De Sica: *Metteur en scène*," from an article originally published in Italian (Editions Guanda, 1953), in *Qu'est-ce que le cinéma?* Vol. 4 (Éditions du Cerf, 1962), pp. 73–91; in *Qu'est-ce que le cinéma?* (Cerf, 1975 [single-volume version]), pp. 311–329; translated into English by Hugh Gray in *What Is Cinema?* Vol. 2 (Univ. of California Press, 1971), pp. 61–78, and edited below by Bert Cardullo.

I must confess to the reader that my pen is paralyzed by scruples because of the many compelling reasons why I should not be the one to introduce De Sica to him. First, there is the presumption implied in a Frenchman wanting to teach Italians something about their own cinema in general, and, in particular, about the man who is possibly their greatest director. Besides, when I imprudently accepted the honor of introducing De Sica in these pages, I was particularly conscious of my admiration for *Ladri di biciclette* (1948) and I had not yet seen *Miracolo a Milano* (1951). We in France have, of course, seen *Ladri di biciclette* (1948), *Sciuscià* (1946), and *I bambini ci guardano* (1943), but lovely as *Sciuscià* is, and revealing as it is of the talents of De Sica, it bears, side by side with certain sublime discoveries, traces of the apprentice director. The scenario occasionally succumbs to melodramatic indulgence, and the direction has a certain poetic elegance, a lyrical quality, that today it seems to me De Sica is concerned to avoid. In short, we do not have there as yet the personal style of the director. His complete and final mastery is revealed in *Ladri di biciclette* to such an extent that the film seems to include all the efforts that went into the making of its predecessors.

But can one judge a director by a single film? This film is sufficient proof of the genius of De Sica, but not of the future forms that this genius will take. As an actor, De Sica is no newcomer to the cinema, but one must still call him "young" as a director—a director of the future. In spite of the resemblances we will observe between them, *Miracolo a Milano* differs greatly in inspiration and structure from *Ladri di biciclette*. What will his next film be? Will it reveal trends that appear only of minor importance in the previous works? In short, we are undertaking to speak of the style of a director of the first order on the basis of just two films—one of which seems to conflict with the orientation of the other. This is all right if one does not confuse the role of a critic with that of a prophet. I have no trouble explaining why I admire *Ladri* and *Miracolo* but that is something very different from pretending to deduce from these two films what are the permanent and definitive characteristics of their maker's talent.

Vittorio De Sica (1902–1974).

All the same I would willingly have done that for Rossellini after *Roma, città aperta* (1945) and *Paisà* (1946). What I would have been able to say (and what I actually wrote in France) ran the risk of being modified by Rossellini's subsequent films, but not of being given the lie. The style of Rosellini belongs to a different aesthetic family. The rules of its aesthetics are plain to see. It fits a vision of the world directly adapted to a framework of *mise en scène*. Rossellini's style is a way of seeing, while De Sica's is primarily a way of feeling. The *mise en scène* of the former lays siege to its object from outside. I do not mean without understanding and feeling—but that this exterior approach offers us an essential ethical and metaphysical aspect of our relations with the world. In order to understand this statement one need only compare the treatment of the child in *Germania, anno zero* (1947) and in *Sciuscià* and *Ladri di biciclette*.

Rossellini's love for his characters envelops them in a desperate awareness of man's inability to communicate; De Sica's love, on the contrary, radiates from the people themselves. They are what they are, but lit from within by the tenderness he feels for them. It follows that Rossellini's direction comes between his material and us, not as an artificial obstacle set up between the two, but as an unbridgeable, ontological distance, a congenital weakness of the human being which expresses itself aesthetically in terms of space, in forms, in the structure of his *mise en scène*. Because we are aware of it as a lack, a refusal, an escape from things, and hence finally as a kind of pain, it follows that it is easier for us to be aware of it, easier for us to reduce it to a formal method. Rossellini cannot alter this without himself passing through a personal moral revolution.

By contrast, De Sica is one of those directors whose sole purpose seems to be to interpret their scenarios faithfully, whose entire talent derives from the love they have for their subject, from their ultimate understanding of it. The *mise en scène* seems to take shape after the fashion of a natural form in living matter. Despite a different kind of sensibility and a marked concern for form, Jacques Feyder in France also belongs to this family of directors whose one method of work seems to be to treat their subject honestly. This neutrality is illusory but its apparent existence does not make the critic's task any easier. It divides up the output of the filmmaker into so many special cases that, given one more film, all that has preceded it might be called into question. It is a temptation therefore to see only craftsmanship where one is looking for style, the generous humility of a clever technician meeting the demands of the subject instead of the creative imprint of a true *auteur*.

The *mise en scène* of a Rossellini film can be readily deduced from the images he uses, whereas De Sica forces us to arrive at his *mise en scène* inductively from a visual narrative which does not seem to admit of it. Finally and above all, the case of De Sica is up to now inseparable from his collaboration with Zavattini, even more than is that of Marcel Carné in France with Jacques Prévert. There is no more perfect example in the history of the cinema of a symbiosis of screenwriter and director. The fact that Zavattini collaborates with others, while Prévert has written few stories or scripts for anyone but Carné, makes no difference. On the contrary, what it allows us to conclude is that De Sica is the ideal director for Zavattini, the one who understands him best and most intimately. We have examples of the work of Zavattini without De Sica, but nothing of De Sica without Zavattini. We are therefore undertaking arbitrarily to distinguish that which truly belongs to De Sica and all the more arbitrarily because we have just referred to his at least apparent humility in the face of the demands of the scenario.

We must likewise refuse to separate, as something against nature, what talent has so closely joined. May De Sica and Zavattini forgive us—and, in advance, the reader, who can have no interest in my scruples and who is waiting for me to get on with my task. I would like it understood, however, for my own peace of mind, that I aim only to attempt a few critical statements which the future will doubtless call into question; they are simply the personal testimony of a French critic writing in 1951 about work full of promise, the qualities of which are particularly resistant to aesthetic analysis. This profession of humility is in no sense just an oratorical precaution or a rhetorical formula. I beg the reader to believe that it is first and foremost the measure of my admiration.

It is by way of its poetry that the realism of De Sica takes on its meaning, for in art, at the source of all realism, there is an aesthetic paradox that must be resolved. The faithful reproduction of reality is not art. We are repeatedly told that it consists in selection and interpretation. That is why up to now the "realist" trends in cinema, as in other arts, consisted simply in introducing a greater measure of reality into the work: but this additional measure of reality was still only an effective way of serving an abstract purpose, whether dramatic, moral, or ideological.

In France, "naturalism" goes hand in hand with the multiplication of novels and plays *à thèse*. The originality of Italian neorealism, as compared with the chief schools of realism that preceded it and with the Soviet cinema, lies in never making reality the servant of some *a priori* point of view. Even the Dziga Vertov theory of the "Kino-eye" only employed the crude reality of everyday events so as to give it a place on the dialectical spectrum of montage. From another point of view, theater (even realist theater) used reality in the service of dramatic and spectacular structure. Whether in the service of the interests of an ideological thesis, of a moral idea, or of a dramatic action, realism subordinates what it borrows from reality to its transcendent needs. Neorealism knows only immanence. It is from appearance only, the simple appearance of beings and of the world, that it knows how to deduce the ideas that it unearths. It is a phenomenology.

In the realm of means of expression, neorealism runs counter to the traditional categories of spectacle—above all, as regards acting. According to the classic understanding of this function, inherited from the theater, the actor expresses something: a feeling, a passion, a desire, an idea. From his attitude and his miming the spectator can read his face like an open book. In this perspective, it is agreed implicitly between spectator and actor that the same psychological causes produce the same physical effect and that one can without any ambiguity pass backwards and forwards from one to the other. This is, strictly speaking, what is called acting.

The structures of the *mise en scène* flow from it: décor, lighting, the angle and framing of the shots, will be more or less expressionistic in their relation to the behavior of the actor. They contribute for their part to confirm the meaning of the action. Finally, the breaking up of the scenes into shots and their assemblage is the equivalent of an expressionism in time, a reconstruction of the event according to an artificial and abstract duration: dramatic duration. There is not a single one of these commonly accepted assumptions of the film spectacle that is not challenged by neorealism.

First, the performance: it calls upon the actor to *be* before expressing himself. This requirement does not necessarily imply doing away with the professional actor but it normally tends to substitute the man in the street, chosen uniquely for his general comportment, his ignorance of theatrical technique being less a positively required condition than a guarantee against the expressionism of traditional acting. For De Sica, Bruno was a silhouette, a face, a way of walking. Second, the setting and the photography: the natural setting is to the artificial set what the amateur actor is to the professional. It has, however, the effect of at least partly limiting the opportunity for plastic compositions available with artificial studio lighting.

But it is perhaps especially the structure of the narrative which is most radically turned upside down. It must now respect the actual duration of the event. The cuts that logic demands can only be, at best, descriptive. The assemblage of the film must never add anything to the existing reality. If it is part of the meaning of the film as with Rossellini, it is because the empty gaps, the white spaces, the parts of the event that we are not given, are themselves of a concrete nature: stones which are missing from the building. It is the same in life: we do not know everything that happens to others. Ellipsis in classic montage is an effect of style. In Rossellini's films it is a lacuna in reality, or rather in the knowledge we have of it, which is by its nature limited.

Thus, neorealism is more an ontological position than an aesthetic one. That is why the employment of its technical attributes like a recipe does not necessarily produce it, as the rapid decline of American neorealism proves. In Italy itself not all films without actors, based on a news item, and filmed in real exteriors, are better than the traditional melodramas and spectacles. On the contrary, a film like *Cronaca di un amore* (1950), by Michelangelo Antonioni can be described as neorealist (in spite of the professional actors, of the detective-story-like arbitrariness of the plot, of expensive settings, and the baroque dress of the heroine) because the director has not relied on an expressionism outside the characters; he builds all his effects on their way of life, their way of crying, of walking, of laughing. They are caught in the maze of the plot like laboratory rats being sent through a labyrinth.

The diversity of styles among the best Italian directors might be advanced as a counter argument, and I know how much they dislike the word neorealist.

Zavattini is the only one who shamelessly admits to the title. The majority protest against the existence of a new Italian school of realism that would include them all. But that is a reflex reaction of the creator to the critic. The director as artist is more aware of his differences than his resemblances. The word neorealist was thrown like a fishing net over the postwar Italian cinema and each director on his own is doing his best to break the toils in which, it is claimed, he has been caught. However, in spite of this normal reaction, which has the added advantage of forcing us to review a perhaps too easy critical classification, I think there are good reasons for staying with it, even against the views of those most concerned.

Certainly the succinct definition I have just given of neorealism might appear on the surface to be given the lie by the work of Lattuada with its calculated, subtly architectural vision, or by the baroque exuberance, the romantic eloquence of De Santis, or by the refined theatrical sense of Visconti, who makes compositions of the most down-to-earth reality as if they were scenes from an opera or a classical tragedy. These terms are summary and debatable, but can serve for other possible epithets which consequently would confirm the existence of formal differences, of oppositions in style. These three directors are as different from one another as each is from De Sica, yet their common origin is evident if one takes a more general view and especially if one stops comparing them with one another and instead looks at the American, French, and Soviet cinema.

Neorealism does not necessarily exist in a pure state and one can conceive of it being combined with other aesthetic tendencies. Biologists distinguish, in genetics, characteristics derived from different parents, so-called dominant factors. It is the same with neorealism. The exacerbated theatricality of Malaparte's *Il Cristo proibito* (1950) may owe a lot to German expressionism, but the film is nonetheless neorealist, radically different from the realist expressionism of a Fritz Lang.

But I seem to have strayed a long way from De Sica. This was simply that I might be better able to situate him in contemporary Italian production. The difficulty of taking a critical stand about the director of *Miracolo a Milano* might indeed be precisely the real indication of his style. Does not our inability to analyze its formal characteristics derive from the fact that it represents the purest form of neorealism, from the fact that *Ladri di biciclette* is the ideal center around which gravitate, each in his own orbit, the works of the other great directors? It could be this very purity which makes it impossible to define, for it has as its paradoxical intention not to produce a spectacle which appears real, but rather to turn reality into a spectacle: a man is walking along the street and the onlooker is amazed at the beauty of the man walking.

Until further information is available, until the realization of Zavattini's dream of filming eighty minutes in the life of a man without a cut, *Ladri di biciclette* is without a doubt the ultimate expression of neorealism. Though this *mise en scène* aims at negating itself, at being transparent to the reality it reveals, it would be naive to conclude that it does not exist. Few films have been more carefully put together, more pondered over, more meticulously elaborated, but all this labor by De Sica tends to give the illusion of chance, to result in giving dramatic necessity the character of something contingent. Better still, he has succeeded in making dramatic contingency the very stuff of drama. Nothing happens in *Ladri di biciclette* that might just as well not have happened. The worker could have chanced upon his bicycle in the middle of the film, the lights in the auditorium would have gone up, and De Sica would have apologized for having disturbed us, but after all, we would be happy for the worker's sake.

The marvelous aesthetic paradox of this film is that it has the relentless quality of tragedy while nothing happens in it except by chance. But it is precisely from the dialectical synthesis of contrary values, namely artistic order and the amorphous disorder of reality, that it derives its originality. There is not one image that is not charged with meaning, that does not drive home into the mind the sharp end of an unforgettable moral truth, and not one that to this end is false to the ontological ambiguity of reality. Not one gesture, not one incident, not a single object in the film is given a prior significance derived from the ideology of the director.

If they are set in order with an undeniable clarity on the spectrum of social tragedy, it is after the manner of the particles of iron filings on the spectrum of a magnet—that is to say, individually; but the result of this art in which nothing is necessary, where nothing has lost the fortuitous character of chance, is in effect to be doubly convincing and conclusive. For, after all, it is not surprising that the novelist, the playwright, or the filmmaker should make it possible for us to hit on this or that idea, since they put them there beforehand, and have seeded their work with them. Put salt into water, let the water evaporate in the fire of reflection, and you will get back the salt. But if you find salt in water drawn directly from a stream, it is because the water is salty by nature. The workman, Bruno, might have found his bike just as he might have won in the lottery—even poor people win lotteries. But this potential capacity only serves to bring out more forcefully the terrible powerlessness of the poor fellow. If he found his bike, then the enormous extent of his good luck would be an even greater condemnation of society, since it would make a priceless miracle, an exorbitant favor, out of the return to a human order, to a natural state of happiness, since it would signify his good fortune at still being poor but able to make a living.

It is clear to what an extent this neorealism differs from the formal concept which consists of decking out a formal story with touches of reality. As for the technique, properly so called, *Ladri di biciclette,* like a lot of other films, was shot in the street with nonprofessional actors but its true merit lies elsewhere: in not betraying the essence of things, in allowing them first of all to exist for their own sakes, freely; it is in loving them in their singular individuality. "My little sister reality," says De Sica, and she circles about him like the birds around Saint Francis. Others put her in a cage or teach her to talk, but De Sica talks with her and it is the true language of reality that we hear, the word that cannot be denied, that only love can utter.

To explain De Sica, we must go back to the source of his art, namely to his tenderness, his love. The quality shared in common by *Miracolo a Milano* and *Ladri di biciclette,* in spite of differences more apparent than real, is De Sica's inexhaustible affection for his characters. It is significant then, in *Miracolo a Milano,* that none of the bad people, even the proud or treacherous ones, are antipathetic. The junkyard Judas who sells his companions' hovels to the vulgar Mobbi does not stir the least anger in the onlookers. Rather would he amuse us in the tawdry costume of the "villain" of melodrama, which he wears awkwardly and clumsily: he is a good traitor. In the same way the new poor, who in their decline still retain the proud ways of their former fine neighborhoods, are simply a special variety of that human fauna and are not therefore excluded from the vagabond community—even if they charge people a *lira* a sunset. And a man must love the sunset with all his heart to come up with the idea of making people pay for the sight of it, and to suffer this market of dupes.

Besides, none of the principal characters in *Ladri di biciclette* is unsympathetic. Not even the thief. When Bruno finally manages to get his hands on him, the public would be morally disposed to lynch him, as the crowd could have done earlier to Bruno. But the spark of genius in this film is to force us to swallow this hatred the moment it is born and to renounce judgment, just as Bruno will refuse to bring charges. The only unsympathetic characters in *Miracolo a Milano* are Mobbi and his acolytes, but basically they do not exist. They are only conventional symbols. The moment De Sica shows them to us at slightly closer quarters, we almost feel a tender curiosity stirring inside us. "Poor rich people," we are tempted to say, "how deceived they are." There are many ways of loving, even including the way of the inquisitor. The ethics and politics of love are threatened by the worst heresies. From this point of view, hate is often more tender, but the affection De Sica feels for his creatures is no threat to them; there is nothing threatening or abusive about it. It is courtly and discreet gentleness, a liberal generosity, and it demands nothing in return. There is no admixture of pity in it even for the poorest or the most wretched,

Miracle in Milan, dir. Vittorio De Sica, 1951.

because pity does violence to the dignity of the man who is its object. It is a burden on his conscience.

The tenderness of De Sica is of a special kind and for this reason does not easily lend itself to any moral, religious, or political generalization. The ambiguities of *Miracolo a Milano* and *Ladri di biciclette* have been used by the Christian Democrats and by the Communists. So much the better: a true parable should have something for everyone. I do not think De Sica and Zavattini were trying to argue anybody out of anything. I would not dream of saying that the kindness of De Sica is of greater value than the third theological virtue [in addition to charity, the other two virtues are faith and hope] or than class consciousness, but I see in the modesty of his position a definite artistic advantage. It is a guarantee of its authenticity while, at the same time, assuring it a universal quality.

This penchant for love is less a moral question than one of personal and ethnic temperament. As for its authenticity, this can be explained in terms of a naturally happy disposition developed in a Neapolitan atmosphere. But these psychological roots reach down to deeper layers than the consciousness cultivated by partisan ideologies. Paradoxically and in virtue of their unique quality, of their inimitable flavor, since they have not been classified in the categories of either morals or politics, they escape the latter's censure, and the Neapolitan charm of De Sica becomes, thanks to the cinema, the most sweeping message of love that our times have heard since Chaplin. To anyone who doubted the importance of this love, it is enough to point out how quick partisan critics were to lay claim to it. What party indeed could afford to leave love to the other? In our day there is no longer a place for unattached love but since each party can with equal plausibility lay claim to being the proprietor of it, it means that much authentic and naïve love scales the walls and penetrates the stronghold of ideologies and social theory.

Let us be thankful to Zavattini and De Sica for the ambiguity of their position—and let us take care not to see it as just intellectual astuteness in the land of Don Camillo, a completely negative concern to give pledges on all sides in return for an all-around censorship clearance. On the contrary it is a positive striving after poetry, the stratagem of a person in love, expressing himself in the metaphors of his time, while at the same time making sure to choose such of them as will open the hearts of everyone. The reason why there have been so many attempts to give a political exegesis to *Miracolo a Milano* is that Zavattini's social allegories are not the final examples of this symbolism, these symbols themselves being simply the allegory of love. Psychoanalysts explain to us that our dreams are the very opposite of a free flow of images. When these express some fundamental desire, it is in order perforce to cross the threshold of the super-ego, hiding behind the mark of a two-fold symbolism, one general, the other individual. But this censorship is not something negative. Without it, without the resistance it offers to the imagination, dreams would not exist.

There is only one way to think of *Miracolo a Milano,* namely as a reflection, on the level of a film dream, and through the medium of the social symbolism of contemporary Italy, of the warm heart of Vittorio De Sica. This would explain what seems bizarre and inorganic in this strange film: otherwise it is hard to understand the gaps in its dramatic continuity and its indifference to all narrative logic.

In passing, we might note how much the cinema owes to a love for living creatures. There is no way of completely understanding the art of Flaherty, Renoir, Vigo, and especially Chaplin unless we try to discover beforehand what particular kind of tenderness, of sensual or sentimental affection, they reflect. In my opinion, the cinema more than any other art is particularly bound up with love. The novelist in his relations to his characters needs intelligence more than love; understanding is his form of loving. If the art of a Chaplin were transposed into literature, it would tend to lapse into

Miracle in Milan, dir. Vittorio De Sica, 1951.

sentimentality; that is why a man like André Suarès [1866–1926], a man of letters *par excellence,* and evidently impervious to the poetry of the cinema, can talk about the "ignoble heart" of Chaplin when this heart brings to the cinema the nobility of myth.

Every art and every stage in the evolution of each art has its specific scale of values. The tender, amused sensuality of Renoir, the more heartrending tenderness of Vigo, achieve on the screen a tone and an accent which no other medium of expression could give them. Between such feelings and the cinema there exists a mysterious affinity that is sometimes denied even to the greatest of men. No one better than De Sica can lay claim to being the successor to Chaplin. I have already remarked how as an actor he has a quality of presence, a light which subtly transforms both the scenario and the other actors to such an extent that no one can pretend to play opposite De Sica as he would opposite someone else. We in France have not hitherto known the brilliant actor who appeared in Camerini's films. He had to become famous as a director before he was noticed by the public. By then he no longer had the physique of a young leading man, but his charm survived, the more remarkable for being the less easy to explain. Even when appearing as just a simple actor in the films of other directors, De Sica was already himself a director since his presence modified the film and influenced its style.

Chaplin concentrates on himself and within himself the radiation of his tenderness, which means that cruelty is not always excluded from his world; on the contrary, it has a necessary and dialectic relationship to love, as is evident from *Monsieur Verdoux* (1947). Charlie is goodness itself, projected onto the world. He is ready to love everything, but the world does not always respond. On the other hand, De Sica the director infuses into his actors the power to love that he himself possesses as an actor. Chaplin also chooses his cast carefully but always with an eye to himself and to putting his character in a better light. We find in De Sica the humanity of Chaplin, but shared with the world at large. De Sica possesses the gift of being able to convey an intense sense of the human presence, a disarming grace of expression and of gesture which, in their unique way, are an irresistible testimony to man. Ricci (*Ladri di biciclette*), Totò (*Miracolo a Milano*), and Umberto D., although greatly differing in physique from Chaplin and De Sica, make us think of them.

It would be a mistake to believe that the love De Sica bears for man, and forces us to bear witness to, is a form of optimism. If no one is really bad, if face to face with each individual human being we are forced to drop our accusation, as was Ricci when he caught up with the thief, we are obliged to say that the evil which undeniably does exist in the world is elsewhere than in the heart of man, that it is somewhere in the order of things. One could say it is in society and be partly right. In one way *Ladri di biciclette*, *Miracolo a Milano*, and *Umberto D.* (1952) are indictments of a revolutionary nature. If there were no unemployment it would not be a tragedy to lose one's bicycle. However, this political explanation does not cover the whole drama. De Sica protests the comparison that has been made between *Ladri di biciclette* and the works of Kafka on the grounds that his hero's alienation is social and not metaphysical. True enough, but Kafka's myths are no less valid if one accepts them as allegories of social alienation, and one does not have to believe in a cruel God to feel the guilt of which Joseph K. is culpable. On the contrary, the drama lies in this: God does not exist; the last office in the castle is empty. Perhaps we have here the particular tragedy of today's world, the raising of a self-deifying social reality to a transcendental state.

The troubles of Bruno and Umberto D. have their immediate and evident causes but we also observe that there is an insoluble residue comprised of the psychological and material complexities of our social relationships, which neither the high quality of an institution nor the good will of our neighbors can dispose of. The nature of the latter is positive and social, but its action proceeds always from a necessity that is at once absurd and imperative. This is, in my opinion, what makes this film so great and so rich. It renders a two-fold justice: one by way of an irrefutable description of the wretched condition of the proletariat, another by way of the implicit and constant appeal of a human need that any society whatsoever must respect. It condemns a world in which the poor are obliged to steal from one another to survive (the police protect the rich only too well) but this imposed condemnation is not enough, because it is not only a given historical institution that is in question or a particular economic set-up, but the congenital indifference of our social organization, as such, to the fortuitousness of individual happiness. Otherwise Sweden could be the earthly paradise, where bikes are left along the sidewalk both day and night.

De Sica loves mankind, his brothers, too much not to want to remove every conceivable cause of their unhappiness, but he also reminds us that every man's happiness is a miracle of love whether in Milan or anywhere else. A society that does not take every opportunity to smother happiness is already better than one which sows hate, but the most perfect still would not create love, for love remains a private matter between man and man. In what country in the world would they keep rabbit hutches in an oil field? In what other would the loss of an administrative document not be as agonizing as the theft of a bicycle? It is part of the realm of politics to think up and promote the objective conditions necessary for human happiness, but it is not part of its essential function to respect its subjective conditions. In the universe of De Sica, there lies a latent pessimism, an unavoidable pessimism we can never be grateful enough to him for, because in it resides the appeal of the potential of man, the witness to his final and irrefutable humanity.

I have used the word love. I should rather have said poetry. These two words are synonymous or at least complementary. Poetry is but the active and creative form of love, its projection into the world. Although spoiled and laid waste by social upheaval, the childhood of the shoeshine boy has retained the power to transform his wretchedness in a dream. In France, in the primary schools, the children are taught to say, "Who steals an egg steals a bull." De Sica's formula is, "Who steals an egg is dreaming of a horse." Totò's miraculous gift, which was handed on to him by his adopted grandmother, is to have retained from childhood an inexhaustible capacity for defense by way of poetry.

The piece of business I find most significant in *Miracolo a Milano* is that of Emma Gramatica rushing toward the spilled milk. It does not matter who else scolds Totò for his lack of initiative and wipes up the milk with a cloth, so long as the quick gesture of the old woman has as its purpose to turn the little catastrophe into a marvelous game, a stream in the middle of a landscape of the same proportion. And so on to the multiplication tables, another profound terror of one's childhood, which, thanks to the little old woman, turns into a

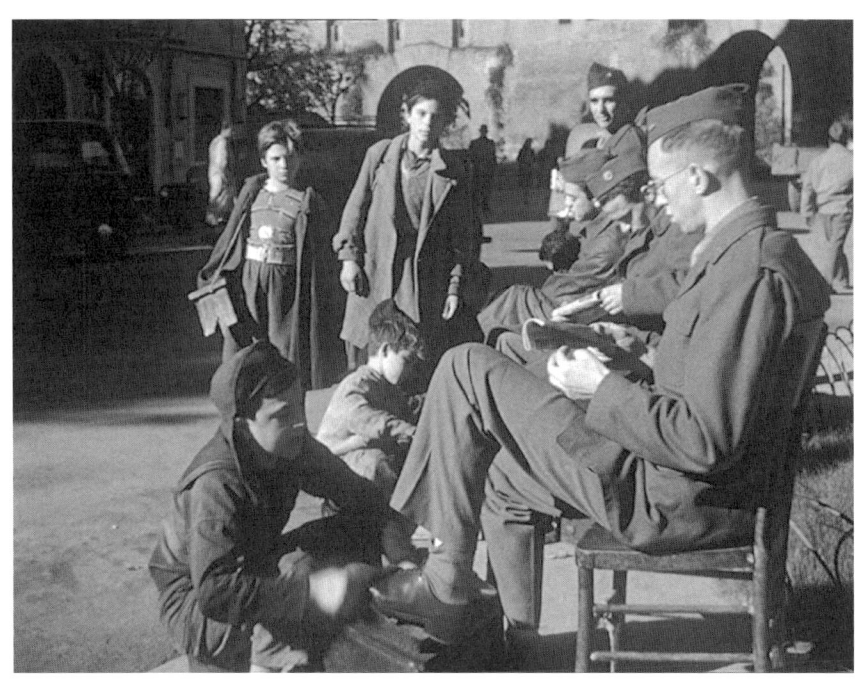

Shoeshine, dir. Vittorio De Sica, 1946.

dream. City dweller Totò names the streets and the squares "four times four is sixteen" or "nine times nine is eighty-one," for these cold mathematical symbols are more beautiful in his eyes than the names of the characters of mythology.

Here again we think of Charlie; he also owes to his childhood spirit his remarkable power of transforming the world to a better purpose. When reality resists him and he cannot materially change it—he switches its meaning. Take, for example, the dance of the rolls, in *The Gold Rush* (1925), or the shoes in the soup pot, with this proviso that, always on the defensive, Charlie reserves his power of metamorphosis for his own advantage, or, at most, for the benefit of the woman he loves. Totò on the other hand goes out to others. He does not give a moment's thought to any benefit the dove can bring him, his joy lies in his being able to spread joy. When he can no longer do anything for his neighbor he takes it on himself to assume various shapes, now limping for the lame man, making himself small for the dwarf, blind for the one-eyed man. The dove is just an arbitrarily added possibility, to give poetry a material form, because most people need something to assist their imaginations. But Totò does not know what to do with himself unless it is for someone else's benefit.

Zavattini told me once: "I am like a painter standing before a field, who asks himself which blade of grass he should begin with." De Sica is the ideal director for a declaration of faith such as this. There is also the art of the playwright who divides the moments of life into episodes which, in respect of the moments lived, are what the blades of grass are to the field. To paint every blade of grass one must be the Douanier Rousseau. In the world of cinema one must have the love of a De Sica for creation itself.

Chapter Eight

"A Saint Becomes a Saint Only After the Fact: *Heaven over the Marshes*"

"Un saint ne l'est qu'après: *La fille des Marais*," *Cahiers du cinéma*, n. 2 (May 1951), pp. 46–48, in *Qu'est-ce que le cinéma?* Vol. 4 (Éditions du Cerf, 1962), pp. 60–64; translated into English by Bert Cardullo.

Italian film not only has good directors, it also has excellent cinematographers, among whom Aldo Tonti (aka G. R. Aldo) is probably one of the best in the world. To be sure, a cinematographer's art may lie in the direction of self-effacement, and Tonti has given us evidence of this. But it seems that in the last few years, more and more plastic composition has become the rule. This has become a way of integrating into realism a vivid and ornate theatricality, which is no less characteristic not only of Italian film but also of Italian artistic sensibility in general. One could even argue that this synthesis is more radically new than the neorealism of *Bicycle Thieves* (1948), which has always been present, as we know, in Italian film, even if not to so great an extent. Opposed to it was the public's more pronounced taste for spectacles with magnificent sets and mammoth crowds.

In *La terra trema* (1948), for instance, one sees very well how Luchino Visconti, whose wonderful *Ossessione* (1942) had initiated the rebirth of Italian realistic cinema, strives to create a necessarily grand synthesis between the most rigorous verisimilitude, on the one hand, and the most plastic composition, on the other—a plasticity that necessarily completely transforms the verism. Whereas the taste for spectacular grandeur expressed itself in the past through the fame of the star, the magnitude of the set, or the number of wild animals deployed, it has come today to be totally subordinate to the most modest, down-to-earth subject matter. Visconti's fishermen are real fishermen, but they have the bearing of tragic princes or operatic leads, and the cinematography confers on their rags the aristocratic dignity of Renaissance brocade.

Using the same cinematographer as Visconti did in *La terra trema*—the amazing Aldo—Augusto Genina has been no less concerned to play the game of realism in *Heaven over the Marshes* (1949). His peasants are as authentic as were Georges Rouquier's in *Farrebique* (1946). Whereas three quarters of Italian films, even those made in studios with professional actors, are post-synchronized, Genina recorded the sound on the spot, and his peasants really say … what they say. When one considers the enormous difficulty of getting nonprofessional actors to speak as naturally as they behave (see, for example, *Farrebique*), one can appreciate the additional amount of work that Genina imposed on himself in order to obey the dictates of realism, right down to the least discernible details. If this were a minor work, one could regard these details as superfluous. But they are, in fact, part of a coherent aesthetic whole whose essential elements are laid down in the initial script.

Heaven over the Marshes is a film about the circumstances that led to the canonization of little Maria Goretti, who was murdered at the age of fourteen by the boy whose sexual advances she had resisted. These factors made me fear the worst. Hagiography is already a dangerous exercise in itself, but, granted, there are some saints made to appear on stained-glass windows and others who seem destined for the painted plaster of Saint-Sulpice Church, whatever their standing in paradise might be. And the case of Maria Goretti doesn't seem to be *a priori* any more promising than that of Saint Thérèse of Lisieux. Less even, for her biography is devoid of extraordinary events; hers is the life of the daughter of a poor family of farmhands in the Pontine marshes near Rome at the turn of the century. No visions, no voices, no signs from heaven: her regular attendance at catechism and the fervor of her first Holy Communion are merely the commonplace signals of a rather commonplace piety. Of course, there is her "martyrdom," but we have to wait until the last fifteen minutes of the film before it occurs, before "something finally happens."

And even this martyrdom: what is it when you take a close look at it and judge the psychological motives behind it? A banal sex crime, a trivial news item devoid of dramatic originality: "Young Peasant Stabs Unwilling Girl to Death." And why? There is not a single aspect of this crime that doesn't have a natural explanation. The resistance of the girl is perhaps nothing but an exaggerated physiological response to the violation of her sense of decency,

Heaven over the Marshes, dir. Augusto Genina, 1949.

the reflex action of a frightened little animal. It's true that she invokes divine will and the threat of hellfire to resist Alessandro. However, it is not necessary to have recourse to the subtleties of psychoanalysis to understand how the imperatives of catechism and the mysticism of first Holy Communion could kindle the imagination of a frightened adolescent.

Even if we take for granted that Maria's Christian upbringing can't be made to substitute for her real, unconscious motives in determining behavior, that behavior still isn't convincing, for we sense that she does indeed love Alessandro. So why all this resistance, which can only have tragic consequences? Either it is a psychological reaction that is stronger than the heart's desire, or it really is the obedience to a moral precept; but isn't this taking morality to an absurd extreme, since it leads to the downfall of two beings who love each other? Moreover, before she dies, Maria asks Alessandro to forgive her for all the trouble she has caused him, that is, for driving him to kill her.

It should not be surprising, therefore, that, at least in France, this saint's life has disappointed the Christians even more than it has the non-believers. The former don't find in it the requisite religious apologetics, and the latter don't find in it the necessary moral apologetics. All that we have here is the senseless crushing of a poor child's life—there are no unusual mitigating circumstances. Maria Goretti is neither Saint Vincent de Paul, nor Saint Teresa of Avila, nor even Bernadette Soubirous. But it is to Genina's credit that he made a hagiography that doesn't prove anything, above all not the sainthood of the saint. Herein lies not only the film's artistic distinction but also its religious one. *Heaven over the Marshes* is a rarity: a good Catholic film.

What was Genina's starting point? It was not simply to reject all the ornament that comes with the subject matter—the religious symbolism and, it goes without saying, the supernatural element of traditional hagiographies (a film such as Léon Carré's *Monsieur Vincent* [1947] also avoids these stumbling blocks). He set out to achieve much more than this: his goal was to create a phenomenology of sainthood. Genina's *mise en scène* is a systematic refusal not only to treat sainthood as anything but a fact, an event occurring in the world, but also to consider it from any point of view other than the external one. He looks at sainthood from the outside, as the ambiguous manifestation of a spiritual reality that is absolutely impossible to prove.

The apologetic nature of most hagiographies supposes, by contrast, that sainthood is conferred *a priori*. Whether it be Saint Thérèse of Lisieux or Saint Vincent de Paul, we are told the life of a saint. Yet, good logic dictates, as does good theology, that a saint becomes a saint only after the fact: when he is canonized; during his lifetime, he is simply *Monsieur Vincent*. It is only by the authoritative judgment of the Holy See that his biography becomes a hagiography. The question raised in film as in theology is the retroactiveness of eternal salvation, since, obviously, a saint does not exist as a saint in the present: he is simply a being who becomes one and who, moreover, risks eternal damnation until his death. Genina's bias in favor of realism made him go as far as to prohibit in any of his images the supposition of his protagonist's "sainthood," so afraid was he of betraying the spirit of his endeavor. She is not, and she must not be, a saint whose martyrdom we witness, but rather the little peasant girl Maria Goretti, whose life we see her live. The camera lens is not the eye of God, and microphones could not have recorded the voices heard by Joan of Arc.

This is why *Heaven over the Marshes* will be disconcerting to viewers who are used to an apologetics that confuses rhetoric with art and sentiment with grace. In a way, Genina plays devil's advocate by playing servant to the only filmic reality possible. But just as canonization hearings are won against the public prosecutor Satan, Maria Goretti's sainthood is served in the only valid manner possible by a film that expressly sets out not to demonstrate it. In short, Genina tells us: "This is Maria Goretti, watch her live and die. *On the other hand,* you know she is a saint. Let those who have eyes to see, read by transparence the evidence of grace in her life, just as you must do at every moment in the events of your own lives." The signs that God sends to his people are not always supernatural. A serpent in a bush is not the devil, but the devil is still there as well as everywhere else.

Chapter Nine

"Neorealism, Opera, and Propaganda" (*Forbidden Christ*)

"Néo-réalisme, opera et propagande (*Le Christ interdit*)," *Cahiers du cinéma*, n. 4 (July–August 1951), 46–51. Translated into English by Bert Cardullo.

The fact that Curzio Malaparte's public personality is an object of scandal does not make a review of *Forbidden Christ* (1950) an easy task. The angry contempt that this picture's author inspires is certainly often based on unfavorable prejudice, which was reflected by his exclusion from the list of honorees at this year's Cannes Film Festival. But, conversely, I fear that the effort at critical objectivity necessary to overcome this prejudice may make me go to the opposite extreme. In short, I do not want the little moral respect I have for Mr. Malaparte to prompt me to declare that *Forbidden Christ* is, "after all," a masterpiece. For I believe that such indeed is the paradox of this astonishing film: that it should so deeply bear the mark of a personality which is almost deprived of nobility and that it should be a great film all the same.

I must perhaps first make a distinction between the explicit content of this work and its aesthetic realization, between its ideological "message" and the form in which that message is cast. But this distinction seems to introduce a second paradox, because *Forbidden Christ* is a thesis film, that is, a genre that is difficult to defend even when one agrees with the thematic intention of the author, and all the more so when one has strong reasons to disagree with it. Let me try, then, to explain these two paradoxes.

The value of *Forbidden Christ* certainly proceeds in the first place from its author's personality. Its success follows in a line of outstanding films from Cocteau's *Blood of a Poet* (1930) to Welles's *Citizen Kane* (1941) and up to Malraux's *Man's Hope* (1945). This success once again demonstrates *a contrario* the professional rigidity, technical onerousness, and other similar problems that weigh negatively on film production throughout the world, such that perhaps it is a good practice to ignore everything that surrounds the making of cinema if one is going to be able to make a good film.

We have been told that Malaparte had a good assistant. Perhaps. We had also been told the same thing about Orson Welles. But if Malaparte's assistant had had some genius, he would not have waited until *Forbidden Christ* to show it. It is nevertheless plausible that he knew his job to perfection and that he was extremely useful to Malaparte, in that he allowed the director to do his work without having to go through a burdensome apprenticeship. This was true of Welles as well, who was lucky to have the cinematographer Gregg Toland as his collaborator on *Citizen Kane*. It is simply childish, however, to ignore the obvious in this case: that Curzio Malaparte remains the one and only author of *Forbidden Christ*, and that this author was until this film a writer who had never seen a camera.

It is unthinkable, though, that a novelist could become from one day to the next a virtuoso accordionist or an extremely talented painter if he hadn't first gone to some music or fine arts school. The great neoclassical artist Jean-Auguste-Dominique Ingres himself had to learn how to play the violin, if only to play it badly. We are always told about filmmaking that the enormity of its technical demands makes it the opposite of all the "individual" arts: music could be played only on a pipe if you so desired; painting can be done on a piece of cardboard with just a few colors; and poetry can be written in a small room on a piece of scrap paper. Still, although the material contingencies of filmmaking have a heavy influence on the production system, they weigh less than a feather at the level of the directing.

It was indeed miraculous that Jean Cocteau found Charles, the Viscount of Noailles, to finance the making of *The Blood of a Poet*, but Cocteau learned how to make a movie faster than how to clean his pipe. It is precisely the technical complexity of filmmaking, which is dialectically opposed to the simplicity and realism of the cinematic image, that frees the author-director from all constraints and allows him to dispense with useless initiations to the profession. Learning how to write takes a long time; learning how to make a film is immediate: all you have to do is go to the movies. For the rest, the assistants, the photographers, the sound engineers, and the electricians are there. From a strictly aesthetic point of view, there is no art whose exercise is simpler than this one. It is Christopher Columbus's egg, and a golden egg, to be sure: an utterly brilliant discovery that seems obvious only after the fact.

The honest pessimists will admit that *Forbidden Christ* is an extraordinary film, but they will invoke the charm and daring of ignorance to explain its creation. They will say that its strange beauty originates, in fact, from an indifference to the rules of directing on the part of an intelligent writer who has a visual talent, but they will warn us against the limitations of such success. Cocteau says that Chaplin admired a certain cut of the camera in *The Blood of a Poet* because it was completely heretical. But this was only an editing error that the author would not have permitted himself in his second film. One could phrase the matter as follows: "If the heavens, helped by masochistic or unconscious capitalists, were to sting novelists and poets with the cinematic venom, we would be graced with many a thrilling film, but their general benefit for the art of cinema could only be illusory. Ultimately, cinema is made by the likes of André Berthomieu and René Clair. Exceptions like Cocteau and Malaparte just confirm the rule."

I would answer, quite the contrary, that these filmic exceptions all have an aesthetic significance of exceptional importance, that the absence of follow-up films on the part of the author is beside the point, and that the only thing one should deduce from such an absence is the victorious revenge of routine. *Citizen Kane* happened to triumph over Hollywood and to force a lasting reconsideration of technical habits and routines; even *The Blood of a Poet* has had some influence, though it may be owed entirely and exclusively to Cocteau. And although it is true that, for various reasons, *Man's Hope* has not had a direct influence on film production, one can very well discern in it *a posteriori* its prophetic quality.

As early as 1936, André Malraux had posited the principles of both neorealism—which was to triumph ten years later—and the film adaptation of novels, a vein that is far from exhausted. The prewar critics who saw in *Man's Hope* only the fluke of individual genius, without any resonance apart from Malraux's literary work, thus seriously underestimated this film's aesthetic significance. Relatively speaking, and of course without granting to *Forbidden Christ* the intrinsic as well as extrinsic importance of *Man's Hope,* it is nonetheless possible to situate the originality of Malaparte's film in the context of contemporary cinema in general and of Italian neorealism in particular.

I have underlined in connection with Augusto Genina's *Heaven over the Marshes* (1949) the efforts of Italian filmmakers to "go beyond" neorealism and in fact to go back through neorealism to the theatrical and spectacular tradition that is dialectically opposed to it. Neorealism has not been the flash in the pan to which some skeptics thought they could reduce it, but it is true that this style is now nearing its limits. After De Sica's *Bicycle Thieves* (1948), which is to Italian neorealism what Racine's *Phaedra* (1677) is to French neoclassicism, neorealism probably has more of a past than a future, at least in its pure form of the dramaturgy of everyday events. It is significant that it is precisely De Sica who should have made *Miracle in Milan* (1951), thus moving from the realistic style of Lumière to the fantastic one of Méliès. Onto the solid and vital staff of realism, Italian filmmakers obviously have tried to graft different styles: Visconti with *La terra trema* (1948), Antonioni in *Story of a Love Affair* (1950), Genina in *Heaven over the Marshes,* and Lattuada with *The Mill on the Po* (1949)—all of these venture down divergent paths, but neorealism is their common crossroads in the movement away from the formalist tradition against which postwar Italian cinema seemed to be directly reacting.

It is in such an evolution, beginning in neorealism but diverging from it, that one must first situate *Forbidden Christ,* which is one of the most significant examples of this trend. In this respect, and with regard to Italian cinema, Malaparte more or less consciously goes back to a certain theatrical vein, a particular cinematic *bel canto,* inspired by Giovanni Pastrone's *Cabiria* (1914) as it were, but more generally by the Italian artistic temperament itself. This remark is made to appease those who are reluctant to acknowledge in Malaparte too much cinematic creativity, but I should add immediately that *Forbidden Christ* has an absolute originality of its own, such that there is little point in trying to reduce it to any earlier artistic manifestations or traditions.

Starting from neorealism, whose essential characteristics (natural settings, realistic make-up and costumes, nonprofessional walk-ons, etc.) he respects, Malaparte uses it with a certain freedom that verges on fantasy. Although real, his landscapes are as fantastic as the day after the end of the world. Bruno Baldi's village and the relativistic treatment of the architecture, as well as the characters, seem issued directly from a de Chirico painting. If this universe of stone, of earth, and of men is nevertheless as real as it would be in a documentary, its *time* and its *space* are as unreal and artificial as those of nightmares and tragedies. The action proceeds not at all according to logical or psychological necessity, but as it would in the world of parables. The living beings are therefore there when it is *necessary, where* it is necessary, according to a transcendent causality that owes nothing to chance or accident. They do not step into the shot, they *appear* in it.

The concrete duration of the action itself is indiscernible, just as it is within the twenty-four-hour framework of a classical tragedy. The geographical space is equally stylized, reduced to dramatic areas or locations where events polarized by destiny take place: the countryside around the village, which shows the lunar face of a planet devastated by history; the squares, the walls, the streets, the houses—all of these are not those of a village like any other with its days and its nights, but part of a labyrinth conniving with the

Forbidden Christ, dir. Curzio Malaparte, 1950.

minotaur that Bruno has come to fight. The living beings who inhabit it are, like him, masked in enigma, remoteness, silence. Even the eyes of love look inward to leave this loved one to his loneliness. Tragic convention reigns in this film, then, and it does so with crushing efficiency. Unlike the theater, the cinema invents here a visible, concrete Mount Olympus that is as true as light and sun. One need mention only two scenes in order to grasp clearly the role that Malaparte thus gives to space and time in *Forbidden Christ*.

First, the scene at the fair, leading up to the drama of the cross, which is treated as a dramatic *ballet* within the well-specified framework of the market square, with the movement of the crowd that turns away from the stands, the carousels, and the fire-eaters in order to gather in front of the natural proscenium where the cross has been erected. An extraordinarily agile, continuous, and descriptive piece of editing takes us along with the hero, into the crowd. This sequence is then brutally interrupted by a cut to the quick hammering rhythm of the drums of the procession; a series of close-ups dissolves the unity of the previous space and the duration of the action inside it, but brings them back together again in a new rhythm at the other end of the square. The camera next flies over the crowd, which looks like an ant hill; it shows from above the entire dramatic area that it had earlier revealed to us only at ground level. Everything is orchestrated in a relentless choreographic tempo, with a surprisingly rigorous sense of the complementary roles of camera movement, editing, and character placement.

The scene of the suspended execution is less complex but even more significant. It takes place in two different locations: the market square of the village and the countryside around it. The announcement of the event causes some commotion in the population, as the women gather in a chorus and overwhelm the hero with their silent reprobation. After forgiveness is granted, everybody goes back to the village. The return of Bruno is filmed from very high up; he enters the square where, in expectation of the murder, all life seems as though it has coagulated into motionless human groups. Time itself seems suspended: it is no longer that of everyday life, of reality, but that of tragedy. When destiny is vanquished, life can resume: as Bruno appears, the church's bell strikes the hour, and suddenly it is as if nothing had happened; time flows again, indifferent to the hero as well as to the one who was to be his victim, dogs bark, and men's lives resume, oblivious to the gods.

Malaparte evidences this exceptional feeling for stylization not only in these scenes but also in the dialogue. Take, for instance, the conversation on the bed where the fiancée admits that she is having an affair with Bruno's brother, as the position of their bodies seems to offer them up for crucifixion on the very diagonals of the screen. Let's not dwell on it here, but there are few works in which one can witness such a masterful control of the plastic significance of cinematic space and the figurative significance of screen time. Malaparte may be "neorealist" if one judges him by the currency or relevance of his subject matter and the very substance of his film, but this realism expresses itself in *Forbidden Christ* in the aesthetics of dream, tragedy, and opera. Let me now judge this film in comparison with the rest of the world's cinematic output during the 1950–1951 season.

Forbidden Christ is a film with a thesis or, more accurately, a propaganda film. The whole aesthetic of the picture is thus geared toward eloquent rhetoric. The problem is that didacticism, apologetics, and politics still remain the major scandals—and virtual unknowns—of the cinema. Novels, paintings, and plays with a thesis have themselves not survived the nineteenth century. The least we can say about the current attempts to restore the genre, in art as in literature, is that they are hardly convincing. Only the screen has provided the twentieth century with unquestionable instances of a propagandistic art that can sustain comparison with any of the classical aesthetic categories. But it also appears that the wonderful conjunction of politics and art that established the grandeur of the Soviet cinema from 1925 to the mid-1930s is a well-kept secret, partially and episodically retrieved by contemporary Soviet

Forbidden Christ, dir. Curzio Malaparte, 1950.

cinema in a chance scene, or part of it, but never on the scale of whole works with their concepts intact. It would be childish, however, to remain blind to the current ideological needs of art. It does not matter if communism is the direct cause of this blindness or reactionism: the cinema cannot afford to ignore its own propagandistic power, even less so today, in 1951, than in 1925. The ideas of our time will use it, with or without artistic merit—and use it with all efficiency.

But whatever we think—and I think mostly bad things—about what Curzio Malaparte wants to tell us, he says it with eloquence. It has generally been admitted that his film contains some beautiful moments of "silent cinema," only to be followed by disparaging comments about this picture's endless wordiness. That would amount to a genuine misunderstanding, though, because Malaparte's fundamental originality in *Forbidden Christ* lies precisely in the relationship he introduces between word and image. The crucial moment of any film adaptation of a novel, which Malraux aptly called "the transition to dialogue," becomes here the transition to speechifying.

Let me stress that, paradoxically, such speechifying even haunted the silent Soviet cinema. How could an ideological cinema do totally without words, which still remain the surest way, if not to persuade viewers, at least to communicate ideas to them? After all, speeches—the harangues of a meeting or an assembly—are the capital events of political life. A silent revolution would be an historical monster. But filming the facial expressions of a mute orator would be a ridiculous act whose horror is surpassed only by the addition of the sound of his voice. Useful and economical in political reality, speeches are among the most terrifying stumbling blocks of propaganda films. Should cinema, then, renounce the recourse to speech in a genre that really cannot not do without it? It is for this aesthetic contradiction that Malaparte seems to have found an aesthetically satisfying solution.

People talk a lot in *Forbidden Christ,* but their speeches are a lot like opera-singing: the dialogue has no pretense to dramatic or psychological realism; it is a kind of ideological *bel canto* prepared for by the orchestration of the images. Yet it is the stylization of these images that elevates the words to the highest level. There is no discrepancy, then, between the film's speeches and its visual expression, but there is a dialectical alternation between two modes of eloquence, one of them having in itself no more importance than the libretto of an opera. To be sure, the ideas of Curzio Malaparte are as meaningless as his talent is great, and this distinction is made possible precisely because we are dealing here with the aesthetics of propaganda; but the fact that such a distinction is possible at all is already a achievement, for the traditional curse of authors who have a thesis to defend is that they usually fail on both counts: that is, on the levels of both art and propaganda.

Perhaps we should demand nothing more from ideological cinema than a kind of formalism that is open to the defense of any idea or action. This, after all, is what we expect from a good lawyer; it does remain, however, that a lawyer with a solid case is more convincing to us. It is Emile Zola's declaration "J'accuse" (1898) that has become famous, not Jean-Herold Paquis's Fascist diatribes during the war, even if Paquis was not the worst of Cicero's students. This is why *Forbidden Christ* is a failure with regard to its author's explicit intentions. But the mediocrity of Malaparte's cause should not blind us to the strength of his plea. The film's admirable technique deserves to be praised all the more since it seems to me to be independent of its political content.

It is thus legitimate to distinguish in *Forbidden Christ* between two radically different levels of expression: that of artistic form, which is akin, as we have seen, to the structures of tragedy and fantasy; and that of ideological discourse. The latter of itself does not fit into any of the traditional aesthetic categories: it borrows from them only their efficacy, even as the opera libretto does from the singers in tandem with the orchestra. And the prosaicism if not persuasiveness of the ideological discourse—of the ideas—benefits from the lyrical stylization of the story; as such, the text exists only in the mode of the recitative, the duet, and the chorus.

I would happily compare *Forbidden Christ* to the final experiments of Sergei Eisenstein. The obvious formalism of *Alexander Nevsky* (1938) and of *Ivan the Terrible* (1944) had only the most accidental of relationships with these films' historical theses. (It may be necessary to recall here that Eisenstein has made his self-criticism of *Ivan the Terrible* only in regard to its screenplay and historicism, and not at all in regard to the directing—as some people too often think.) With the different kind of genius Eisenstein obviously had, he tried to find, just as Malaparte is doing in his film, a new solution to the demands of propaganda in a certain expressiveness or theatricalization of the *mise en scène* that was akin to opera. The result was absolutely great, but it was also clearly a dead end, because Eisenstein, as he was paradoxically turning away from realism, went back to the German expressionism of the 1920s with his production of *The Battleship Potemkin* (1925), thus reneging on twenty years of cinematic evolution. The cunning, if not the genius, of Curzio Malaparte is to perform the same operation all over again, starting from neorealism and similarly shortchanging the evolution of cinema. His propaganda piece known as *Forbidden Christ* is to contemporary film what Gian Carlo Menotti's opera *The Consul* (1950) is to the lyric repertoire.

Chapter Ten

"The Road to Hope"

"*Le chemin de l'espérance (Il cammino della speranza)*," *Cahiers du cinéma*, n. 20 (February 1952), in *Qu'est-ce que le cinéma?* Vol. 4 (Éditions du Cerf, 1962), pp. 65–67; translated into English by Bert Cardullo.

The Road to Hope (1950) is one of the most beautiful postwar Italian films on the eminently epic, and hence cinematic, theme of the journey to the Promised Land. Some Sicilians, who have been reduced to unemployment by the closing down of the sulfur mines, leave with their families for France, where a crooked labor recruiter has promised them they will find work. The road is long, from the snows of Mount Etna to those of the Saint Gothard Pass [in the Alps on the border between France and Italy]. Abandoned by their guide, hunted down by the police, chased by the farm workers whose strike they have unwittingly broken to earn a few *lire*, the survivors of this illegal emigration finally get to see the Promised Land from the top of a pass in the Alps, which an officer of the Alpine police will compassionately allow them to descend.

This "European" happy ending should not mislead us as to the real ending called for by the film: Sisyphuses to their misery and their despair, these Sicilians cannot but be driven back once more up the symbolic slopes of Mount Etna because of the social chaos that awaits them below. Thus the Promised Land is in fact just an absurd paradise where only grapes of wrath can grow. One can only regret Pietro Germi's concessionary and timid attitude toward this wonderful subject, which he doesn't always treat with the necessary rigor. A nasty crime story, complete with sentimental complication, needlessly encumbers the film, apparently for the edification of all the housewives of the world. His only excuse for this strand, and almost a valid one, is the taciturn beauty of Elena Varzi, whose stubborn brow bears the mark of the saber of destiny.

The Road to Hope, dir. Pietro Germi, 1950.

Pietro Germi is a young director in whom some Italian critics would like to see a brilliant hope for the future. It's possible, if he isn't consumed first by formalism or by a harking back to Eisensteinian rhetoric, to which Germi's *In the Name of the Law* (1949) and above all his recent *Il brigante di Tacca del Lupo* (1952) dangerously testify more than does *The Road to Hope*. But if *The Road to Hope* is a far cry from the masterpieces of neorealism, it can at least pride itself on indicating more clearly than other films the shift that has occurred in Italian filmmaking, the transformation from a neorealism of war, if you will (*Rome, Open City* [1945], *Paisan* [1946], *Shoeshine* [1946], and other films inspired by the Liberation and its aftermath), to a neorealism of peace, to which De Sica's *Bicycle Thieves* (1948) stands as the unforgettable introduction.

The fact is that the social reality of postwar Italy remains essentially dramatic, or even more precisely: tragic. The fear of misery because of unemployment plays the role of a fateful menace in the lives of the people. Living means trying to escape from this predicament. Working and, through work, keeping one's basic human dignity, the right to minimal happiness and love—these are the sole concerns of the protagonists of Renato Castellani's *Two Cents' Worth of Hope* (1951), just as they are of the protagonists of *The Road to Hope* or *Bicycle Thieves*. Of this fundamental theme, upon which screenwriters can fashion a thousand variations, one could say that it is the negative of the theme that inspires perhaps more than half of all American films.

The Road to Hope, dir. Pietro Germi, 1950.

Many scripts, most of them written for American comedies, are in fact built on the pursuit of wealth or at least on the obsession with success, which for women means the conquest of some Prince Charming who is the heir to an industrial tycoon. Conversely, the neorealistic protagonist does not dream at all of asserting himself through ambition: he simply tries not to let himself be overcome by misery. Because unemployment can make him lapse into nothingness, "two cents' worth of hope" are enough to buy his happiness. So, as one might have surmised, the documentary substance of Italian neorealism achieves the dignity of art only insofar as it rediscovers in itself the great dramatic archetypes upon which our empathy is, and always will be, founded.

Chapter Eleven

"*Two Cents' Worth of Hope*"

"*Deux sous l'espoir*," *France-Observateur* (July 1952), in *Qu'est-ce que le cinéma?* Vol. 4 (Éditions du Cerf, 1962), pp. 68–72; translated into English by Bert Cardullo.

The Italian critics have said that neorealism doesn't exist, and the French critics that it won't last. I think that in reality only Cesare Zavattini and Roberto Rossellini have unabashedly embraced the term, although each has attached a different meaning to it. If you want to hurt any other Italian filmmaker, all you have to do is congratulate him on his contribution to neorealism. In truth the Italians are more irritated than pleased with the success they have had under this generic label; consequently, each one defends himself against the term's suggestion of a unified movement. There are probably two related reasons for this. The first is completely psychological and quite understandable: the irritation of any artist who is conscious of his uniqueness, which the critics attempt to smother with an historical classification. Neorealism throws apples and oranges into the same bag. There is at least as much difference, for example, among Alberto Lattuada, Luchino Visconti, and Vittorio De Sica as there is among Marcel Carné, Jean Renoir, and Jacques Becker. Yet with the term "neorealism," the critics often seem to be implying that Italian film exists as a movement, as a collective sensibility, rather than as a series of individual talents. One can understand the filmmakers' reaction.

But more important still than these natural reactions of artistic pride, it seems to me, is the bias against "realism." When neorealism first astonished the world, critics praised everything that was documentary about it, its sense of social reality—in short, everything that made it look like a news report. The Italian filmmakers rightly realized the danger that lay in that kind of praise.

The prestige of a documentary could only be accidental and minor. Once the exoticism of authentic documentaries, on the one hand, and the bias in their favor due to the war, on the other, had worn off, the popularity of Italian film would not have lasted if it had been grounded only in realism. Indeed, art aims to go beyond reality, not to reproduce it. And this is even truer of film because of its technical realism, its ability to reproduce reality so easily. The Italian directors, then, continue to resist as much as they can when the critics try to place the yoke of neorealism around their necks.

We often marveled in France at the success of Italian film production during the years 1946 and 1947, as if it were a sort of miracle, or at the very least the dazzling result of favorable, though precarious, circumstances: the sudden fertilization by the Liberation of an old and minor tendency in Italian film [the realist or "verismo" style from the years 1913–1916, inspired by the writings of Verga and Zola]. But such unforeseen brilliance could only be that of a nova, and as such couldn't last. Besides, a type of filmmaking that would lay more stress on the material photographed than on the subject treated, on the pictorial rather than on the narrative—that would substitute reality for the imagination—would sooner or later have to lose its luster.

Bicycle Thieves (1948) was the first great work to prove, not only that neorealism could survive very well without the themes of the Liberation, that its subject matter was by no means directly linked to the war or its aftermath, but also that neorealism's apparent lack of "story," of plot or action, was not in the least a sign of its inferiority to the structures of classical film narrative. De Sica and Zavattini's film has at once the accidental freedom of life seen through a window and the relentless force of ancient tragedy. For those who still have doubts about the present and future vigor of neorealism, Renato Castellani's *Two Cents' Worth of Hope* (1951), which received the Grand Prize this year at the Cannes Film Festival, presents another irrefutable argument. This pure masterpiece, although its tone is quite different from that of *Bicycle Thieves*, proves once again that the Italian cinema has managed to discover a new relationship between the realistic calling of film and the eternal demands of dramatic poetry.

Two Cents' Worth of Hope is the story of an unemployed Romeo by the name of Antonio. After being discharged from military service, he goes back to his native village, where his mother and young sisters are as poverty-stricken as when he left them. With fierce determination he looks for work, but life is tough and unemployment is the common lot of many men his age. Because he is ready to take anything, even the dirtiest of jobs, he will from time to time find employment; most often it will be for a very short period, although sometimes there's a chance it will last. But then there is Juliet. Her

Two Cents' Worth of Hope, dir. Renato Castellani, 1951.

name is Carmela, she is fifteen or sixteen years old, and she is the daughter of a respectable firecracker manufacturer who doesn't want to hear about the possibility of an unemployed son-in-law.

In fact, though, Antonio has only a very slight weakness for this girl who is enamored of him. He had forgotten her while he was in the army. He tries to get rid of her, since he has enough worries for the moment trying to feed his family. But Carmela clings to Antonio with incredible patience and cunning; she looks for every opportunity to arouse him and to compromise them both in the eyes of the village and her parents. The principal result of her plotting is that Antonio loses the jobs he had so painfully managed to find, among them a peculiar one as the private blood donor to the anemic child of a Neapolitan bourgeoise. Thus, not only does Antonio not want Carmela at all, but also her indiscreet attentions to him jeopardize the marriage she dreams of, since, without a job, Antonio can't even think of marrying her.

Carmela's love strategy has paradoxical results, however. Even though he has many reasons to hate her, Romeo finally begins to be attracted to Juliet. He's not going to let it be said that his life has been poisoned to such an extent by a girl he does not even love. So many problems at least deserve a wife, but her father, the firecracker manufacturer, refuses to give his blessing. He accuses Antonio of trying to force his way into an honorable and relatively well-off family. Mad with wounded dignity, Antonio strips Carmela bare on the village square: he will take her naked, just as she was born; her only dowry will be the two cents' worth of hope that enable poor people to go on living.

Two Cents' Worth of Hope, dir. Renato Castellani, 1951.

One can see that this story doesn't have the tragic ending of *Romeo and Juliet* [a version of which Castellani (1913–1985) went on to make in 1954: *Giulietta e Romeo*]. But one cannot help thinking of their love story in connection with this film, not only because of certain precise analogies, such as the antagonism between the families, but also, and above all, because of the extraordinary poetry of the sentiments and the passions, the thoroughly Shakespearean imagination that inspires them.

One can easily understand why and how neorealism has managed to triumph over its aesthetic contradictions in this marvelous film. Castellani is one of those whom the label "neorealist" irritates. And yet, his film completely observes the canons of neorealism: it is a remarkable report on rural unemployment in the Vesuvian region of contemporary Italy. All the characters are naturally drawn from the premises (especially Antonio's mother, an incredible gossip who is toothless, loud, and delightfully sly). The script's structure, for its part, is typically neorealistic: the episodes are not causally connected, or, in any event, they lack dramatic necessity. The narrative is rhapsodic, and the film would last two more hours with no effect whatsoever on its unity. This is because the events don't stretch along an *a priori* continuum; they follow one another accidentally, like events in real life.

But it goes without saying that the reality of *Two Cents' Worth of Hope* is that of poetry itself, and that freer, less obvious harmonies are substituted in this tale for dramatic necessities. I mean "tale" here in the Oriental sense,

Romeo and Juliet, dir. Renato Castellani, 1954.

which suggests a simple, leisurely story, more or less loosely organized. Thus, Castellani perfectly realizes the paradox of giving us one of the most beautiful, most pure love stories in the history of film, evoking Marivaux and Shakespeare in the process, while at the same time he gives us the most exact account, the most ruthless indictment, of Italian rural poverty in 1951.

Chapter Twelve

"*Umberto D.*: A Great Work"

"Un grande œuvre: *Umberto D.*," *France-Observateur* (October 1952), in *Qu'est-ce que le cinéma?* (Cerf, 1975 [single-volume version]), pp. 331–335; translated into English by Hugh Gray in *What Is Cinema?* Vol. 2 (Univ. of California Press, 1971), pp. 79–82, and edited below by Bert Cardullo.

Until I saw *Umberto D.* (1952), I considered *Ladri di biciclette* (1948) as having reached the uttermost limits of neorealism so far as the concept of narrative is concerned. It seems to me today that *Ladri di biciclette* falls far short of the ideal Zavattini subject. Not that I consider *Umberto D.* superior. The unmatchable superiority of *Ladri di biciclette* still resides in the paradox of its having reconciled radically opposite values: factual freedom and narrative discipline. But the authors only achieve this by sacrificing the continuum of reality. In *Umberto D.* one catches a glimpse, on a number of occasions, of what a truly realist cinema of time could be, a cinema of "duration."

These experiments in continuous time are not new in cinema. Alfred Hitchcock's *Rope* (1948), for example, runs for eighty uninterrupted minutes. But there it was just a question of action such as we have in the theater. The real problem is not the continuity of the exposed film but the temporal structure of the incident. *Rope* could be filmed without a change of focus, without any break in the shots, and still provide a dramatic spectacle, because in the original play the incidents were already set in order dramatically according to an artificial time—theatrical time—just as there is musical time and dance time.

In at least two scenes of *Umberto D.* the problem of subject and script take on a different aspect. In these instances it is a matter of making "life time"—the simple continuing to be of a person to whom nothing in particular happens—take on the quality of a spectacle, of a drama. I am thinking in particular of when Umberto D. goes to bed, having retired to his room thinking he has a fever and, especially, of the little servant girl's awakening in the morning. These two sequences undoubtedly constitute the ultimate in "performance" of a certain kind of cinema, at the level of what one would call "the invisible subject," by which I mean the subject entirely dissolved in the fact to which it has given rise. Whereas when a film is taken from a story, the latter continues to survive by itself like a skeleton without its muscles; one can always "tell" the story of the film.

The function of the subject is here no less essential than the story but its essence is reabsorbed into the scenario. To put it another way, the subject exists before the working scenario, but it does not exist afterward. Only the "fact" exists which the subject had itself forecast. If I try to recount the film to someone who has not seen it—for example, what Umberto D. is doing in his room or the little servant Maria in the kitchen, what is there left for me to describe? An impalpable show of gestures without meaning, from which the person I am talking to cannot derive the slightest idea of the emotion that gripped the viewer. The subject here is sacrificed beforehand, like the wax in the casting of the bronze.

At the scenario level this type of subject corresponds, reciprocally, to the scenario based entirely on the behavior of the actor. Since the real time of the narrative is not that of the drama but the concrete duration of the character, this objectiveness can only be transformed into a *mise en scène* (scenario and action) in terms of something totally subjective. I mean by this that the film is identical with what the actor is doing and with this alone. The outside world is reduced to being an accessory to this pure action, which is sufficient to itself in the same way that algae deprived of air produce the oxygen they need. The actor who gives a representation of a particular action, who "interprets a part" always, in a measure, directs himself because he is calling more or less on a system of generally accepted dramatic conventions which are learned in conservatories. Not even these conventions are any help to him here. He is entirely in the hands of the director in this complete replica of life.

True, *Umberto D.* is not a perfect film like *Ladri di biciclette*, but this is perhaps understandable since its ambition was greater. Less perfect in its entirety but certainly more perfect and more unalloyed in some of its parts—those in which De Sica and Zavattini exhibit complete fidelity to the aesthetic of neorealism. That is why one must not accuse *Umberto D.* of facile sentimentality, some measure of modest appeal to social pity. The good qualities and even, for that matter, the defects of the film are far beyond any categories

Umberto D., dir. Vittorio De Sica, 1952.

of morality or politics. We are dealing here with a cinematographic "report," a disconcerting and irrefutable observation on the human condition. One may or may not find it to one's taste that this report should be made on the life of a minor functionary boarding with a family or on a little pregnant servant; but, certainly, what we have just learned about this old man and this girl as revealed through their accidental misfortunes above all concerns the human condition. I have no hesitation in stating that the cinema has rarely gone such a long way toward making us aware of what it is to be a man. (And also, for that matter, of what it is to be a dog.)

Hitherto dramatic literature has provided us with a doubtless exact knowledge of the human soul, but one which stands in the same relation to man as classical physics to matter—what scientists call macrophysics, useful only for phenomena of considerable magnitude. And certainly the novel has gone to extremes in categorizing this knowledge. The emotional physics of a Proust is microscopic. But the matter with which this microphysics is concerned is on the inside. It is memory. The cinema is not necessarily a substitute for the novel in this search after man, but it has at least one advantage over it, namely, that it presents man only in the present: to the "time lost and found" of Proust there corresponds in a measure the "time discovered" of Zavattini; this is, in the contemporary cinema, something like Proust in the present indicative tense.

A conspiracy of silence, a sullen and obstinate reticence, is building up against *Umberto D.*, however, and as a result even the good that has been written about it seems to condemn the film with faint praise—though it is a kind of mute ill humor or even contempt (to which no one is prepared to admit in view of the illustrious past of its makers) that in secret animates the hostility of more than one critic. There will certainly be no "Battle of *Umberto D.*" And yet it is one of the most revolutionary and courageous films of the last two years—not only of the Italian cinema but of European cinema as a whole, a masterpiece to which film history is certainly going to grant a place of honor, even if for the moment an inexplicable failure of attention or a certain blindness on the part of those who love the cinema allows it only a reluctant and ineffective esteem.

If there are lines outside theaters showing Christian-Jaque's *Adorables créatures* (1952) or Henri Verneuil's *Le fruit défendu* (1952), it is perhaps in part because the brothels have been closed; all the same, there should be a few thousand of people in Paris who expect other pleasures from film. For the Paris public to be properly shamed, must *Umberto D.* leave the marquees before it has had the kind of run it deserves?

Umberto D., dir. Vittorio De Sica, 1952.

The chief reason for the misunderstandings that have arisen about *Umberto D.* lies in comparing it with *Ladri di biciclette*. Some will say with some semblance of reason that De Sica "returns to neorealism" here, after the poetico-realist interlude of *Miracolo a Milano*. (*Miracolo a Milano* [1951] itself created only audience discord. In the absence of the general enthusiasm that greeted *Ladri di biciclette*, the originality of the scenario, the mixture of the fantastic and the commonplace, and the penchant of our time for political cryptography stirred up around this strange film a sort of *succès de scandale*.) This is true, but only if one hastens to add that the perfection of *Ladri di biciclette* was only a beginning, though it was first regarded as a culmination. It took *Umberto D.* to make us understand what it was in the realism of *Ladri di biciclette* that was still a concession to classical dramaturgy. Consequently what is so unsettling about *Umberto D.* is primarily the way it rejects any relationship to traditional film spectacle.

Of course, if we take just the theme of the film, we can reduce it to a seemingly "populist" melodrama with social pretensions, an appeal on behalf of the middle class: a retired minor official reduced to penury decides against suicide because he can neither find someone to take care of his dog nor pluck up enough courage to kill it before he kills himself. This final episode is not the moving conclusion to a dramatic series of events. If the classical concept of "construction" still has some meaning here, the sequence of events which De Sica reports obeys a necessity that has nothing to do with dramatic structure. What kind of causal relationship could you establish between a harmless angina for which Umberto D. will be treated in hospital, his landlady's turning him out on the street, and his thinking of suicide? The notice to vacate was served irrespective of the angina. A "dramatic author" would have made the angina acute in order to establish a logical and a pathetic relationship between the two things. Here, on the contrary, the period in hospital is in effect hardly justified by the real state of Umberto D.'s health; rather than making us pity him for his unhappy lot, it is really a rather cheerful episode.

That is not where the question lies, though. It is not his real poverty that moves Umberto D. to despair, though it is in a very real sense a contributing factor, but only in the degree that it shows him just how lonely he is. The few things which Umberto D. must rely on others to do for him are all it takes to alienate his few human contacts. To the extent that it is indeed the middle class that is involved, the film reports the secret misery, the egoism, the lack of fellow-feeling which characterizes its members. Its protagonist advances step by step further into his solitude: the person closest to him, the only one to show him any tenderness, is his landlady's little maid; but her kindness and her good will cannot prevail over her worries as an unwed mother-to-be. Through his one friendship, then, there runs the motif of despair.

But here I am now lapsing back into traditional critical concepts, though I am talking about a film whose originality I set out to prove. If one assumes some distance from the story and can still see in it a dramatic patterning, some general development in character, a single general trend in its component events, this is only after the fact. The narrative unit is not the episode, the event, the sudden turn of events, or the character of its protagonists; it is the succession of concrete instants of life, no one of which can be said to be more important than another, for their ontological equality destroys drama at its very basis. One wonderful sequence to which I refer above—it will remain one of the high points of film—is a perfect illustration of this approach to narrative and thus to direction: the scene in which the maid gets up.

The camera confines itself to watching her doing her little chores: moving around the kitchen still half asleep, drowning the ants that have invaded the sink, grinding the coffee. The cinema here is conceived as the exact opposite of that "art of ellipsis" to which we are much too ready to believe it devoted. Ellipsis is a narrative process; it is logical in nature and so it is abstract as well; it presupposes analysis and choice; it organizes the facts in accord with the general dramatic direction to which it forces them to submit. On the contrary, De Sica and Zavattini attempt to divide the event up into still smaller events and these into events smaller still, to the extreme limits of our capacity to perceive them in time. Thus, the unit event in a classical film would be "the maid's getting out of bed"; two or three brief shots would suffice to show this. De Sica replaces this narrative unit with a series of "smaller" events: she wakes up; she crosses the hall; she drowns the ants; and so on.

But let us examine just one of these. We see how the grinding of the coffee is divided in turn into a series of independent moments: for example, when she shuts the door with the tip of her outstretched foot. As it goes in on her the camera follows the movement of her leg so that the image finally concentrates on her toes feeling the surface of the door. Have I already said that it is Zavattini's dream to make a whole film out of ninety minutes in the life of a man to whom nothing happens? That is precisely what "neorealism" means for him. Two or three sequences in *Umberto D.* give us more than a glimpse of what such a film might be like; they are fragments of it that have already been shot. But let us make no mistake about the meaning and the value realism has here. De Sica and Zavattini are concerned to make cinema the asymptote of reality—but in order that it should ultimately be life itself that becomes spectacle, in order that life might in this perfect mirror be visible poetry, be the self into which film finally changes it.

Chapter Thirteen

"In Italy"

"En Italie," chapter by André Bazin in André Bazin et alia, *Cinéma 53 à travers le monde* (Éditions du Cerf, 1954), pp. 85–100. Translated into English by Bert Cardullo.

The 1951–1952 season had ended on a triumphant note for Italian neorealism with the wonderful *Two Cents' Worth of Hope* (1951), by Renato Castellani. Another masterpiece opened the 1952–1953 season, *Umberto D.* (1952), by Cesare Zavattini and Vittorio De Sica. Unfortunately, the film was released under deplorable conditions at the end of September and was insufficiently supported by the critics, who were still napping after the holidays, so that it enjoyed absolutely no success. Violently attacked in Italy for para-political reasons, *Umberto D.* consequently not find the welcome in Paris that it deserved. For this, shame on the critics' children and grandchildren up to the seventh generation!

In the Zavattini and De Sica oeuvre, *Miracle in Milan* (1951) was a parenthetical work. It was an excursion into fantasy, related to realism and in its service perhaps, but generally following a different path from the one defined by *Shoeshine* (1946) and *Bicycle Thieves* (1948). With *Umberto D.*, this director and screenwriter return to pure neorealism, in which they attempt to eliminate all concessions to the traditional concept of cinematic dramaturgy.

Now an eccentricity of Zavattini's is his claim that Italian cinema must, contrary to all evidence, "transcend" neorealism. This is a perilous and paradoxical position after the success of *Bicycle Thieves,* which represented the pinnacle from which any artist could only descend. But *Umberto D.* proves that the undeniable perfection of *Bicycle Thieves* does not delimit the neorealist aesthetic; indeed, for this reason *Umberto D.* may even be superior to *Bicycle Thieves.* This latest film succeeds, rather than in the strict application

Shoeshine, dir. Vittorio De Sica, 1946.

of the laws of neorealist form, in creating an almost miraculous equilibrium between neorealism's revolutionary conception of screenwriting and the exigencies of classical storytelling. Where one would never have believed that such a compromise could exist, these film artists have arrived at an ideal synthesis between the necessary rigor of tragedy and the spontaneous fluidity of daily reality. For Zavattini, however, this success did not come without sacrificing a part of his aesthetic theory, which we all know would create a cinematic "spectacle" of ninety minutes in the life of a man to whom nothing ever happens. An impossible task, perhaps, except in a theoretical film that would reflect reality like a two-way mirror, but such a deeply aesthetic notion is as inexhaustible as nature itself.

From this point of view, *Umberto D.* tries to go, and succeeds in going, much further than *Bicycle Thieves* did; two or three of its scenes, in fact, more than suggest the complete neorealism that Zavattini visualizes. Disagreement will inevitably arise, because the film's socio themes and its sentiment may make some people consider it a plea for old-age pensions, while others dismiss it as nothing but a populist melodrama. There will always be the carping critic who wants to mock De Sica's "faint heart," yet it is clear that the real film here is much more than the sum of its parts.

First let's look at the film's "action." A retired bureaucrat, reduced to half-misery and demoralized by the threat of losing his room, decides against committing suicide because he cannot find a home for his dog or muster up the courage to kill the animal, either. But this final scene is not the pathetic conclusion (also, what conclusion are we talking about, since the old man has to live on?) of a *dramatic chain* of events. If the events happen to be dramatic, they are so in themselves and not with regard to a pre-established "action." Granted, the succession of these events, sometimes only moments, is not incoherent. One can see some progress in it, but this progress is accidental as it were: the opposite of *necessary* or *inevitable* and tragically transcendent. To wit: Umberto D. is suffering from angina, and his illness fills up a lot of time in the film; it will land him in the hospital, but his hospitalization has almost no consequences for the action and, after his recovery, the protagonist finds himself in the same situation as before. The basic unit of the film is thus not a scene, an event, a *coup de théâtre;* its mainspring is not even the protagonist's character: the story is only a succession of concrete moments of life, none of which can be said to be more important than the others.

Indeed, the story of *Umberto D.*—if one can still speak in this instance of a story or plot—is as much about the times when "nothing happens" as it is about dramatic events, such as the protagonist's failed suicide. De Sica dedicates more than one reel to showing us Umberto D. in his room, closing his shutters, arranging various objects, looking at his tonsils, going to bed, taking his temperature. Too many pills for a sore throat, I have to say! Enough pills for suicide … The sore throat plays its small role in the plot, but the most beautiful sequence in the film—and one of the highest achievements in the history of cinema—is the awakening of the pregnant little maid. Rigorously avoiding dramatic italicizing, the scene perfectly illustrates Zavattini's conception of narrative and hence of *mise en scène.*

Early in the morning, the young girl gets up, comes and goes in the kitchen, drowns the ants that are swarming in the sink, grinds the coffee, closes the door with the tip of her toe … and all these "irrelevant" actions are reported to us with meticulous temporal continuity. This scene is without any dramatic "usefulness," as the camera limits itself to filming the young woman during her habitual morning activities. Cinema becomes here the very opposite of the art of ellipsis, which one can too easily think it was made for. Ellipsis implies analysis and choice; it organizes facts according to the dramatic sense they must be submitted to. De Sica and Zavattini try, by contrast, to divide the event up into smaller events, and those into even smaller events, up to the limit of our perception of duration.

I mentioned to Zavattini that this last scene sustains our unflagging interest, whereas Umberto D.'s bedroom scene does not succeed in the same way. "You see," he told me, "that the aesthetic principle is not in question, but only its application. The more screenwriters reject genres of action and spectacle and try to make a story conform to the continuity of everyday life, the more choosing from among the infinite events of someone's life becomes a delicate, problematic issue. The fact that you were bored by Umberto D.'s sore throat, yet moved to tears by my little heroine's coffee grinder, only proves that I chose the second time what I, and perhaps you, had not conceived of before."

This is an uneven film, certainly, and one that does not satisfy the soul as much as *Bicycle Thieves*, but *Umberto D.* is also a film whose weaknesses are due only to its ambitions. Nonetheless, we should no longer be mistaken about the concept of "realism" in film art: the purpose of De Sica and Zavattini is to make of cinema an asymptote of reality, in the process almost making of life itself a spectacle—life *in itself* at last, even as the cinema alters it. This places a film like *Umberto D.* not only in the forefront of neorealism, but at the very edge of the invisible avant-garde, which I, in my own small way, hope to promote.

The year began with a misunderstood masterpiece (De Sica's *Umberto D.*), and it ended with an accursed masterpiece, Roberto Rossellini's *Europe '51* (aka *The Greatest Love,* 1952). Just as critics had reproached De Sica for making a social melodrama, they accused Rossellini of indulging in a confused, indeed reactionary, political ideology. They were once again wrong for the most part, for they were passing judgment on the subject without taking into consideration the style that gives it its meaning and its aesthetic value.

A young, rich, and frivolous woman loses her only son, who commits suicide one evening when his mother is so preoccupied with her social life that she sends him to bed rather than be forced to pay attention to him. The poor woman's moral shock is so violent that it plunges her into a crisis of conscience that she initially tries to resolve by dedicating herself to humanitarian causes, on the advice of a cousin of hers who is a Communist intellectual. But little by little she gets the feeling that this is only an intermediate stage beyond which she must go if she is to achieve a mystical clarity all her own, one that transcends the boundaries of politics and even of social or religious morality. Accordingly, she looks after a sick prostitute until the latter dies, then aids in the escape of a young criminal from the police. This last initiative causes a scandal, and, with the complicity of an entire family alarmed by her behavior, the woman's husband, who understands her less and less, decides to have her committed to a sanitarium. If she had become a member of the Communist

Europe '51, dir. Roberto Rossellini, 1952.

party or had entered a convent, bourgeois society would have had fewer objections to her actions, since the Europe of the early 1950s is a world of political parties and social organizations.

From this perspective, it is true that Rossellini's script is not devoid of naïveté, even of incoherence or at any rate pretentiousness. One sees the particulars that the author has borrowed from Simone Weil's life, without in fact being able to recapture the strength of her thinking. But these reservations don't hold up before the whole of a film that one must understand and judge on the basis of its *mise en scène*. What would Dostoyevsky's *The Idiot* be worth if it were to be reduced to a summary of its plot? Because Rossellini is a true director, the form of his film does not consist in the ornamentation of its script: the form is supplied by its very substance.

The author of *Germany, Year Zero* (1947)—in which a boy also kills himself—is profoundly haunted in a personal way by the horror of the death of children, even more by the horror of their suicide, and it is around his heroine's authentic spiritual experience of such a suicide that the film is organized. The eminently modern theme of lay sainthood then naturally emerges; its more or less skillful development by the script matters very little: what matters is that each sequence is a kind of meditation or filmic song on this fundamental theme as revealed by the *mise en scène*. The aim is not to demonstrate but to show. And how could we resist the moving spiritual presence of Ingrid Bergman, and, beyond the actress, how could we remain insensitive to the intensity of a *mise en scène* in which the universe seems to be organized along spiritual lines of force, to the point that it sets them off as manifestly as iron fillings in a magnetic field? Seldom has the presence of the spiritual in human beings and in the world been expressed with such dazzling clarity.

Granted, Rossellini's neorealism here seems very different from, if not the opposite of, De Sica's. However, I think it wise to reconcile them as the two poles of one and the same aesthetic school. Whereas De Sica investigates reality with ever more expansive curiosity, Rossellini by contrast seems to strip it down further each time, to stylize it with a painful but nonetheless unrelenting rigor, in short to return to a classicism of dramatic expression in acting as well as in *mise en scène*. But, on closer examination, this classicism stems from a common neorealistic revolution. For Rossellini, as for De Sica, the aim is to reject the categories of acting and of dramatic expression in order to force reality to reveal its significance solely through appearances. Rossellini does not make his actors *act*, he doesn't make them express this or that feeling; he compels them only to be a certain way before the camera. In such a *mise en scène*, the respective places of the characters, their ways of walking, their movements on the set, and their gestures have much more importance than the feelings they show on their faces, or even than the words they say. Besides, what "feelings" could Ingrid Bergman "express"? Her drama lies far beyond any psychological nomenclature. Her face only outlines a certain property of suffering.

Europe '51 gives ample indication that such a *mise en scène* calls for the most sophisticated stylization possible. A film like this is the very opposite of a realistic one "drawn from life": it is the equivalent of austere and terse writing, which is so stripped of ornament that it sometimes verges on the ascetic. At this point, neorealism returns full circle to classical abstraction and its generalizing quality. Hence this apparent paradox: the best version of the film is not the dubbed Italian version, but the English one, which employs the greatest possible number of original voices. At the far reaches of this realism, the accuracy of exterior social reality becomes unimportant. The children in the streets of Rome can speak English without our even realizing the implausibility of such an occurrence. This is reality through style, and thus a reworking of the conventions of art.

Story of a Love Affair, dir. Michelangelo Antonioni, 1950.

Story of a Love Affair, dir. Michelangelo Antonioni, 1950.

Michelangelo Antonioni belongs to the same artistic family as Rossellini, albeit with perhaps a more conscious intelligence of cinematic means. Antonioni's fame in France is not yet equal to his talent. His first film, a tense and cutting work, which recalls the rigor of Bresson and the sensitivity of Renoir, was *Story of a Love Affair* (1950). It revealed, in addition to its outstanding director, an astonishing actress: Lucia Bosé. Since then, Antonioni has made two very good films that have not been released in France: *The Lady without Camelias* (1953), a satire on beauty pageants, and above all *I Vinti* (*The Vanquished*; aka *Youth and Perversion*, 1952), whose release in France might be prevented for stupid reasons of censorship.

The Lady without Camelias, dir. Michelangelo Antonioni, 1953.

The Italian critics themselves are divided and hesitant about *The Lady without Camelias*, but I saw *I Vinti* at the Venice Film Festival, and the film completely fulfills the early hopes that I had about its director. Its purpose is to evoke the moral situation of postwar youth on the basis of three true stories, one Italian, one English, and one French—each of which chronicles a senseless murder. The French portion is the one causing all the film's troubles, as it is (too closely) inspired by the actual murder on which it's based. The three parts of *I Vinti* are unequal, and the Italian one could have been made by any director with a little talent, but the French part is excellent and the

English wonderful. The latter reaches the extreme purity of a kind of stylized realism, stripped bare of any element borrowed from the charms of the edited or plastic image: this is a true chess game of reality where the actors' behavior, and the environment in which they are placed, are the only signs of a hidden truth.

The Vanquished, dir. Michelangelo Antonioni, 1952.

Italian cinema, however, was not as high on the honor roll of international film festivals this season as in the previous one. I must nevertheless single out among the films that have not yet been released in Paris an appealing work by Mario Soldati titled *The Provincial Woman* (1953; aka *The Wayward Wife*), after a short story by Alberto Moravia. This endeavor is interesting, for the Italians consider Soldati one of their best novelists, and his work in the cinema, usually quite commercial, has had little to do so far with his work as a talented writer. A strange fellow who looks like Groucho Marx, he is indeed also the director of the comedy *O.K. Nero* (1951). With this picture, it is a little as if François Mauriac were making a living by making a movie in imitation of the French comic strip *Les Pieds Nickelés*.

But in Italy writers and filmmakers don't live in separate worlds: I can see a brief but significant confirmation of this in the six-minute cinematic short titled *It Is the Sun's Fault* (1951), written and directed by the novelist Alberto Moravia. It is a brief but grating love story set in high society. Now, in *The Provincial Woman*, the novelist Soldati directs a short story by the same Moravia, the author of *Agostino* (1944). Its title tells all. This is the story of an Italian Emma Bovary, who married a professor who is neither handsome nor rich, and who is blackmailed by a Romanian countess—who is more of a procuress than a countess. The provincial woman is the too-beautiful Gina Lollobrigida. In view of the potential of its authors, this interesting film, made with intelligence and a definite sense of novelistic depth, is nonetheless somewhat disappointing and does not come up to the level, say, of Rossellini's moral rigor or Antonioni's visual style.

The Wayward Wife, dir. Mario Soldati, 1953.

The Wayward Wife, dir. Mario Soldati, 1953.

At the same Cannes Film Festival where *The Provincial Woman* was screened, Vittorio De Sica was showing his latest film: *Stazione Termini* (*Terminal Station*; aka *Indiscretion of an American Wife*, 1953). He himself had the cunning and taste to sing the praises of Clouzot's *The Wages of Fear* (1953) at the Festival's preliminary press conference, in a discreet way of alleviating the jury's subsequent guilt for not singling out *Stazione Termini* for the Cannes honor roll. And all in all, the exclusion of *Stazione Termini* by the Cannes judges was as justified as the absence of *Umberto D.* from the honor roll of 1952 was a scandal.

The weaknesses of the film were unfortunately contained in the premises of its making. *Stazione Termini* is the result of an American mortgage contracted by De Sica after his trip to the United States, where he was supposed to make a film. This trip was twice unlucky as, on the one hand, the project never materialized and, on the other hand, it was nearly the cause of a falling out between the director and his screenwriter Zavattini, who was not able to go because the American embassy rejected his visa application. To the great satisfaction of all those who admire Italian cinema and who love these two wonderfully complementary personalities, the quarrel, which lasted for two years, finally

Indiscretion of an American Wife, dir. Vittorio De Sica, 1953.

seems to have given way to a new, trustful collaboration since a certain letter from De Sica to Zavattini, which the latter published in *Cinema Nuovo* and which was later reprinted in *Cahiers du cinéma*. Both are now working on their next film: *Gold of Naples* (1954).

Whatever Zavattini's personal feelings might have been during that period, he nevertheless worked on the screenplay of *Stazione Termini*. But the conditions of the film's production inevitably steered it toward a compromise between the demands of neorealism and the American conception of romance. Selznick, the producer, probably wanted an "Italian film" in which one could find the external signs of neorealism, but a film also adapted to the tastes of an American audience—*and* to the greater glory of Mrs. Selznick, aka Jennifer Jones. Zavattini had initially written a fundamentally Italian story in which the ultimate parting of the two lovers was the result of a social imperative—the ban on divorce in Italy. Granted, this ban would have had little significance for the Americans, since divorce is legal in the United States. But from Zavattini's dialogue, as well, very little was left after its rewriting by Truman Capote. Therefore, the film is what it had to be: divided between two opposite inclinations, that of neorealism, with a *mise en scène* detailing life in a big Roman train station at 7 P.M., and that of sentiment, with any social element reduced to the role of setting—active, to be sure, but ultimately subordinated to a sentimental story and to our interest in the two stars of the film, Montgomery Clift and Jennifer Jones.

That said, it would be profoundly unfair to treat *Stazione Termini* as just a mediocre or failed film. First, within the warped framework imposed by the producer, De Sica has nevertheless been able to suggest psychological and social truths that are movingly accurate and clinically sharp. I particularly like the young American nephew of the female protagonist, who is so precisely yet discreetly typified with his proud, juvenile incomprehension. One can sense in this fourteen-year-old boy—whom a dozen *carabinieri* trail behind like live toy soldiers in a kid's world—the frankness and severity of a simultaneously liberal and puritanical civilization: the great American one. The role of this secondary character, who embodies both the moral and social conscience of the heroine, is a beautiful and intelligent creation. But beyond these partial successes, which would fully satisfy many another filmmaker, *Stazione Termini* evidences from beginning to end an ease and class of *mise en scène*, and an elegant sensitivity, that are the true marks of a great director.

With the De Sica-Zavattini collaboration, on the one hand, and on the other, the Rossellini and Antonioni films, I have delineated the aesthetic domain of neorealism, whose inclinations can be both extremely rigorous and extremely contradictory. Between these two poles, the year has offered us some other

Indiscretion of an American Wife, dir. Vittorio De Sica, 1953.

films that are not without their own concessions and are a mixture of various influences. But although they are less purely representative of the neorealist school, they nevertheless possess value.

By order of merit, I should perhaps mention first *The Road to Hope* (1950), by Pietro Germi, a young filmmaker who is one of the great hopes of the new Italian cinema. In this film a group of miners and their families secretly leave their village in Sicily—whose sulfur mines have just closed down, depriving all the workers of their jobs—for a promised land where, they are told, there is work for everybody: France. They sell what little furniture they have, collect their raggedy clothes, pay the would-be smuggler who has offered to take them to the border and sneak them across, and then they leave: a miserable army rich only in hope. Abandoned halfway by their so-called guide and questioned by the Italian police, who order them to go back to Sicily (compulsory residence in one place is common in Italy), most of them decide to continue on with their journey anyway. Those who did not give up arrive at the border, where professional smugglers, who are used to this kind of emigration, make them cross at night during a snowstorm. At dawn, the Promised Land is before them. The survivors may finally be able to find work as unskilled laborers, or even, with a little luck, as miners.

The screenplay of *The Road to Hope*, which is wonderful in its general outline, is unfortunately weakened by some melodramatic contrivances and political compromises. One of the two love stories is akin less to neorealism than to cheap soap-opera romance, despite the appealing characters played by Raf Vallone and Elena Varzi. Moreover, the last ten minutes of the film recall much too visibly Lindtberg's *The Last Chance* (1945) without duplicating its eloquence. *The Road to Hope* is also marred by inexplicable flaws that are difficult to explain precisely: does the problem lie in the screenplay, or in the very print I saw of the film, which seems to be in a rather sorry state? These awkwardnesses remain secondary, however, and do not really compromise the narrative line of this simple odyssey of misery, whose extremity truly verges on the absurd.

In the Name of the Law, dir. Pietro Germi, 1949.

Still, I would mostly reproach Pietro Germi—whose *In the Name of the Law* (1949) was seen in France—for his inclination toward aestheticism and even a certain taste for visual rhetoric, which sometimes takes the place in *The Road to Hope* of a profound and heartfelt commitment to the subject matter. His latest film, *The Bandit of Tacca del Lupo* (1952), presented in Venice, unfortunately confirms these fears, which continue to prevent me from ranking Germi among the foremost Italian movie directors.

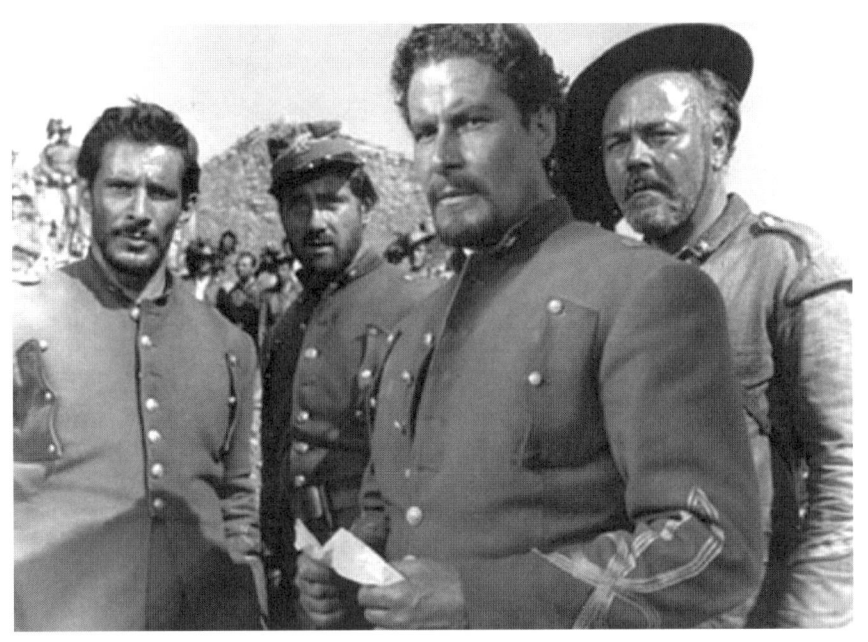

The Bandit of Tacca del Lupo, dir. Pietro Germi, 1952.

By contrast, it is its conscious epic ambition that gives Giuseppe De Santis's *No Peace among the Olives* (1950) its originality and power, despite the film's baroque excesses. With *Tragic Hunt* (1947) and *Bitter Rice* (1949), De Santis had completed the first two works in an epic anthology on the subject of Earth Woman. Less pure and with less formal creativeness than *Tragic Hunt*, less successful in its parallel treatment of the erotic and peasant themes, *No Peace among the Olives* is nevertheless an appealing film, a strange one even in the excess or imbalance of some of its ambitions. The romanticism of De Santis, his unbridled lyricism, often upsets the very elementary plausibility of the screenplay to exult in some kind of delirious baroqueness.

This is the story of a shepherd who, absent during the war, is robbed by a rich landowner and who, upon his return, takes back the sheep that belong to him. But nobody will dare testify in his favor, because the mighty landowner holds in his power all the shepherds of the region. Even Lucia, in love with the shepherd, will finally forsake him; even as he is sent to jail, she agrees to get engaged to the villain, who is her parents' creditor. But the shepherd escapes from prison and comes back to get his revenge. Hiding in a wild and mountainous terrain, he is this time protected by his friends and helped by Lucia. The film climaxes, on the one hand, with a lascivious dance by Lucia

Bitter Rice, dir. Giuseppe De Santis, 1949.

Tragic Hunt, dir. Giuseppe De Santis, 1947.

Bitter Rice, dir. Giuseppe De Santis, 1949.

No Peace among the Olives, dir. Giuseppe De Santis, 1950.

Bosé, which recalls that of Silvana Mangano in *Bitter Rice* (not to speak of Eleonora Rossi Drago in Clemente Fracassi's *Sensualità* [1952], which, like *Bitter Rice,* explores the same vein of—let us call it—agricultural eroticism); and, on the other hand, with the revolt of the shepherds, whose gathered herds stream down the mountains into the legs of the *carabinieri*. The villain deservedly ends up at the bottom of a ravine.

If we limit *No Peace among the Olives* to its plot, this film is merely a kind of peasant melodrama writ large, where nothing is spared: neither the rape of the poor young shepherdess by the rich landowner, nor the final triumph of a latent natural justice that is one step ahead of social justice. But it is obvious that the primal simplicity of this story is intentional on the part of its author, who has conceived his film both as a fresco and as an epic. Documentary realism is thus combined with narrative as well as visual stylization. The care given to the otherwise realistic photography proves my point, for each image is composed as a tableau: women strike poses of *Pietàs* or of *Madonnas*; the actors look as though they had just stepped out of a Michelangelo fresco; and the walk-ons themselves play the role of the ancient chorus. To be sure, one must acknowledge that the result is somewhat grotesque. One is hard put to discover any synthesis between the formal ambitions of the *mise en scène* and the childishness of the screenplay.

No Peace among the Olives, dir. Giuseppe De Santis, 1950.

As for the presence of Lucia Bosé, it has mostly to do with an erotic obsession that is purely its own justification. But in a hundred places of this baroque endeavor, a cinematic genius that cannot leave us indifferent reveals itself. The film was released in Paris, by the way—in a small theater on the outskirts of the city—three years after its making (and *after* it was released in the French provinces) only in a dubbed version. It goes without saying that this stupid exploitation has added quite a few misunderstandings to all those that the film already contained.

As though he had achieved with *No Peace among the Olives* the epitome of his baroque delirium and had therefore freed himself from it, De Santis evidences in *Rome, Eleven O'Clock* (1952) a remarkable sense of dramatic construction as it relates to the *mise en scène*. The film was inspired by a true story, which unfortunately loses force on account of the triviality of its theme. The staircase of a building has collapsed under the weight of two hundred unlucky young women who have come to apply for a typist's job. One is dead and many others are severely injured. The film begins at dawn as the line of applicants is already forming. Almost imperceptibly, De Santis isolates eight or nine of the candidates, whose past and reasons for being there we progressively learn. We will witness a few hours from their individual destinies, which are more or less changed forever by the horrible accident.

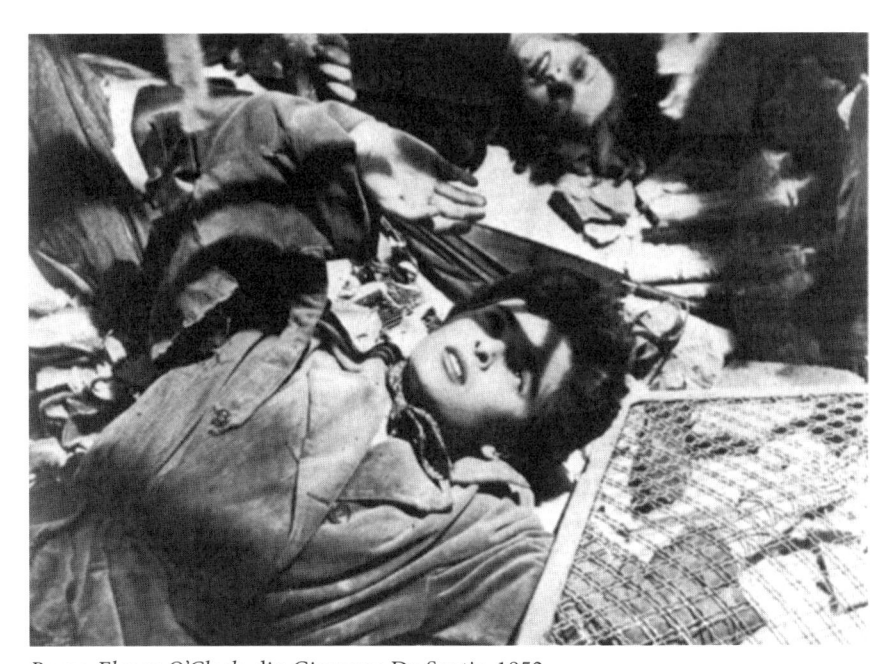

Rome, Eleven O'Clock, dir. Giuseppe De Santis, 1952.

In *Rome, Eleven O'Clock* De Santis and his screenwriters have skillfully been able to avoid the artifice of films consisting of such sketches and to interweave the various, exemplary destinies they have chosen without interrupting the flow of the narrative. But the director plays the game of neorealism only partially here. Whereas his screenplay delves into the social present for its essential component, the violence of the stairway collapse, he nevertheless does not deprive the film of a skilled yet finally traditional dramatic construction. Neither does he want to deprive this endeavor of the advantages of a spectacular cast: Lucia Bosé, Carla del Poggio, Elena Varzi, Léa Padovani, Raf Vallone, and Massimo Girotti are the impressive stars.

Almost at the same time, Augusto Genina was making another film about the same true story: *Three Forbidden Tales* (1952). I shall mention it here only for the sake of thoroughness and because a comparison with the film by De Santis makes the concessions of *Rome, Eleven O'Clock* appear like so many ascetic choices. A wily old filmmaker, Genina is capable of the best (*Heaven over the Marshes* [1949]) as well as the less than good. *Three Forbidden Tales* does not even try to hide the fact that it consists only of sketches: three of them, in fact, one being indecent, one provocative, and one melodramatic. The film is so skillfully made that it verges on craftiness, but in the end its narrative strands are too arbitrarily connected to the real tragedy that is the work's pretext.

With *Altri Tempi* (*Times Gone By*, 1952), Alessandro Blasetti has assuredly taken even less trouble than Genina to link up his seven sketches. But at least he is honest about it. The sole common denominator of his film is its evocation of the end of the nineteenth century. The tone varies, as do the length and subject matter of the tales that Blasetti tells us with relentless vigor. Still, he is able to balance tragedy, realism, morality, sentiment, and irony, not to speak of music and song. Moreover, he has a welcome preference for the comic touch, as displayed in the best of the stories, "The Judgment of Phryne." A mediocre lawyer, who can't find clients, is appointed to do *pro bono* work on a hopeless case—that of a young woman who killed her mother-in-law with rat poison. He finds brilliant inspiration in the rather low neckline of his client (Gina Lollobrigida): he will have her plead guilty in the name of beauty, and in this small dusty court he will get the same indulgence from the jury for her as the ancient Greek courtesan Phryne got from her jurors. Blasetti's intelligence, which found in Vittorio De Sica's acting talent (as the attorney) a charming complicity, was that he chose to keep his lawyer a professional mediocrity, even in his final triumph. This is what gives the lawyer's chance inspiration all its savor. One is reminded here of the work of both Georges Courteline and Marcel Pagnol. Or perhaps simply of the great tradition of Neapolitan farce,

Three Forbidden Tales, dir. Augusto Genina, 1952.

Times Gone By, dir. Alessandro Blasetti, 1952.

for which De Sica will no doubt find renewed inspiration in his forthcoming film, *Gold of Naples*.

Since I am dealing now with comic neorealism, I should not forget *Cops and Robbers* (1951), which garnered its authors (Steno [Stefano Vanzino] and Mario Monicelli) the prize for best screenplay at the 1952 Cannes Film Festival. In truth, I find this award a little excessive (especially when one considers that *Umberto D.* did not even make it to the honor roll). But the film did have humor and verve. It provided its two stars, Totò and Aldo Fabrizi, who are the Italian Fernandel and Raimu, with something better than an excuse for silly antics: a substantial plot, one that even went quite far in the direction of satirical realism. A police officer (Fabrizi), who is also a father with a family, arrests the Totò character, who is a thief and even more so a father with a family. The prisoner escapes and the policeman is forced to run after him. He catches him but in the process makes the acquaintance of Totò's family. Understanding being the first step toward love, our policeman takes a liking to the prisoner, who will then himself have to drag this law enforcer back to prison. Totò will even decide not to run away anymore, so as not to cause the policeman any further trouble. This is the recognizable theme of an excellent social farce, which the screenwriters managed to stuff with thousands of little realistic details that are all absolutely credible.

Sunday in August, dir. Luciano Emmer, 1950.

I did not want to end this chronicle of the neorealist year-in-film on a negative note. But how can I keep silent about a film by Luciano Emmer, whose art documentaries had put him, at the age of twenty, in the foreground of the world's top documentary makers? His first feature film, *Sunday in August* (1950), confirmed the promise that his documentary shorts had shown, even though this picture, in my opinion, had something a little too intellectual, too ingeniously aesthetic, about it to leave me satisfied. It would be better for Luciano Emmer's reputation if he were to forget as soon as possible his second feature film, which is the disastrous result of an impossible co-production. On the theme of the "Italians in Paris," Emmer tries in vain to depict for the benefit of these two nations the material and psychological aspects of superficial tourism. But how could he possibly have survived the handicap of a ridiculous and monstrous dubbing, which makes the French speak Italian in the Italian version and the Italians speak French (with a Marseilles accent!) in the French version? The failure of Emmer's *Paris Is Always Paris* (1951) on the French market will, I hope, serve as a lesson for producers who would still be attracted by such two-headed monsters.

Of course, the idea of such a book [in which this chronicle first appeared] implies a bit of mental gymnastics, as the coincidences or absurdities of distribution prevent the film season in France from coinciding with the film

Sunday in August, dir. Luciano Emmer, 1950.

The White Sheik, dir. Federico Fellini, 1952.

The White Sheik, dir. Federico Fellini, 1952.

season throughout the rest of the world. Therefore, I deem it necessary, after this review of the main films released during the 1952–1953 season (festival premières included), to remind the reader briefly of the oversights and anomalies of an exploitation that sometimes recalls the state of King Ubu's Poland. At least two films should have been released a long time ago with all the acclaim that their merits deserve. First, a film by Alberto Lattuada: *The Overcoat* (1952). Adapted from the famous short story by Gogol, this film is probably Lattuada's best and should have won the prize for best screenplay at the 1952 Cannes Film Festival.

Second, if the French distributors knew their job well, they also would not have failed to release a delightful little comic film—*The White Sheik*—by the screenwriter Federico Fellini, presented at the 1952 Venice Film Festival, and which I personally find superior to *I vitelloni* (1953) by the same author. *The White Sheik* has been praised to the hilt by the Italians this year. It is a charming and sensitive satire on the success of comic strips in popular newspapers. The hero of one of them, the "White Sheik," seduces a young provincial woman who is on her honeymoon in the big city; she then leaves her husband to go in search of her mythic lover. The delightful and intelligent Brunella Bovo (who played the little maid in *Miracle in Milan*) is the naïve protagonist of this wonderful little adventure.

It is equally the case that the same distributors who release first-rate works years after their making flood the French market with third-rate Italian movies, which we could very well do without. Take for instance *The Grandson of the Three Musketeers*, the many miserable imitations of *Cabiria* (1914), the low-budget versions of *Quo Vadis?* (1901, 1913), or even the many ridiculous melodramas that have more in common with cheap romanticism than with neorealism. Any defense of French national cinema has always argued against the American B-movies that invade our screens at the expense of native films or good foreign pictures. I would not hesitate to write that today we are also facing an Italian peril. It is perhaps less wide-ranging and less powerful from an economic point of view, but it is far more depressing from an aesthetic perspective. For whereas American B-movies very often retain some technical virtues and a certain dramatic poetry that is characteristic of the Hollywood system, bad Italian movies, by contrast, are like bad French movies, if not worse: they are moronic and shoddy; nothing saves them. If the Italian cinema has occupied since the war a top ranking in world cinema, it owes that ranking exclusively to its genuine works of art and not at all to its current commercial production, which is far worse than mediocre. But I trust that intelligent advertising and smart exporting on the part of Italian film distributors will remedy this situation.

Chapter Fourteen

"Is the Italian Cinema Going to Disown Itself?"

"Le cinéma italien va-t-il se renier?" *Radio-Cinéma-Télévision* (December 1954), in *Qu'est-ce que le cinéma?* Vol. 4 (Éditions du Cerf, 1962), pp. 100–103. Translated into English by Bert Cardullo.

If I had had to define Italian neorealism three or four years ago, I think I would not have failed to hold as essential several of its characteristics, among them the contemporary relevance of its themes and the realism of its language. These two fundamental characteristics were indeed essential elements in the first masterpiece of the new Italian school, Roberto Rossellini's *Paisà* (1946).

PRESENT-TENSE FILMS IN WHICH THE CHARACTERS SPEAK THEIR OWN LANGUAGE

If one does indeed consider neorealism, according to Zavattini's definition, as a conversion of life into cinema—a way that the filmmaker has, no longer to imagine stories in the margins of everyday reality, but rather to throw light on that reality, to illuminate it from within in order to make of it an object to witness and to love—cinema, just like life, could exist only in the present tense of the indicative. Italian films (neorealist ones at least) thus never use the flashbacks that flourish in American, English, and French movies.

But, less theoretically perhaps, one of the revolutions in taste imposed by neorealism on the international filmgoing audience has to do with the convention of languages. It has become intolerable in a film to hear foreigners speak to each other in the language of the viewer, against all plausibility. (I am excluding dubbing here, which is a convention that precedes a film and is external to it.) One can sometimes see on television how retrospectively ridiculous this is when one watches French films from the mid-1930s, in which Germans speak to their countrymen in the language of La Fontaine with a Teutonic accent. Jean Renoir is to be credited, yet again, with the obliteration of this convention in *La grande illusion* (1937). This film prefigured, as in other respects, the postwar cinema, notably *Paisà* and Leopold Lindtberg's *The Last Chance* (1945). I think that André Cayatte, for his part, was wrong in his *Lovers of Verona* (1948) when he returned to the convention of universal French in the realistic setting of Venice.

Romeo and Juliet, dir. Renato Castellani, 1954.

HISTORICAL NEOREALIST FILMS?

And yet, Renato Castellani claims today that his Italian actors must speak English, and in verse, in the equally realistic setting of Verona. He also wants to have neorealistic blood flow in the veins of theatrical conventions. If his *Romeo and Juliet* (1954) calls for some critical reservations, it is not in this particular respect, however. Castellani has perfectly succeeded in the paradoxical alliance of neorealism and theater, and this perhaps calls for further reflection. All the more so since that reflection will complement the one inspired by any viewing of some of the latest Italian productions. One of the most remarkable films at the last Cannes Film Festival, for example—Carlo Lizzani's *Chronicle of Poor Lovers* (1954), after Vasco Pratolini's novel—told about the life of some people living on a small street in Florence in 1924. At the last neorealist conference in Parma a year ago, some participants insisted on the necessity of making such "historical neorealist films." Is neorealism therefore going to decline or disown itself?

Chronicle of Poor Lovers, dir. Carlo Lizzani, 1954.

Chronicle of Poor Lovers, dir. Carlo Lizzani, 1954.

Chronicle of Poor Lovers, dir. Carlo Lizzani, 1954.

ITALIANS WHO SPEAK ENGLISH

Lizzani's film already proves that this is not the case, and it is perhaps useful to remember that *1860* (1934), the film made by Alessandro Blasetti twelve years before *Paisà*, is often mentioned as the precursor of postwar Italian cinema. Confining neorealism to present-day events would indeed amount to limiting its development and future. Beyond the present-day relevance of its subject matter, neorealism is a way of seeing or presenting people and events with a maximum of "presence" or faithfulness and of life. It is filmmaking in the present tense of the indicative mood, but it does not exclude the historical present.

More: it is possible that this temporal liberty coincides with more paradoxical liberties and that the geographical realism of language itself is not always essential. This personally struck me when I saw Rossellini's *Europe '51* (1952), whose best version was unquestionably the English one (just as the best version of De Sica's *Stazione Termini* [1953] was the American one), despite the enormous implausibilities it entailed. Ultimately it was more important that Ingrid Bergman speak with her own voice, in English, in this picture than to hear Castellani's street kids speak in the (dubbed) language of Shakespeare. Among the conflicts between two realisms, that is, the purely linguistic one regarding the heroine's dialogue and the social one of the secondary characters, the former prevailed.

THE MATURITY OF A STYLE: GIVING NEW MEANING TO CONVENTIONS

Must we conclude, nevertheless, that the whole neorealist endeavor is impure and see in it the evidence of its own weakness? Quite the contrary: for my part, I see in this development evidence for the maturity of neorealism, which is from now on capable of reinstituting the conventions necessary to style, not *in* but *through* reality. *Europe '51*, for instance, is a "modern tragedy." Tragedy implies the tragic style, which is a purification of events and passions, a kind of abstraction through intensity and nobility. Rossellini achieved this in *Europe '51* in his *mise en scène* and in his directing of the actors; but he also created a modern feeling in the film, beyond the present-day relevance of its subject matter, through a neorealist treatment. This neorealism has become, in a way, internal to the characters and their relationships—something like a neorealism of souls. (Robert Bresson's *Diary of a Country Priest* [1951] is not so far away from the same concern.)

In such a context, some primitive characteristics of the Italian school become, if not obsolete, at least insignificant. Paradoxically, neorealism, ceasing to be an external respect for the real, can be defined at its highest level only as a style. Its starting point was a hatred for conventions, yet it may return to them legitimately after their initial and necessary proscription. Shall I say, then, in a paraphrase of Pascal, that true neorealism is poking fun at realism?

Chapter Fifteen

"*La Strada*"

"*La strada,*" *Esprit*, 23.226 (May 1955), pp. 847–851, in *Qu'est-ce que le cinéma?* Vol. 4 (Éditions du Cerf, 1962), pp. 122–128; translated into English by Bert Cardullo.

The vitality of the Italian cinema is confirmed for us once again by this wonderful film of Federico Fellini's. And it is doubly comforting to declare that the rest of the critics have been nearly unanimous in singing the praises of *La strada* (1954). Perhaps without this support, which hasn't hesitated to enlist snobbism on its side, the film would have had some difficulty in bringing itself to the attention of an inundated and undiscerning public.

Fellini has made one of those very rare films about which it can be said, one forgets that they are movies and accepts them simply as works of art. One remembers the discovery of *La strada* as an aesthetic experience of great emotion, as an unanticipated encounter with the world of imagination. I mean that this is less a case of a film's having known how to attain a certain intellectual or moral level than of its having made a personal statement for which the cinema is most surely the necessary and natural form, but which statement nevertheless possesses a virtual artistic existence of its own. It is not a film that is called *La strada;* it is *La strada* that is called a film.

In connection with this idea, Chaplin's last film also comes to mind, although in many ways it is quite different from *La strada*. One could just as well say of *Limelight* (1952) that its only adequate embodiment was the cinema, that it was inconceivable through any other means of expression, and that, nonetheless, everything in it transcended the elements of a particular art form. Thus *La strada* confirms in its own way the following critical premise: to wit, that the cinema has arrived at a stage in its evolution where the form itself no longer determines anything, where filmic language no longer calls

La Strada, dir. Federico Fellini, 1954.

attention to itself, but on the contrary suggests only as much as any stylistic device that an artist might employ.

Doubtless it will be said that only the cinema could, for example, endow Zampanò's extraordinary motorcycle caravan with the significance of living myth that this simultaneously strange and commonplace object attains here. But one can just as clearly see that the film is in this case neither transforming nor interpreting anything for us. No lyricism of the image or of montage takes it upon itself to guide our perceptions; I will even say that the *mise en scène* does not attempt to do so—at least not the *mise en scène* from a technically cinematic point of view. The screen restricts itself to showing us the caravan better and more objectively than could the painter or the novelist. I am not saying that the camera has photographed the caravan in a very plain manner—even the word "photographed" is too much here—but rather that the camera has simply *shown* the caravan to us, or even better, has enabled us to see it.

Surely it would be excessive to pretend that nothing can be created by virtue of cinematic language alone, of its abrasive intrusion on the real. Without even taking into account almost virgin territory such as color and the wide screen, one can say that the degree of relationship between technique and subject matter depends in part on the personality of the director. An Orson Welles, for instance, always creates by means of technique. But what one can say without question is that henceforth advances in the cinema will not necessarily be tied to the originality of the means of expression, to the formal composition of the image or of the images in relation to one another. More precisely, if there is a formal originality to *La strada,* it consists in the film's always staying just this side of the cinema.

That is to say, nothing that Fellini shows us owes any supplementary meaning to the manner in which it is shown; nevertheless, what we see couldn't be seen anywhere but on the screen. It is in this way that the cinema achieves fruition as the art of the real. One knows, of course, that Fellini is a great director, but he is a great director who doesn't cheat on reality. If the camera doesn't *see* it, it isn't in his film. It wouldn't be in his film, in any case, if he hadn't first acknowledged the fullness of its being in the world.

In this sense *La strada* doesn't depart at all from Italian neorealism. But there is a misunderstanding on this subject that requires clarification. *La strada* has been received in Italy with some reservation by the critical guardians of neorealist orthodoxy. These critics are situated on the Left, which in France is called "Progressivist," although this term is misleading, since the Italian critics are both more Marxist and more independent than the French Progressivists. There are certainly Communist critics in France as well, and some of them are cultivated, intelligent, and well-informed, but their point of reference seems to me to be only marginally that of Marxism. The tactics and the watchwords of the Party do play a clearer role in their writing, however, when the work of art in question draws its substance from the political arena, for then Party ideology takes over in spite of everything in the work that resists it. The criticism consequently does no more than render a good or bad judgment on the work according to whether its author's political views are "correct" or "incorrect." As for Progressivist criticism, it is either equivalent to the worst Communist criticism in slavishness and intellectual emptiness, or else it isn't Marxist and in that case has some scope.

In Italy, by contrast, it is Marxist criticism that occasionally gives evidence of a certain independence with regard to the interests of the Party, and without sacrificing the stringency of its aesthetic judgments. I am naturally thinking of the group around Luigi Chiarini and Guido Aristarco at *Cinema Nuovo.* In the last two years their criticism has, I dare say, rediscovered the concept of neorealism, which was held in so little regard at one time, and is attempting to define the term and give it an orientation. (Cesare Zavattini is the figure whose work most conforms to neorealism's ideal, which conceives of a film, not as a fixed and tame reality, but as a work in progress, an inquiry that begins with certain givens and then proceeds in a particular direction.)

I don't feel that I have the competence necessary to give a clear description of the evolution of neorealism as seen by these Marxist critics, but I also don't believe that I am distorting matters to call neorealism, as they define it, a substitute term for "socialist realism," the theoretical and practical sterility of which, fortunately, no longer needs to be demonstrated. In fact, as far as one can trace it through the various tactical changes in the Party line on art that have occurred, socialist realism has never created anything very convincing in itself. In painting, where its influence is easy to determine because it stands in opposition to the whole course of modern art, we know that it hasn't produced any results. In literature and in cinema, the situation is confused, since we are dealing here with art forms from which realism has never been eliminated. But even if there are good films and good novels that don't contradict the precepts of socialist realism, it is still rather doubtful that these precepts had anything to do with the success of these works of art. On the other hand, one can well see the extent to which such precepts have eviscerated many other works.

The truth is that theories have never produced masterpieces and that creative outpourings have a deeper source in History and in men. Italy had the good fortune, like Russia around 1925, to find itself in a situation where cinematic genius began to flourish, and this genius was moving in the direction of social progress, of human liberation. It is natural and legitimate that the most conscientious among the creators and judges of this important movement are anxious today to keep it from falling apart; they would like neorealism to continue along the revolutionary path it set out on around 1945. And surely neorealism can, at least in the cinema, be a valuable substitute for socialist realism. The number of successful neorealist films and their oneness in diversity supply the Marxist aesthetician with food for productive thought, which is the way it should be. If the time comes, however, when such thought outstrips production itself, then neorealism will be in danger. Happily, we are not yet at that point. Nevertheless, I am worried about the intolerance that Marxist criticism is beginning to show toward those who dissent from, let us call it, socialist neorealism—namely, Rossellini and Fellini (who was Rossellini's assistant and in many ways remains his disciple).

"Italy is ever and adamantly the country of Catholicism: whoever is not on the side of Peppone must be in league with Don Camillo." [Don Camillo, an eccentric Roman Catholic village priest, and Peppone, the village's militant Communist mayor, conduct a running war to gain the favor of the local populace in a series of novels (later filmed) by Giovannino Guareschi (1908–1968).] In response to this criticism from the Left, Italian Catholics run to the defense of those neorealist films whose ambiguity lends itself to Catholic coloration. The Congress of Varese, it could be said, is doing battle here with the Congress of Parma. [These were various congresses held in the 1890s by the Catholics, on the one hand, and the Italian Socialist Party, on the other.] Needless to say, the results of this Catholic effort have been rather pitiful.

Because of it, however, Rossellini and Fellini find themselves in a very difficult situation. It is true that their recent films could not be perceived as socially oriented. These films are not concerned at all with the transformation of social institutions; they aren't even genuine social documents. Their makers, as Italian citizens, don't flirt with Communism, but neither do they let themselves be taken in by the Christian Democrats. The result for Rossellini is that he is denounced by both sides. As for Fellini, his case is still under litigation, although the success of *La strada* gives him the benefit of a favorable reception from both sides at the same time—a reception marred, though, by uneasiness and pronounced reservations on the part of the Marxists.

Of course, political bias is just one part of a critic's make-up, with greater or lesser weight attached to it depending on his personality. It may even occur that a critic will set aside his political bias: we have seen Chiarini, for example, defend Rossellini's *Flowers of St. Francis* (1950), whereas *Cinema Nuovo* was divided over *Senso* (1954), which was directed by the Communist Visconti. But the precedent set by such instances certainly does not contribute to a softening of theoretical positions when these are synonymous with political distrust. Thus both the Marxists and the Christian Democrats threaten to evict Fellini from the neorealist pantheon as each defines it, and to hurl him out into the darkness already inhabited by Rossellini.

Obviously everything depends on the definition we give to neorealism from the start. Definition or no definition, however, it seems to me that *La strada* doesn't contradict *Paisan* (1946) or *Open City* (1945) at all, any more than it does *Bicycle Thieves* (1948), for that matter. But it is true that Fellini [who co-scripted *Paisan* and *Open City*] has taken a route different from that of Zavattini [who wrote *Bicycle Thieves*]. Together with Rossellini, Fellini has opted for a neorealism of the person. To be sure, Rossellini's early films, *Paisan* and *Open City* among them, identified moral choice with social consequence, because these two spheres had been equated during the Resistance. But his *Europe '51* (1952) to some degree retreated from social responsibility into the realm of spiritual destiny. What in this film and in *La strada* nonetheless remains neorealist and can even be considered one of neorealism's genuine achievements, is the aesthetic that informs the action, an aesthetic that French ecclesiastic and film critic Amédée Ayfre has judiciously described as phenomenological.

One can see very well, for example, that in *La strada* nothing is ever revealed to us from inside the characters. Fellini's point of view is the exact opposite of the one that would be taken by psychological realism, which claims to analyze character and finally to uncover feelings. Yet anything can happen in the quasi-Shakespearean world of *La strada*. Gelsomina and the *artiste* known as the Fool have an air of the marvelous about them which baffles and irritates Zampanò—but this quality is neither supernatural nor gratuitous, nor even "poetic"; instead, it comes across simply as another property of nature. Furthermore, to return to psychology, the very being of these characters is precisely in their not having any, or at least in their possessing such a malformed and primitive psychology that a description of it would have nothing more than pathological interest. But they do have a soul. And *La strada* is nothing but their experience of their souls and the revelation of this before our eyes.

La Strada, dir. Federico Fellini, 1954.

Gelsomina learns from the Fool that she has a place in the world. Gelsomina the idiot, homely and useless, discovers one day through this tightrope walker and clown that she is something other than a reject, an outcast; better, that she is irreplaceable and that she has a destiny, which is to be indispensable to Zampanò. The most powerful event in the film is, without question, Gelsomina's breakdown after Zampanò murders the Fool. From this point on, she is beset by an agony situated in that instant in which the Fool, who had virtually conferred her being onto her, ceased to exist. Little mouse-like cries escape uncontrollably from her lips at the sight of her dead friend: "The Fool is sick, the Fool is sick."

The stupid, obstinate, and brutish Zampanò can't realize how much he needs Gelsomina, and above all he can't sense the eminently spiritual nature of the bond that unites the two of them. Terrified by the poor girl's suffering and at the end of his patience, he abandons her. But just as the death of the Fool had made life unbearable for Gelsomina, so too will Zampanò's abandonment of her and then her death make life unbearable for him. Little by little this mass of muscles is reduced to its spiritual core, and Zampanò ends up being crushed by the absence of Gelsomina from his life. He's not crushed by remorse over what he did, or even by his love for her, but rather by overwhelming and incomprehensible anguish, which can only be the response of his soul to being deprived of Gelsomina.

Thus one can look at *La strada* as a phenomenology of the soul, perhaps even of the communion of saints, and at the very least as a phenomenology of the reciprocal nature of salvation. Where these slow-witted individuals are concerned, it is impossible to confuse ultimate spiritual realities with those of intelligence, passion, pleasure, or beauty. The soul reveals itself here beyond psychological or aesthetic categories, and it reveals itself all the more, precisely because one can't bedeck it with the trappings of conscience. The salt of the tears that Zampanò sheds for the first time in his sorry life, on the beach that Gelsomina loved, is the same salt as that of the infinite sea, which will never again be able to relieve its own anguish at the sufferings of men.

Chapter Sixteen

"Cruel Naples" (*Gold of Naples*)

"Naples cruelle" (*L'Or de Naples*), *Cahiers du cinéma*, n. 48 (June 1955), pp. 47–52, in *Qu'est-ce que le cinema?* Vol. 4 (Éditions du Cerf, 1962), pp. 104–111; translated into English by Bert Cardullo.

As strange as it might seem on first consideration, Vittorio De Sica is an accursed filmmaker. I may sound paradoxical, or I may seem to be looking for an argument, because my statement increases in ambiguity when you simultaneously consider the popularity of De Sica the actor and the critical importance assigned to *Bicycle Thieves* (1948). However, all we have to do is to reflect a little to realize that *Miracle in Milan* (1952) has enjoyed critical but not popular success and that *Umberto D.* (1952) hasn't enjoyed any success at all. The conditions under which the latter film was released in Paris, moreover, amounted to a guarantee of failure. The festival prize lists are also quite significant in this regard. The year *Umberto D.* was shown in Cannes (at a matinee screening), the jury preferred to honor *Cops and Robbers* (1951; dir. Mario Monicelli).

In 1953, the jury underlined the Hollywood-style immorality of De Sica's *Stazione Termini* (*Terminal Station*, aka *Indiscretion of an American Wife*, 1953) by deciding to ignore it; this year again, the audience and the jury have coldly received *Gold of Naples* (1954), and De Sica wasn't even awarded a tiny tin palm. In the end the film is going to be released in Paris only at the cost of cutting two of its six original episodes, including the best one, or at least the most significant. In the meantime, however, De Sica's popularity as an actor continues to grow thanks to films like *Bread, Love, and Jealousy* (1954; dir. Luigi Comencini).

It is fashionable among young critics to drag De Sica's name through the mud, and I grant that he occasionally deserves some serious condemnation. But before condemning him, one should at least try to understand why the festival juries, half the traditional critics, and the public in general ignore or despise not so much his most ambitious films, like *Umberto D.*, as his compromised projects such as *Stazione Termini* and *Gold of Naples*. For it is indeed quite strange that, even when De Sica resigns himself, for reasons far too obvious, to making a film with stars and vignettes and built around clever tricks and purple passages, everything turns out as though he had again been far too ambitious for a festival audience. The criticisms I have heard people make of his work at Cannes are thus not at all justified. Granted, *Gold of Naples* is a prostituted film, but it is still so classy that it seems prudish and boring to those who admire our own *Adorable Creatures* (1952; dir. Christian-Jaque) or bourgeois psychological dramas tailor-made by good French craftsmen.

Everything, then, depends on your point of reference. Absolutely speaking, or compared with his own work and with what we like of other Italian films, De Sica has not hesitated in *Gold of Naples* to make deplorable concessions. But compared with what the public and often even the critics know—or don't know—of Italian cinema, his film remains a monument to austerity. One must nonetheless reproach De Sica first with betraying neorealism here by pretending to serve it. In fact, *Gold of Naples* is an essentially theatrical film, through the twists of its plot as well as through the decisive importance it accords to acting. Certainly, the movie's episodes can be considered "short stories" or "novelettes," but their skillful and rigorous construction deprives them of the dramatic indeterminacy that constitutes neorealism. The incidents and the characters proceed from the action in *Gold of Naples,* they don't precede it. De Sica has succeeded in regenerating the structure of conventional drama or the dramatic novel through certain elements borrowed from neorealism. By multiplying the picturesque and unexpected touches, he wraps his dramatic construction in a coral-like cover of small facts that deceive us as to the make-up of the rock underneath. Neorealism being in essence a denial of dramatic categories, De Sica substitutes for them a micro-dramaturgy that suggests the absence of action. In the process, however, he evidences only a superior theatrical cunning.

This is why the episode I prefer is perhaps the one that people generally deem the most offensive: I mean the card game, because it is also the sketch whose scenic resources are the least camouflaged. This story of a monomaniacal baron whom the baroness forbids to gamble yet who ends up gambling away his jacket and glasses with the concierge's son, is a farce conceived for acting effects. There are limits to the ambition of this genre but these limits are

Gold of Naples, episode "Pizza on Credit," dir. Vittorio De Sica, 1954.

acceptable, especially when you consider that what De Sica adds to the genre considerably increases its aesthetic value. It is always better to give more than you had promised rather than to fail to live up to the promises you have made.

Conversely, I much admire—without liking it very much—the sketch that the filmmakers undoubtedly prefer: I refer to the burial of a child (unfortunately cut by the French distributor). De Sica and Zavattini wanted to give a guarantee of neorealism here; unlike other episodes, which are artfully constructed, this one appears to be a reconstituted scene from a news bulletin. De Sica limits himself to following the funeral procession of the dead child. The mother's behavior, the wretched exhibition she displays all along the way in order to give her child's last voyage a solemnity that is both tragic and joyous—this never crystallizes into "action," yet manages to hold our interest from beginning to end. Such an astonishing bravura passage in principle belongs to the same aesthetic family as the maid's wake-up scene in *Umberto D*. Why do I feel embarrassed by it, then? Probably because of the moral contradiction between the subject matter and the almost unseemly cleverness-by-understatement with which the sequence is handled. Such control over the means and ends, when the situation of the characters calls for sympathy and even pity, is somewhat irritating. Think by comparison of the simple, efficient, and sincere lyricism of Jules Dassin in *Rififi* (1955) during the return of the inhabitants of Saint-Etienne with the child.

As you can see, my reservations are not small. They won't prevent me, however, from acknowledging the merits of *Gold of Naples* from a relative point of view. If the film was not successful at Cannes, that must be because it nonetheless contains something good and worthy. We must explain the paradox of its failure not by the shortcomings that I have just mentioned and that on the contrary should have contributed to its success, but by the upholding at its very core of a union of form and content, which justifies a certain admiration.

First and foremost, craft is craft, and one had better realize this before criticizing its use. I apologize to our Hitchcocko-Hawksians, whom I am going to shock, but it is Hitchcock whom I can't help thinking of here. Of course, De Sica's skill does not bring itself to bear on the same elements of the *mise en scène* as Hitchcock's. The structuring of the image plays only a secondary role (although there is an unforgettable find in *Gold of Naples*: the elevator in the baron's house). The *mise en scène* is practically identified here with the directing of the actors, but you have to consider that the result is the same in that nothing in the picture seems likely to escape from the filmmaker's control.

Although there are fifty kids scattered like a flight of birds in the frame, for example, each of them seems to be making at every instance exactly the gesture that needs to be made, paradoxically even when that gesture must be unexpected. It *is* in fact unexpected, and that is the amazing part. De Sica relies on a certain margin of freedom and spontaneity that his walk-ons give him, but this man and his power are such that not a single discordant or approximate note is struck in the crowd. God and the Devil submit to that power. This director's self-assurance verges on obscenity during the scene of the baron's card game. Before De Sica, filmmakers had managed to make children play-act, but even the most gifted child is capable after all of only two or three expressions, which the director then strives to justify. For the first time, one can see here a ten- or eleven-year-old express in ten minutes a gamut of feelings whose variety equals that of his grown-up partner, in this case De Sica himself.

Gold of Naples, episode "The Racketeer," dir. Vittorio De Sica, 1954.

As for the professional actors, it would be an understatement to say that De Sica brings out the best in them: he reconstitutes them entirely. Not through the facile device of giving the professional a role that is different from the part he usually plays, but by somehow revealing in him another actor, a richer one who is more imbued with the character he is playing. Take, for instance, the extraordinary acting of Silvana Mangano, but take also the acting of Totò in the story of the racketeer. When you consider that it has become a commonplace of French criticism to maintain that our own Fernandel is a dramatic actor who too seldom finds work as one, all you can do is burst out laughing. Fernandel at his best looks like nothing more than an industrious clown alongside the simplicity and intelligence evidenced here by his Italian rival. God knows, however, that their usual antics are pretty much alike.

Nonetheless, everything happens in this film as though De Sica had the power of endowing his nonprofessional actors with the skill of experienced performers and his established stars with the spontaneity of common people. Of course, I'm not saying that this is my personal ideal, but it is, at least implicitly, the one which almost all filmmakers would strive to attain if it were in their power to get close to it. De Sica achieves it so perfectly that the audience, which is used to approximations of the ideal, perhaps feels more ill at ease than pleased in front of it.

I don't think, either, that in general the qualities of the script have been properly appreciated. Whatever one may think of the choice of subjects, it goes without saying that each of these could have been treated in a different way. Yet, the construction of all the episodes, and particularly of their dénouements, is amazingly intelligent. As a general rule, each story calls for an ending in, say, the style of Marcel Pagnol, that is, a false and moving one. Naturally, the average French filmmaker would substitute for such an ending one in Charles Spaak's style, that is, a true-to-life and pessimistic conclusion. The ambitious filmmaker would reject both the "good" and the "bad" endings and, in an act of supreme daring, would not end the story at all. De Sica and Zavattini manage to go them all one better.

The story seems at first to be moving toward a happy ending. We expect a surprise, and it comes with an unexpected development in the action, which makes us believe that in fact there will be no ending. Then, in the last few seconds, the script uncovers the most unexpected yet most necessary ending, which is the dialectical synthesis of all the endings that it had rejected. This is not due to the cleverness of an inventive screenwriter who seeks to surprise us at all costs, but rather to a constructive determination that throws a far more illuminating light on the whole action. The device presupposes such a dramatic strictness that it sometimes goes unnoticed even by the most attentive viewers, who cannot even imagine that the filmmaker might have aimed so high.

The ending of the episode entitled "Theresa," for example, was incorrectly interpreted by almost everyone. This is the nearly Dostoyevskian story of a young and rich Neapolitan bourgeois who decides to marry a prostitute to punish himself for having let a young woman die of love for him. This marriage, which must necessarily, and according to his own wishes, destroy his happiness, endanger his wealth, and ruin his reputation, takes place without the poor girl's understanding the game that she is being made to play (this is almost the plot of Bresson's *The Ladies of the Bois de Boulogne* [1946] in reverse). When she discovers that she is present only to remind her husband of his sin, her despair is immense. In his masochistic madness, the man hadn't even considered any of the most humanly plausible propositions: first, that his prostitute could make a nice and sweet wife, if only out of her gratitude to him, or second, that she could summon up enough female dignity to reject such a hateful game. Projecting onto the whole world his desire for castigation, he can see the woman he has chosen as true only to the *a priori* moral ideal of the prostitute, that is, as a diabolical and wicked being.

This summary clearly indicates the two possible endings: (1) the man, longing for unhappiness, finds happiness in spite of himself with a good girl (the Marcel Pagnol ending); (2) the prostitute, her female pride injured, prefers going back to the street in spite of her dreams of bourgeois respectability, comfort, and fidelity (the Spaak ending). Well, after her awful wedding night, the girl does run away; then, in the street, she thinks the situation over and goes back. I have heard people account for this third ending with psychological explanations that vary more or less according to the following: after she has run away out of wounded pride, the poor woman finds herself alone on the street in the rain and realizes all that she is going to lose; resigned, she silences her dignity and returns to bourgeois society, which is the ideal of every "self-respecting" prostitute.

This explanation, however, suggests that the viewer has not carefully watched the last two shots. Primarily because Silvana Mangano's face, carefully lit by a street lamp, expresses a whole range of feelings, the final one of which is neither resignation nor envy but rather hatred, which is moreover confirmed by the way she knocks on the door to ask her husband for admittance. The only plausible explanation, then, is that she had left on account of the blow to her pride, and that she comes back for the same reason, after some deep reflection. She has understood that flight is a doubly absurd solution, since it will deprive her of the material advantages of marriage as well as the consolations of revenge. Her return is therefore neither resigned nor submissive; it is an even higher manifestation of her femininity than flight, for it proves she thought that even a prostitute had the right to be loved. And now she's going to prove something even greater: that she is capable of avenging herself.

Thus matters finally get settled according to the man's will, but for moral reasons that are exactly the opposite of those he imagines. The girl is going to take her expected place in the unbelievable scheme of things; toward her husband she's now going to behave according to the conventional idea of a prostitute, because she will have ceased to be one passively. She will thus affirm her womanhood through hatred. Fulfilling the man's wish, she will then bring him to his doom, not because prostitutes will be prostitutes but out of deliberate choice, as a free woman of the world. You will recognize that this ending is not only unexpected and brilliant (provided that you at least see it), but also and above all that it retroactively raises the action from the primitive level of psycho-sociology to the higher plane of morality and even metaphysics.

Gold of Naples seems to me to contain still other important lessons. To the extent that the filmmaker's intention is perhaps more or less deliberately impure, some aspects of the Zavattini-De Sica collaboration come out more clearly. I will first underline the fact that *Gold of Naples* is a film of cruelty—a cruelty that has undoubtedly contributed to disconcerting the festival audience, which is used to associating good humor with southern European verve. Naples in this sense is nothing but a super-Marseilles.

I myself have made rather naïve statements in the past about De Sica's kindheartedness. And it is true that sentimentalism drips profusely from his films. But much will be forgiven him here for the authenticity of his cruelty. Granted, goodness in art can quickly become revolting. Chaplin's tramp may indeed look so good to those who don't discern the ambiguity in his heart. Goodness in itself does not signify anything, but its close and almost inevitable association with cruelty has a moral and aesthetic meaning that psychology alone cannot account for. Am I wrong? It seems to me that such kind cruelty, or cruel kindness, is far more than simply the invention of De Sica and Zavattini.

In any case, what seems very clear to me is that the director's talent essentially proceeds from his talent as an actor, and that this talent is not neorealistic by nature. If the collaboration between Zavattini and De Sica has been so successful, this is perhaps due to the attraction of opposites. In this marriage, the writer has brought the realistic temperament and the director the knowledge of theatrical exploitation. But these two artists were too intelligent or too gifted just to add the latter to the former: they subtly combined the two or, if I may be permitted such an image, they emulsified them. Theatricality and realism are so subtly mixed in their work that their aesthetic suspension gives the illusion of a new body, which would then be neorealism. But its stability is uncertain, and we can very well see in *Gold of Naples* how a great deal of the theatricality precipitates to the bottom—or is it the foundation?—of the *mise en scène*.

Chapter Seventeen

"In Defense of Rossellini"

"Défense de Rossellini," a letter to the editor of *Cinema nuovo* (August 1955), in *Qu'est-ce que le cinéma?* Vol. 4 (Éditions du Cerf, 1962), pp. 150–160; in *Qu'est-ce que le cinéma?* (Cerf, 1975 [single-volume version]), pp. 347–357; translated into English by Hugh Gray in *What Is Cinema?* Vol. 2 (Univ. of California Press, 1971), pp. 93–101, and edited below by Bert Cardullo.

AN OPEN LETTER TO GUIDO ARISTARCO, EDITOR-IN-CHIEF OF *CINEMA NUOVO*

I have been meaning to write these comments for some time now, but month after month I have deferred doing so, put off by the importance of the problem and its many ramifications. I am also aware that I lack theoretical preparation, as compared with the seriousness and thoroughness with which Italian critics on the left devote themselves to the study of neorealism in depth. Although I welcomed neorealism on its first arrival in France and have ever since continued to devote to it the unstinting best of my critical attentions, I cannot claim to have a coherent theory to rival your own, nor can I pretend to be able to situate the phenomenon of neorealism in the history of Italian culture as surely as you can. If you take into account, too, the fact that I am bound to look absurd if I try to instruct Italians in their own cinema, you will have the major reasons why I have failed as yet to respond to your invitation to discuss in the pages of *Cinema Nuovo* the critical position which you and your associates have taken on some recent films.

I would like to remind you, before getting to the heart of the discussion, that differences of opinion due to nationality are frequent even among critics of the same generation whom all else would seem to align. We of *Cahiers du cinéma*, for example, have experienced this with the staff of *Sight and Sound*, and I am not ashamed to admit that it was at least in part the high regard in which Lindsay Anderson held Jacques Becker's *Casque d'or* (which was a failure in France in 1952) that led me to reconsider my own view and to see virtues in the film which had escaped me.

It is true that the judgment of a foreigner is apt sometimes to go astray because of a lack of familiarity with the context from which a film comes. For example, the success outside France of films by Duvivier or Pagnol is clearly the result of a misunderstanding. Foreign critics admire in these films a picture of France that seems to them "wonderfully typical," and they confuse this "exoticism" with the value of these films as film. I recognize that these differences are of little consequence and I presume that the success abroad of some Italian films, which I think you are right to hold in low esteem, is based on the same kind of misunderstanding. Nevertheless, I do not think that this is true of the films that have caused us to disagree, nor even with neorealism in general.

To begin with, you will allow that French critics were not wrong, at the very outset, in being more enthusiastic than Italian critics about the films that today are the undisputed glory of the Italian cinema on both sides of the Alps. For my part, I flatter myself that I was one of the few French critics who always linked the rebirth of Italian cinema to "neorealism," even at the time when it was fashionable to say that the term was meaningless. Today I still think it the best term there is to designate what is best and most creative in Italian cinema. But this is also why I am disturbed by the way in which you defend it.

Do I dare suggest, dear Aristarco, that the harsh line taken by *Cinema Nuovo* against certain tendencies in neorealism which you consider regressive prompts me to fear that you are thereby unwittingly putting the knife to what is most alive and rich in your own cinema? I am eclectic enough in what I most admire in Italian cinema, but you have passed some harsh judgments that I am prepared to accept: you are an Italian. I can understand why the success in France of Luigi Comencini's *Pane, Amore e Fantasie* (*Bread, Love, and Dreams*, 1953) annoys you; your reaction resembles mine to Duvivier's films on Paris. But, on the other hand, when I find you hunting for fleas in Gelsomina's tousled hair, or dismissing Rossellini's last film as less than nothing I am forced to conclude that under the guise of theoretical integrity you are in the process of nipping in the bud some of the liveliest and most promising offshoots of what I persist in calling neorealism.

You tell me you are amazed at the relative success which Rossellini's *Viaggio in Italia* (*Voyage in Italy*, 1953) has had in Paris, and even more so by the

Voyage in Italy, dir. Roberto Rossellini, 1953.

almost unanimous enthusiasm of the French critics for it. As for *La strada* (1954), you are well aware of what a success it has been. These two films have come just at the right moment to restore Italian cinema not only in the interest of the general public but also in the esteem of the intellectuals—for interest in Italian film has flagged in the past year or two. The reasons for their success are in many ways very different. Nevertheless, far from their having been felt here as a break with neorealism and still less as a regression, they have given us a feeling of a creative inventiveness deriving directly from the spirit which informs the Italian school. I will try to tell you why.

But first I have to confess to a strong dislike for a notion of neorealism that is based, to the exclusion of all else, on what is only one of its present aspects, for this is to submit its future potential to *a priori* restrictions. Perhaps I dislike it so because I haven't enough of a head for theory. I think, however, that it is because I prefer to allow art its natural freedom. In sterile periods theory is a fruitful source for the analysis of the causes of the drought, and it can help to create the conditions necessary for the rebirth. But when we have had the good fortune to witness the wonderful flowering of Italian cinema over the past ten years, is there not more danger than advantage to be gained if we try to lay down a law that we say is imposed by theory?

Not that we do not have to be strict. On the contrary, an exacting and rigorous criticism is needed—now more than ever, I think. But its concern should be to denounce commercial compromise, demagoguery, the lowering of the level of the ambitions, rather than to impose *a priori* aesthetic standards on artists. As I view it, a director whose aesthetic ideals are close to your own but who sets to work assuming that he can include only ten or twenty percent of these ideals in any commercial script he may happen to shoot, has less merit than a man who for better or worse makes films that conform to his ideal, even if his concept of neorealism differs from yours. In the first of these two films, you are content objectively to record that the film is at least in part free of compromise by according it two stars in your critique, but you consign the second film to aesthetic hell, without right of appeal.

In your view Rossellini would, doubtless, be less to blame if he had made something like *Stazione Termini* (*Terminal Station;* aka *Indiscretion of an American Wife*, 1953) or *Umberto D.* (1952) rather than his own *Giovanna d'Arco al rogo* (*Joan of Arc at the Stake*, 1954) or *La Paura* (*Fear*, 1954). It is not my intention to defend the author of *Europe '51* (1952) at the expense of Lattuada or De Sica; the policy of compromise is defensible, up to a point. I am not going to try to define it here, but it does seem to me that Rossellini's independence gives his work—whatever one may think of it on other grounds—an integrity of style and a moral unity only too rare in cinema, which compel us to esteem it even before we admire it.

But it is not on such methodological grounds as these that I hope to defend him. Instead, I will direct my argument on his behalf at the assumptions on which the discussion is based. Has Rossellini ever really been a neorealist and is he one still? It would seem to me that you admit that he has been a neorealist. How indeed can there be any question of the role played by *Roma, città aperta* (1945) and *Paisà* (1946) in the origin and development of neorealism? But you say that a certain "regression" is already apparent in *Germania, anno zero* (1947), that it is decisive beginning with *Stromboli* (1950) and *The Flowers of St. Francis* (1950), and that it has become catastrophic in *Europe '51* and *Viaggio in Italia*.

But what is it, in essence, that you find to blame in this aesthetic itinerary? Increasingly less concern for social realism, for chronicling the events of daily life, in favor, it is not to be denied, of an increasingly obvious moral message—a moral message that, depending on the degree of his malevolence, a person may identify with either one of the two major tendencies in Italian politics. I refuse to allow the discussion to descend to this dubious level. Even if Rossellini had in fact Christian-Democrat leanings (and of this there is no proof, public or private, so far as I know), this would not be enough to exclude him *a priori* from the possibility of being a neorealist artist. But let that pass.

It is true, nonetheless, that one does have a right to reject the moral or spiritual postulate that is increasingly evident in his work, but even so to reject this would not imply rejection of the aesthetic framework within which this message is manifest, unless the films of Rossellini were in fact films *à thèse*—that is, unless they were mere dramatizations of *a priori* ideas. But in point of fact there is no Italian director in whose work aim and form are more closely linked, and it is precisely on this basis that I would characterize Rossellini's neorealism.

If the word has any meaning—whatever the differences that arise over its interpretation, above and beyond a minimal agreement—in the first place it stands in opposition to the traditional dramatic systems and also to the various other known kinds of realism in literature and film with which we are familiar, through its claim that there is a certain "wholeness" to reality. Neorealism is a description of reality conceived as a whole by a consciousness disposed to see things as a whole. Neorealism contrasts with the realist aesthetics that preceded it, and in particular with naturalism and verism, in that its realism is not so much concerned with the choice of subject as with a particular way of regarding things. If you like, what is realist in *Paisà* is the Italian Resistance, but what is neorealist is Rossellini's direction—his presentation of the events, a presentation that is at once elliptical and synthetic.

To put it still another way, neorealism by definition rejects analysis, whether political, moral, psychological, logical, or social, of the characters and their actions. It looks on reality as a whole, not incomprehensible, certainly, but inseparably one. This is why neorealism, although not necessarily antispectacular (though spectacle is to all intents and purposes alien to it), is at least basically antitheatrical in the degree that stage acting presupposes on the part of the actor a psychological analysis of the emotions to which a character is subject and a set of expressive physical signs that symbolize a whole range of moral categories.

This does not at all mean that neorealism is limited to some otherwise indefinable "documentarianism" [or supposed attitude of impersonal objectivity]. Rossellini is fond of saying that a love not only for his characters but for the real world just as it is lies at the heart of his conception of the way a film is to be directed, and that it is precisely this love that precludes him from putting asunder what reality has joined together: namely, the character and the setting. Neorealism, then, is not characterized by a refusal to take a stand *vis-à-vis* the world, still less by a refusal to judge it; as a matter of fact, it always presupposes an attitude of mind: it is always reality as it is visible through an artist, as refracted by his consciousness—but by his consciousness as a whole and not by his reason alone or his emotions or his beliefs—and reassembled from its distinguishable elements.

I would put it this way: the traditional realist artist—Zola, for example—analyzes reality into parts, which he then reassembles in a synthesis the final determinant of which is his moral conception of the world, whereas the consciousness of the neorealist director filters reality. Undoubtedly, his consciousness, like that of everyone else, does not admit reality as a whole, but the selection that does occur is neither logical nor is it psychological; it is ontological, in the sense that the image of reality it restores to us is still a whole—just as a black and white photograph is not an image of reality broken down and put back together again "without the color" but rather a true imprint of reality, a kind of luminous mold in which color simply does not figure. There is ontological identity between the object and its photographic image.

Voyage in Italy, dir. Roberto Rossellini, 1953.

I may perhaps make myself better understood by an example from *Viaggio in Italia*. Admittedly the public is easily disappointed by the film in that the Naples which it depicts is incomplete. This reality is only a small part of the reality that might have been shown, but the little one sees—statues in a museum, pregnant women, an excavation at Pompeii, the tail-end of the procession of the early Christian martyr Saint Januarius—has the quality of wholeness which in my view is essential. It is Naples "filtered" through the consciousness of the heroine. If the landscape is bare and confined, it is because the consciousness of an ordinary bourgeoise itself suffers from great spiritual poverty. Nevertheless, the Naples of the film is not false (which it could easily be with the Naples of a documentary three hours long). It is rather a mental landscape at once as objective as a straight photograph and as subjective as pure personal consciousness. We realize now that the attitude which Rossellini takes toward his characters and their geographical and social setting is, at one remove, the attitude of his heroine toward Naples—the difference being that his awareness is that of a highly cultured artist and, in my opinion, an artist of rare spiritual vitality.

I apologize for proceeding by way of metaphor, but I am not a philosopher and I cannot convey my meaning any more directly. I will therefore attempt one more comparison. I will say this of the classical forms of art and of traditional realism, that they are built as houses are built, with brick or cut stones. It is not a matter of calling into question either the utility of these houses or the beauty they may or may not have, or the perfect suitability of bricks to the building of houses. The reality of the brick lies less in its composition than it does in its form and its strength. It would never enter your head to define it as a piece of clay; its peculiar mineral composition matters little. What does count is that it have the right dimensions. A brick is the basic unit of a house. That this is so is proclaimed by its appearance.

One can apply the same argument to the stones of which a bridge is constructed. They fit together perfectly to form an arch. But the big rocks that lie scattered in a ford are now and ever will be no more than mere rocks. Their reality as rocks is not affected when, leaping from one to another, I use them to cross the river. If the service which they have rendered is the same as that of the bridge, it is because I have brought my share of ingenuity to bear on their chance arrangement; I have added the motion which, though it alters neither their nature nor their appearance, gives them a provisional meaning and utility. In the same way, the neorealist film has a meaning, but it is *a posteriori,* to the extent that it permits our awareness to move from one fact to another, from one fragment of reality to the next, whereas in the classical artistic composition the meaning is established *a priori*: the house is already there in the brick.

If my analysis is correct, it follows that the term neorealism should never be used as a noun, except to designate the neorealist directors as a body. Neorealism as such does not exist. There are only neorealist directors—whether they be materialists, Christians, Communists, or whatever. Visconti is neorealistic in *La terra trema* (1948), a call to social revolt, and Rossellini is neorealistic in *The Flowers of St. Francis*, a film that lights up for us a purely spiritual reality. I will only deny the qualification neorealist to the director who, to persuade me, puts asunder what reality has joined together. In my view, then, *Viaggio in Italia* is neorealist—more so than *Gold of Naples* (1954), for example, which I greatly admire but whose realism is basically psychological and subtly theatrical, despite the many realistic touches that aim to take us in.

I would go even further and claim that of all Italian directors, Rossellini has done the most to extend the frontiers of the neorealist aesthetic. I have said that there is no such thing as pure neorealism. The neorealist attitude is an ideal that one can approach to a greater or lesser degree. In all films termed neorealist there are traces still of traditional realism—spectacular, dramatic, or psychological. They can all be broken down into the following components: documentary reality plus something else, this something else being the plastic beauty of the images, the social sense, or the poetry, the comedy, and so on. You would look in vain in the works of Rossellini for some such distinction of event and intended effect. There is nothing in his films that belongs to literature or to poetry, not even a trace of "the beautiful" in the merely pleasing sense of the word. Rossellini directs facts. It is as if his characters were haunted by some demon of movement. His little brothers of Saint Francis seem to have no better way of glorifying God than to run races. And what of the haunting death march of the little urchin in *Germania, anno zero*?

Gesture, change, physical movement constitute for Rossellini the essence of human reality. This means, too, that his characters are more apt to be affected by the settings through which they move than the settings are liable to be affected by their movement. The world of Rossellini is a world of pure acts, unimportant in themselves but preparing the way (as if unbeknownst to God himself) for the sudden dazzling revelation of their meaning. Thus it is with the miracle of *Viaggio in Italia*: unseen by the two leading characters, almost unseen even by the camera, and in any case ambiguous (for Rossellini does not claim that it is a miracle but only the noise and crowd movements that people are in the habit of calling a miracle), its impact on the consciousness of the characters is such, nonetheless, as to prompt the unexpected outpouring of their love for one another.

To my mind, no one has been more successful in creating the aesthetic structure which in consequence of its strength, wholeness, and transparency is better suited to the direction of events than the author of *Europe '51*; the structure that Rossellini has created allows the viewer to see nothing but the event itself. This brings to mind the way in which some bodies can exist in either an amorphous or a crystalline state. The art of Rossellini consists in knowing what has to be done to confer on the facts what is at once their most substantial and their most elegant shape—not the most graceful, but the sharpest in outline, the most direct, or the most trenchant. Neorealism discovers in Rossellini the style and the resources of abstraction.

To have a regard for reality does not mean that what one does in fact is to pile up appearances. On the contrary, it means that one strips the appearances of all that is not essential, in order to get at the totality in its simplicity. The art of Rossellini is linear and melodic. True, several of his films make one think of a sketch: more is implicit in the line than it actually depicts. But is one to attribute such sureness of line to poverty of invention or to laziness? One would have to say the same of Matisse. Perhaps Rossellini is more a master of line than a painter, more a short-story writer than a novelist. But there is no hierarchy of genres, only of artists.

I do not expect to have convinced you, my dear Aristarco. In any event, it is never with arguments that one wins over a person. The conviction one instills in them often counts for more. I shall be satisfied if just my conviction (in which you will find an echo of the admiration for Rossellini of several of my critic-colleagues) serves at least to stimulate your own.

Chapter Eighteen

"De Sica and Rossellini"

"De Sica and Rossellini," *Radio-Cinéma-Télévision* (September 1955); in *Qu'est-ce que le cinéma?* Vol. 4 (Éditions du Cerf, 1962), pp. 112–116; translated into English by Bert Cardullo.

If Zavattini-De Sica and Rossellini do indeed embody what is best and purest in neorealism as the total description of the real, it is true that they also represent its opposite poles and that this opposition has become more and more marked through the years. I will reduce it to these two primary aspects: one has to do with content and the other with style.

FOR ZAVATTINI-DE SICA, HUMAN REALITY IS A SOCIAL PHENOMENON

By temperament, and perhaps also out of conviction, the team of Zavattini-De Sica essentially considers human reality first as a social phenomenon. This does not mean that they are not interested in the individual. Quite the contrary, *Bicycle Thieves* (1948) and *Umberto D.* (1952) are self-evidently pleas on behalf of the human being and his or her individual happiness, but the conditions of this happiness are reduced to a series of factual "prerequisites": unemployment and all its consequences, the State and its economic hypocrisies, etc. In Zavattini, there is, on the one hand, man and his nature, and, on the other hand, all the complex social circumstances that beget suffering and tragedy. I am aware that I am oversimplifying matters here, but I don't think I am misrepresenting the gist of Zavattini's inspiration. For him, neorealism is first and foremost a realism of the relationship of the individual to society. This probably explains the preference, and even fondness, of left-wing critics for Zavattini.

FOR ROSSELLINI, A MORAL PROBLEM

Even though the subject matter of *Paisà* and *Germany, Year Zero* could fool us with regard to Rossellini's ultimate concerns, I think that their true nature was not social, but moral. For the director of *Stromboli* (1950), *The Miracle* (1948), and *Europe '51* (1952), the protagonist of the film must solve for himself an essential moral problem; he must find the answer to a question that will give the world its moral or ethical sense. This does not mean that, compared to Zavattini's concerns, Rossellini's ignore social reality. As with De Sica, a depiction of the historical context accompanies any depiction of the individual; Rossellini gives us a faithful and objective rendering of the shock of a moral event in the context of the social reality encountered by the individual: waves radiate from it and their effect on surrounding objects or obstacles is often reflected back to the source.

Roberto Rossellini (1906–1977).

It may even happen that the cause of the hero's or heroine's moral anguish is of an eminently social nature, as in *Europe '51*. This fools the bourgeois family, which is impervious to anxiety, as well as the priest, for whom spiritual problems must crystallize in *religious* sociology, or the communist militant who believes only in revolutionary efficiency. But it is of course not because Vincent de Paul's sainthood was geared toward alleviating his time's injustices that it was of a social nature. Thus, Rossellini's neorealism can tackle subjects that appear to be related to the traditional ones of the novel, such as individual character analysis—and this is indeed the case in *Voyage in Italy* (1953). But this is done according to aesthetic laws that are precisely the opposite, whether the subject matter be on the surface social or psychological.

Here is the definition of neorealism by Amédée Ayfre: "All the objective, subjective, and social elements of reality are in neorealism never analyzed as such; they are contained in a block of events with all its inextricable blurring: a block in time as well as in space, which spares us not one second, not one gesture. Above all, there is this way in neorealism of taking the opposite stance from that of analysis, of putting an end to the compartmentalized description of man and of the world." This definition seems valid for the films by Zavattini-De Sica as well as for those of Rossellini, in that the former as well as the latter purports to give us a global image of man—one that would not isolate him from his geographical, historical, and social context, and one that also rejects the dramatic organization of the narrative, because narrative is an abstract construct. The plot, if one can still call it that, no longer lies in some action that one could detach from events as if from a skeleton: it is immanent in the events themselves, contained in each instant of each of these events, indissociable from the fabric of life.

ZAVATTINI ANALYZES, ROSSELLINI SYNTHESIZES

But if this general observation applies to the Zavattinian ideal, as materialized for example by De Sica in the sequence of the little maid's getting up in *Umberto D.*, as well in whatever episode from Rossellini's *The Flowers of St. Francis* (1950) or *Voyage in Italy*, I must now point up a difference between the two filmmakers. One could no doubt otherwise characterize the difference in style between Rossellini and De Sica, but it seems to me that the gist of their opposition is that De Sica's directing is based on analysis, whereas Rossellini's is based on synthesis.

Once after a long interview that Zavattini had given to me, I wrote that his cinematic ambition was to be, as it were, the Proust of the present tense of the indicative mood. Let me elaborate. For Zavattini, through De Sica, the idea is to observe our fellow man from closer and closer, to perceive the particular realities that make up his most trivial behaviors, then to capture even smaller realities, as if with a microscope that would magnify human activity more and more and progressively reveal a universe of consciousness, whereas what we usually see there is only an old man tidying up his room or a young girl grinding coffee.

Rossellini, by contrast, would look at his characters from the large end of a telescope. Of course, the distances I am alluding to here are figurative and purely theoretical, in the sense that we have the impression of witnessing events from afar, without being able to intervene, events whose causes we do not all discern and whose latent progression suddenly bursts into heartrending complications, which are both inevitable and unpredictable. This is true for the child's suicide at the beginning of *Europe '51* or for the dénouement of *Voyage in Italy*, which is caused by a "miracle" invisible to the protagonists and of which the camera itself sees almost nothing.

KINDNESS AND LOVE

To conclude, I could perhaps say that neorealism for both Rossellini and De Sica amounts to becoming totally conscious of the human predicament, but that this awareness leads Zavattini to subdivide reality further and further, whereas it leads Rossellini to emphasize the forces which hold that reality together and restrict man's tragic liberty from all sides. From a different point of view, I would say that the progressive approach to the Zavattinian protagonist, his quasi-microscopic description, reveals a sympathetic intent that I would even call kindness. Whereas the Rossellinian distance—through the tension it creates between us and the protagonist, through the denial of psychological participation that this distance implies—imposes on us a relationship that can only be called *love*, but love that is not sentimental and that one could go so far as to call metaphysical.

Chapter Nineteen

"Senso"

"*Senso*," *France-Observateur* (February 1956); in *Qu'est-ce que le cinéma?* Vol. 4 (Éditions du Cerf, 1962), pp. 117–121; translated into English by Bert Cardullo.

The action of *Senso* (1954) takes place in 1866 at the time of the "Risorgimento" [the nineteenth-century movement for the liberation and unification of Italy]. Venice is under Austrian occupation. The performance of a Verdi opera (*Il Trovatore* [1853]) at the Phoenix Theater is the occasion for a patriotic demonstration during which Marquis Ussoni, one of the leaders of the "Resistance," provokes a young Austrian officer, Franz Mahler. Ussoni is arrested upon his exit from the theater. To save him, his cousin, Countess Livia Serpieti, seeks to make the acquaintance of the handsome Austrian lieutenant, who easily takes advantage of the situation in order to try out on the imprudent countess his abilities as a skillful and cynical seducer. The result is that he becomes her lover. Such a limited summary hardly permits me to analyze the at once subtle and elemental dealings that unite for the worst this weak yet lucid young man and this beautiful older woman, who will sacrifice all honor and decency for him and ultimately betray the cause of her friends in the "Resistance," whom she had served as an advisor.

According to impeccable logic, Visconti develops the action on two levels: the historical and the individual. The love relationship of the two protagonists begins and evolves in an irreversibly downward direction, whereas all the values (moral as well as political) that attach to the historical context are progressive and bracing. But this moral-political Manichaeism is not the product of a clever screenwriter's or director's trick: it is inherent in the story from the start, and subsequent events simply conspire to bring it out. To be sure, there are villains (Count Serpieri, for example, who is the typical "collaborator"), but the protagonists are doomed without them, and Franz Mahler, in his refined and clear-eyed ignominy, knows it. Marquis Ussoni, however, is there as proof of the fact that history does not dispose of anyone *a priori*. On the contrary: he digs deep into his family's heritage to find the courage and determination with which to go on. And if she hadn't been blinded by love, Livia herself would perhaps have continued to participate in the triumph of History. But as soon as she is blindfolded, she can but fight in vain against the current as she is dragged down along with her social class to the bottom of the abyss, where she will have only the fatal consolation of joining her lover.

Senso, dir. Luchino Visconti, 1954.

What should be transparent even from my poor summary of the action are both the film's transposition of time from the "Risorgimento" to the Occupation and Resistance of World War II (this transposition is carried very far in its details, especially where the relations between the underground "Resistance" and the official national army are concerned), and its Marxist analysis of a romantic entanglement. From these two points of view, *Senso* would certainly deserve a fuller discussion than I am able to give here. But I must at least point out that the appeal of this ideological perspective is in its never appearing to have been slavishly applied from outside the aesthetic logic of the narrative; on the contrary: the ideological component comes across as an added dimension that naturally attends the revelation of the romantic truth. Nevertheless, I don't think that this breaks any absolutely new ground. In this respect, *Senso* is probably simply adhering to the novelistic aesthetic that originated with Flaubert and that was particularly affirmed by naturalism. The film thus allies itself with a literature that is simultaneously descriptive and critical. Still, and for reasons completely contingent on their source, good examples of Marxist inspiration are so rare that it would be difficult to remain insensitive to this one.

Obsession, dir. Luchino Visconti, 1942.

But let's try to define the style adopted by Visconti in this film. I don't think that, stylistically, *Senso* is essentially different from *Ossessione* (1942) or *La terra trema* (1948), as some of Visconti's own comments might suggest. I recognize, on the contrary, the same fundamental preoccupations in this latest work. Of *La terra trema*, for instance, I would not hesitate to say that Visconti had indulged in the "theatricalization" of doubly realistic material: realistic, in the normal sense, since the film was about a real village and the authentic life of its authentic inhabitants, but also in the restrictive, "miserabilistic" sense. There's nothing less "beautiful," less noble, less spectacular than this poor society of fishermen. Naturally, I don't intend the term "theatrical" in its pejorative sense. I use it instead to suggest the nobility and extraordinary dignity that Visconti's *mise en scène* injected into this reality. These fishermen were not dressed in rags, they were draped in them like tragic princes. Not because Visconti was trying to distort or simply interpret their existence, but because he was revealing its immanent dignity.

Of *Senso* I would conversely say that it reveals the realism of theater. Not only because Visconti gives us this motif from the start with the opera whose action, as it were, leaves the stage for the house, but also because the historical aspect, despite all its ramifications—especially in matters aristocratic and military—is experienced first on the level of décor and spectacle. This is true for all "period films," of course, especially those in color. But starting from this point, Visconti continuously seeks to impose upon this magnificent, beautifully composed, almost picturesque setting the rigor and, most importantly, the unobtrusiveness of a documentary.

Let me give only one example among a hundred. A few moments before battle, the Italian soldiers, who had been hiding behind haystacks, come out and fall in for the attack. The folded-up flag is brought to the commanding officer; brand-new in its protective covering, it must be taken out before it can be unfurled. This detail is barely visible in an extreme long shot in which every element is given the same, strict weight. Now imagine a similar scene shot by Duvivier or Christian-Jaque: the flag would be used as a dramatic symbol or as an integral part of the *mise en scène*. For Visconti, what matters is that the flag is *new* (as new as the Italian army); he calls attention to it, however, not through the framing, but only, where possible, through heightened realism.

Visconti claims that in *Senso* he wanted to show the "melodrama" (read: the opera) of life. If this was his intention, his film is a complete success. *La terra trema* had the magnitude and the nobility of opera; *Senso* has the density and the import of reality. It is possible that Visconti's film satisfies another kind of dialectic. It would hardly take away from the film's achievement if it didn't exclusively satisfy the one described here.

Chapter Twenty

"*Il Bidone*, or the Road to Salvation Reconsidered"

"*Il bidone* ou le salut en question," *France-Observateur* (March 1956); in *Qu'est-ce que le cinéma?* Vol. 4 (Éditions du Cerf, 1962), pp. 129–133; translated into English by Bert Cardullo.

When I heard one of my colleagues cleverly sneer, "It's a swindle!" to a countryman after the screening of this film at the Venice Festival, I didn't feel very proud of being a French critic. But these "wise guys" weren't as harsh as most Italian critics, for I have also heard the most esteemed among them declare that *Il bidone* (*The Swindle*, 1955) definitely proved that those who had praised *La strada* (1954) had been mistaken. For my part, I admit that the Venice screening left me perplexed because I don't understand Italian: some long sequences therefore appeared to me to be doubly questionable. But, far from negating my admiration for *La strada*, *Il bidone* seemed to me to confirm the genius that was manifested in it. Even if Fellini's latest film was relatively unsuccessful, it still suggested a power of invention, a poetic and moral vision, that was by no means inferior to that of *La strada* or even *I vitelloni* (1953).

But *Il bidone* is not an unsuccessful film. I realize this today after seeing it for the third time, subtitled at last, and rid of a few scenes, which were indeed unnecessary. Not that they were unjustified from a certain point of view. But, in fact, the film is now too short, for Fellini had intended to develop these scenes further, which would have been useful to a full understanding of the characters' destinies; for some reason, in the end he gave up on doing so. So the excised scenes were superfluous, and it was better to cut too much than not enough. This is not at all comparable, fortunately, to the mutilations undergone at a certain point by a print of *La strada*, nor is it comparable, even more fortunately, to the mutilations allegedly intended for *Il bidone* by the French distributor: these were supposed to do nothing less than radically transform the meaning of the dénouement.

Augusto, the protagonist of the film, does indeed die for having tried to con his two pals into believing that he has taken pity on the paralyzed girl whose parents the three of them have just swindled. In reality, he wants to keep the money for himself, so that he can help his own daughter pursue her studies. The other swindlers beat him up in revenge and leave him to die alone on a stony hillside. We can see that if Augusto had really let himself be moved by the poor peasant girl, he would have been redeemed and would have died an innocent man, much to the great satisfaction of the Manichaeism that presides over all commercial happy endings.

Does his behavior make him fundamentally good or evil? Fortunately, Fellini never places himself on the level of such moral psychology. His universe dramaturgically remaps the road to salvation. People are what they are—beings—and what they *become*, not what they do; their actions, whether good or evil or filled with purity of intention, don't permit them to be judged any more objectively than subjectively. The purity of the man lies deeper: for Fellini, it is essentially defined by the transparency or the opacity of the soul, or even, if you will, by a certain perviousness to grace. Naturally, those who are perfectly transparent and open to other people's love want to do good and generally do so (although this type of "good" often has very little to do with morality in the strictest sense); but we are dealing here with the consequences of essence, not the causes of action.

So, we may believe that Augusto is saved, just like Zampanò in *La strada*, even though he has intended and done evil right up to the end, because he has at least died in a state of anxiety. His conversation with the paralyzed girl did not move him at all in the psychological sense of the word. Far from making him comprehend the shame of betraying a child's confidence, it doubtless gave him, on the contrary, the courage and determination to swindle his accomplices. At the same time, however, his conversation with the paralyzed girl introduced turmoil to his soul; it made him see, finally, not so much the accidental lie of his actions as the essential imposture of his life.

By contrast, Picasso (whose story was abbreviated in the final version) is a nice, sensitive, sentimental man, always full of good intentions and always ready to take pity on others or on himself. But for all this, Picasso's salvation is probably hopeless. Why does he steal? Because he "looks like an angel"; with a face like his, he couldn't be suspected of anything. Incapable of truly responding to his internal fissures, of bridging them, Picasso is doomed to darkness and to ultimate downfall, despite the gentleness and love he displays toward his wife and child. Picasso's actions do not make him evil, but he *is* lost, just as Augusto is probably saved, despite the fact that he is incapable of pity.

Il bidone, dir. Federico Fellini, 1955.

I haven't used this Christian vocabulary intentionally—although a Christian inspiration is certainly undeniable in Fellini's work—but such a vocabulary is undoubtedly the one that best conveys the nature of the realities that are the object of a film like *Il bidone*. Whether construed as metaphors or as metaphysical truths, the terms salvation or damnation, darkness or transparency of the soul, are the ones that impose themselves on me as I write, since they most accurately express the state of ultimate urgency in which our being is suspended as we otherwise conduct our lives.

Of these swindlers Fellini has said, I think, that they are aging *vitelloni* (overgrown calves). The phrase perfectly describes these second-rate con men whose art resides solely in their huckster's gift of gab; they can't even get rich off their work, unlike the former colleague of theirs who is now a drug dealer and who invites them to celebrate New Year's Eve at his luxurious apartment. This extraordinary sequence, in which the chief device of contemporary cinema, the surprise party, is once again to be found, is the climax of the film. If there can be talk of symbolism at the precise moment in *Il bidone* where realism is at its peak, then one can say that Fellini doubtless wanted to construct an image of hell, and a rather scorching one at that, for these poor devils who will not be able to endure its fire for very long.

I realize that I haven't told much of the "story." This is probably because I surmised that the reader had already read several summaries of it. One reason above all others is that the film doesn't much encourage plot summary. Although full of strange and funny episodes, it goes beyond the merely picturesque. If I dwelt on that aspect, I'd only be treating the accessories. *Il bidone* is built, or rather created, like a novel: from the very inside of the characters. Fellini has certainly never conceived a situation for its narrative logic, nor even less for its dramatic necessity, and he doesn't do so here. The events happen all of a sudden: they are totally unpredictable, yet somehow inevitable, as the ones would have been that Fellini could have substituted for them.

If I had to compare this world to the world of a well-known novelist, it would unquestionably be that of Dostoyevsky, despite all the particulars that separate the two. In the Russian novelist's work, as in Fellini's, events are in fact never anything but the completely accidental instruments through which human souls feel their way, and nothing ever happens that is fundamentally connected with their salvation or damnation. Good and evil, happiness and anguish, are from this point of view nothing more than relative categories in comparison with the absolute alternative in which these protagonists are trapped, and that I can't help but call, even if only metaphorically, salvation or damnation.

Chapter Twenty-one

"The Roof"

"*Il tetto,*" *France-Observateur*, 7.343 (6 December 1956), p. 18; translated into English by Bert Cardullo.

We know how disastrous the state of Italian cinema is: it has been put out of balance economically by super-productions and overpriced casting, and it is artistically torn by the contradictions that exist between the exploitation of the star system and the recipes of neorealism. This crisis does not at all mean that neorealism has run out of steam and that we are witnessing its decadence. Quite the contrary. It is the forsaking of neorealism or its watering down by producers that is the cause of all this. Nevertheless, everything that has mattered in the Italian cinema for the last three years, Fellini to begin with of course, evidences the vitality of an inspiration that seems to be inherent in the particular genius of Italian cinema.

One of the most obvious symptoms of the crisis, after the quasi-exile of Rossellini [as a result of his extra-marital relationship with Ingrid Bergman] is the unemployment of the director Vittorio De Sica. The filmmaker of *Umberto D.* (1952) is not guilty of disingenuousness here. He has repeatedly claimed that he had to have a career as an actor in order to be able from time to time to both produce and direct a film according to his heart's wishes. In this respect, *Gold of Naples* (1954) was a compromise (albeit a very honorable one), as it was based on a neorealist theme. De Sica nevertheless made "an actor's movie." But with *The Roof* (1956), we see him at last try to go back to the pure neorealist formula of *Bicycle Thieves* (1948) and *Umberto D.*

A HOUSE IN ONE NIGHT

The simplicity of this film is such that one can describe its plot completely in just a few sentences. A young couple does not have a private residence. Living under the same roof as the brother-in-law and the parents-in-law turns sour: after an argument, they leave. But where will they find a roof? These two then decide to build on a dumping ground in the area one of those unlawful shacks that Italian jurisprudence tolerates as long as they are erected, roof included, before the arrival of the police. In fact, their idea is to build, in just one night, a small brick house of a few square meters. But if the roof is not laid before dawn, the police will have everything torn down and the unlucky owner will incur a debt of several thousand *lire*. This summary is an indication of the construction of *The Roof*: particularly noteworthy in the first part is the social realism of the film's descriptiveness, whereas the second part is underscored by a suspense that gives the picture a certain dramatic tension. But this tension or suspense is only the scaffolding that supports the small events that constitute the true subject matter of the film, from beginning to end.

The Roof, dir. Vittorio De Sica, 1956.

A WONDERFUL FEMALE DISCOVERY

All things considered, *The Roof* unlike *Umberto D.* for instance, does come in for some criticism. The screenplay is perhaps not as rigorous as one might expect from Cesare Zavattini when he refuses to make any concessions. The film's lack of rigorousness is mainly due to its dramatic simplicity, which borders on the simplistic. But I still have a weakness for *The Roof*, because of the sweetness of the story, its transparence or plainness, and the charm of its romance. Falling back on old principles, De Sica has naturally cast nonprofessional actors in *The Roof*. With Gabriella Palotta, who plays the young woman, he has probably made his most wonderful female discovery. And God knows how felicitous his acting choices have already been in *Miracle in Milan* (1951) and *Umberto D*. Paradoxically, it is good that the young man's presence in De Sica's latest film is not so convincing, as some inequality was necessary here. This much genius in the casting can be bearable only for one actor!

The Roof, dir. Vittorio De Sica, 1956.

Unless you have a particular allergy to the films of De Sica and Zavattini, and despite the small reservations one might have if one happens to be in a picky mood, *The Roof*, then, is an admirable film and should therefore not be missed.

Chapter Twenty-two

"Neorealism Returns: Love in the City"

"Le néo-réalisme se retourne: *L'Amour à la ville*," *Education Nationale* (February 28, 1957) and *Cahiers du cinéma*, 12, #69 (March 1957), pp. 44–46; in *Qu'est-ce que le cinéma?* Vol. 4 (Éditions du Cerf, 1962), pp. 146–149; translated into English by Bert Cardullo.

In truth, and it is a fortunate one, neorealism's existence has preceded its essence, as it were. The concern for neorealist dogma and theory appeared only later among a few directors and critics, more specifically when inspiration appeared to start drying up. Cesare Zavattini himself (the prolific screenwriter who alone accounts for half of Italian cinema) notably advocated extremist film theories at the 1954 Parma Conference. To him, neorealism's purpose is essentially to reveal social reality, to transform into spectacle the human world that surrounds us and that we nevertheless ignore. But paradoxically, this "spectacularization" must modify reality as little as possible; the ideal would be to film things as they are and yet make them speak to our eyes, our ears, and our minds. The art of the filmmaker would consist, if you will, in making things shine from the inside, to release in them a glow, a brilliance that would bring them to our attention, our love, and our reflection.

Pushing these theories even further, however, Zavattini draws from them conclusions with regard to directing and acting—conclusions that were bound to stun my French mind. "I got my inspiration from a trivial event," the screenwriter of *Bicycle Thieves* (1948) says, and the ideal according to him would be not only to reconstitute it in all its details, but also to have it re-enacted in front of the camera by its true protagonists. If the event is a murder, the re-enactment would be by the murderer himself, the victim being of course out of the picture!

Rossellini one day told me that the true Cartesians are not the French, as is commonly believed, but the Italians. The fact is, one would think, like Boileau, that since what is true is not always what is plausible, it is not only permissible but also necessary to betray the truth intelligently sometimes in order to serve it better. This is not the place to examine and criticize in detail Zavattini's theory; I will simply say that such an ideal construction as his could only be born in the mind of a poet, not of a realist.

Love in the City is my real subject here: made in 1953, it has been released in France only now for reasons of distribution and censorship that are equally absurd. The film was banned from exportation because of one of its sketches, the one [titled *Love That Pays*] in which Carlo Lizzani was interviewing prostitutes. So it had to be cut, and the version we are able to see in France has only five episodes. We will just take comfort from the fact that, according to some witnesses, censorship has for once not cut the best episode.

Love in the City, episode "Heaven for Four Hours," dir. Dino Risi, 1953.

For the critic who is interested in neorealism, this film has a particular theoretical interest. Its endeavor is almost experimental and is very much inspired by Zavattini's concept of film as inquiry. Zavattini even kept for himself, as screenwriter and adaptor, the novella *Catherine's Story*, and I think he monitored from up close the making of this episode, which was entrusted to the very young Francesco Maselli, whose talent has since been confirmed elsewhere. Zavattini told me about all this in 1954: it was a work that was very close to his heart and, at the time, he considered it to be the closest to his neorealist ideal.

I must admit right away that the unequal results of the experiment all seem to me, in different respects, paradoxical. After reading the screenplays only, I would have picked Antonioni's script as the winner and Zavattini's as the loser. Michelangelo Antonioni, the director of *Story of a Love Affair* (1950), has chosen an approach that is rather close, I think, to what could have been done on television. The idea in his sketch, *Attempted Suicide*, was to conduct an inquiry into suicide, and a certain number of people who escaped death by their own hand are gathered in front of the camera. Invisible, the filmmaker questions them and they speak. But Antonioni did not play the game completely correctly: he nevertheless spectacularized his approach. Moreover, his method, which is giving such good results on French TV, is perhaps vitiated by the incredible ability of the Italians to perform what they are saying. Whatever one may say about this in the end, here lies one of the

Love in the City, episode "The Italians Turn Their Heads," dir. Alberto Lattuada, 1953.

secrets of neorealism: the performative ability of ordinary Italian citizens. By trying to force his nonprofessionals, through his approach, to remain relatively impassive, Antonioni was in fact going against the Italian temperament.

By contrast, Zavattini seems to owe his episode's success only to the miracle of the same temperament. We know that Zavattini does not stop at subject matter that consists only of trivial events from daily reality; he dreams of having the trivial events in question re-enacted in front of the camera by those who were their protagonists in real life. This is, as I have already noted, the idea not of a realist but of a poet, and the warmest supporters of Zavattini in Italy are hard put to follow him down this particular path. Perhaps they are wrong, in that this unremitting determination to strip filmmaking of all traces of artistic intervention clears the way, ironically, for unexpected and new aesthetic phenomena. I must admit in any case that nothing seems to me *a priori* more absurd than this idea of re-locating the poor woman who had abandoned her child on some wasteland, just to have her minutely re-live in front of the camera the day before and the day *of* her desperate action.

There are two points to make here: first, if this story could in itself be turned into a good screenplay, total faithfulness to it would only damage its potential as compelling drama; second, it seems obvious that only an incredible coincidence could predestine the real protagonist of this event to play her own role in the film. All I can do is remind the reader of the aforementioned maxim put forward by Boileau regarding truth and plausibility. To wit: we know that a murderer does not necessarily look like one. Yet, one is forced to note that reality in this instance transcends every cautionary restriction of art. Not because documenting this particular tale in all its crude and brutal reality would make of art a kind of derisory statement, but, on the contrary, because, given this scenario (even if it were not literally true), no other way of directing could have done it more justice. Indeed, if one had looked all over Italy for a woman of the people able to play the role of Catherine, one would inevitably have had to choose Catherine herself. It remains to be seen whether Zavattini's theories triumphed here or whether their implementation only emphasized with the utmost clarity the ethnic, social, and individual predicaments that make such a neorealism possible in the first place.

The other three episodes of *Love in the City* most assuredly deserve equal criticism. But I shall forsake such criticism because their unequal success seems to me to be less than exemplary of the purpose of this whole endeavor. Let's just say that the Federico Fellini episode (*A Matrimonial Agency*) is good without being purely Fellinian, if only because of the way in which it mixes landscape with character. The Dino Risi episode (*Heaven for Four Hours*) is diabolically skillful, but it is slightly marred by small dramatic, if

Love in the City, epidode "The Italians Turn Their Heads," dir. Alberto Lattuada, 1953.

not demagogic, concessions. As for the Alberto Lattuada sketch (*The Italians Turn Their Heads*), I have to say that it is the one most tampered with during the editing process; but much will be forgiven its creators for a dazzling opening and a sensational musical score. The music of this film on the whole is especially elaborate, most notably in Zavattini's episode, *Catherine's Story*.

Chapter Twenty-three

"The Profound Originality of *I Vitelloni*"

"La profonde originalité des *Vitelloni*," *Radio-Cinéma-Télévision* (October 1957); in *Qu'est-ce que le cinéma?* Vol. 4 (Éditions du Cerf, 1962), pp. 143–145; translated into English by Bert Cardullo.

Without question, few films in the history of cinema have captured their era and exercised their influence more subtly than *I vitelloni* (1953). Chaplin's films operated through the miraculously universal character of the Tramp. Films like *The Threepenny Opera* (1931) owe their audience, and the mark they have left on an entire generation, in part to the particularly successful marriage of music and cinema. By contrast, nothing in *I vitelloni* seemed capable of impressing itself on the viewer's memory: no famous actors; not even, as in *La strada* (1954), a poetically original and picturesque character around which the film is built; no story, or almost none. And yet the term "vitelloni" has become a common word: it now designates an international human type, and what is more, some of the best films each year remind us of Fellini's own (most recently, the American film *The Bachelor Party* [1957], directed by Delbert Mann from a screenplay by Paddy Chayevsky).

Recently I saw *I vitelloni* again, and I was deeply struck right away by the fact that, despite some minor weaknesses, the film had not only not aged, it had even matured with time, as if its message hadn't been able upon initial release to reveal the full scope of its richness, and as if we had needed some time to gauge its importance. Of course, it is true that three subsequent Fellini films have helped to give the earlier one more trenchancy, depth, and nuance:

I vitelloni, dir. Federico Fellini, 1953.

I vitelloni, dir. Federico Fellini, 1953.

La strada, *Il bidone* (1955), and *The Nights of Cabiria* (1957). But I think that everything was already contained in *I vitelloni* and set out there with magisterial genius.

Much has been written about this film's message and its moral and spiritual significance; so I'd prefer to underline what the repercussions of this message are, not exactly for film form (never has the distinction between form and content been revealed to be more artificial than in *I vitelloni*), but for the idea of cinematic "spectacle." From this point of view, the profound originality of *I vitelloni* seems to me to reside in its negation of the norms of storytelling on the screen. In almost all films, our interest is aroused not only by the plot or the action, but also by the development of the characters and the relationship of that development to the chain of events. Granted, neorealism had already changed things by succeeding in interesting us in small events that seemed to have no dramatic import (as in *Bicycle Thieves* [1948] and *Umberto D.* [1952]). Still, the action was carefully portioned out and the main character, whose personality was otherwise given or was determined by his environment, did *evolve* toward a dénouement.

With Fellini, it's different. His protagonists don't "evolve"; they mature. What we see them do on the screen is not only frequently without dramatic value, but also without logical meaning in the narrative chain. Most of the time it is pointless "agitation," which is the opposite of action: stupid strolls along beaches, absurd divagations, ridiculous jokes. And yet, it is through these gestures and activities, which appear so marginal that they are cut in most films, that the characters reveal themselves to us in their innermost essence. Not that they reveal to us what we conventionally call "a psychology." The Fellinian protagonist is not a "character," he is a mode of being, a way of living. This is why the director can define him thoroughly through his behavior: his walk, his dress, his hairstyle, his mustache, his dark glasses. Such antipsychological cinema goes farther and deeper than psychology, however: it goes to the protagonist's soul. This cinema of the soul thus focuses most exclusively on appearances; it is a cinema in which the viewer's gaze is most important. Fellini has made positively ridiculous a certain analytical and dramatic tradition of filmmaking by substituting for it a pure phenomenology of being in which the most commonplace of man's gestures can be the beacons of his destiny and his salvation.

Chapter Twenty-four

"*Cabiria*: The Voyage to the End of Neorealism"

"*Cabiria* ou le voyage au bout du néo-réalisme," *Cahiers du cinéma*, n. 76 (November 1957), p. 2–7; in *Qu'est-ce que le cinéma?* Vol. 4 (Éditions du Cerf, 1962), pp. 134–142; in *Qu'est-ce que le cinéma?* (Cerf, 1975 [single-volume version]), pp. 337–345; translated into English by Hugh Gray in *What Is Cinema?* Vol. 2 (Univ. of California Press, 1971), pp. 83–92, and edited below by Bert Cardullo.

As I sit down to write this article, I have no idea what kind of reception Fellini's latest film will have. I hope it is as enthusiastic as I think it should be, but I do not conceal from myself the fact that there are two categories of viewers who may have reservations about the film. The first is that segment of the general public likely to be put off by the way the story mixes the strange with what seems to be an almost melodramatic naïveté. These people can accept the theme of the whore with a heart of gold only if it is spiced with crime. The second belongs, albeit reluctantly, to that part of the "elite" which supports Fellini almost in spite of itself. Constrained to admire *La strada* (1954) and under even more constraint from its austerity and its "outcast" status to admire *Il bidone* (1955), I expect these viewers now to criticize *Le notti di Cabiria* (1957) for being "too well made": a film in which practically nothing is left to chance, a film that is clever—artful even. Let's forget the first objection; it is important only in the effect it may have at the box office. The second, however, is worth refuting.

The least surprising thing about *Le notti di Cabiria* is not that this is the first time Fellini has succeeded in putting together a masterly script, with an action that cannot be faulted—unmarred by clichés or missing links, one in which there could be no place for the unhappy cuts and the corrections in editing from which *La strada* and *Il bidone* suffered. (The original-language version shown in Paris does, however, reveal the deletion of at least one long scene that was still in the film when it was shown at Cannes, namely the scene of "the visitor of Saint Vincent de Paul" to which I allude later.) Of course, *Lo sceicco bianco* (1952) and even *I vitelloni* (1953) were not clumsy in their construction, but chiefly because, though their themes were specifically Fellinian, they were still being expressed within a framework provided by relatively traditional scenarios. Fellini has finally cast these crutches aside with *La strada*: theme and character alone are the final determinants in the story now, to the exclusion of all else; story has nothing now to do with what one calls plot; I even have doubts that it is proper here to speak of "action." The same is true of *Il bidone*.

It is not that Fellini would like to return to the excuses which drama affords him in his earlier films. Quite the contrary. *Le notti di Cabiria* goes even beyond *Il bidone,* but here the contradictions between what I will call the "verticality" of its author's themes and the "horizontality" of the requirements of narrative have been reconciled. It is within the Fellinian system that he now finds his solutions. This does not prevent the viewer from possibly mistaking brilliant perfection for mere facility, if not indeed for betrayal. All the same, on one score at least Fellini has deceived himself a little: is he not counting on

The Nights of Cabiria, dir. Federico Fellini, 1957.

the character played by François Perier (who to me seems miscast) to have a surprise effect?

Now it is clear that any effect of "suspense" or even of "drama" is essentially alien to the Fellinian system, in which it is impossible for time ever to serve as an abstract or dynamic support—as an *a priori* framework for narrative structure. In *La strada* as in *Il bidone*, time is nothing more than the shapeless framework modified by fortuitous events that affect the fate of his heroes, though never in consequence of external necessity. Events do not "happen" in Fellini's world; they "befall" its inhabitants. That is to say, they occur as an effect of "vertical" gravity, not in conformity to the laws of "horizontal" causality.

As for the characters themselves, they exist and change only in reference to a purely internal kind of time—which I cannot qualify even as Bergsonian, insofar as Bergson's theory of the *Données immédiates de la conscience* contains a strong element of psychologism. Let us avoid the vague terms of a "spiritualizing" vocabulary. Let us not say that the transformation of the characters takes place at the level of the "soul." But it has at least to occur at that depth of their being into which consciousness only occasionally reaches down. This does not mean at the level of the unconscious or the subconscious but rather the level on which what Jean-Paul Sartre calls the "basic project" obtains, the level of ontology. Thus the Fellinian character does not evolve; he ripens or at the most becomes transformed (whence the metaphor of the angel's wings, to which I will shortly return).

A SPURIOUS MELODRAMA

But let us confine ourselves, for the moment, to the structure of the script. I totally reject, then, the *coup de théâtre* in *Le notti di Cabiria* that belatedly reveals Oscar a swindler. Fellini must have been aware of what he was doing because, as if to compound his sin, he makes François Perier wear dark glasses when he is about to turn "wicked." What of it? This is a minor concession indeed and I find it easy to pardon in view of the care Fellini now takes to avoid in this film the grave danger to which a complicated and much too facile shooting script exposed him in *Il bidone*. I find it all the more easy to pardon when it is the only concession he makes in this film; for the rest Fellini communicates the tension and the rigor of tragedy to it without ever having to fall back on devices alien to his universe.

Cabiria, the little prostitute whose simple soul is rooted in hope, is not a character out of melodrama, because her desire to "get out" is not motivated by the ideals of bourgeois morality or a strictly bourgeois sociology. She does not hold her trade in contempt. As a matter of fact, if there were such creatures as pure-hearted pimps capable of understanding her and of embodying not love indeed but just a belief in life, she would doubtless see no incompatibility between her secret hopes and her nighttime activities. Does she not owe one of her greatest moments of happiness—happiness followed consequently by an even more bitter deception—to her chance meeting with a famous film star who because he is drunk and feeling embittered against love proposes to take her home to his luxurious apartment. There was something to make the other girls just die of envy! But the incident is fated to come to a pitiful end, because after all a prostitute's trade commonly destines her only to disappointments; this is why she longs, more or less consciously, to get out of it through the impossible love of some stalwart fellow who will make no demands of her. If we seem now to have reached an outcome typical of bourgeois melodrama, it is in any case by a very different route.

The Nights of Cabiria, dir. Federico Fellini, 1957.

Le notti di Cabiria—like *La strada*, like *Il bidone*, and, in the final analysis, like *I vitelloni*—is the story of *ascesis*, of renunciation, and (however you choose to interpret the term) of salvation. The beauty and the rigor of its construction proceed this time from the perfect economy of its constituent episodes. Each of them, as I have said earlier, exists by and for itself, unique and colorful as an event, but now each belongs to an order of things that never fails to reveal itself in retrospect as having been absolutely necessary. As she goes from hope to hope, plumbing en route the depths of betrayal, contempt, and poverty, Cabiria follows a path on which every stop readies her for the stage ahead. When one pauses and reflects, one realizes that there is nothing in the film, before the meeting with the benefactor of the tramps (whose irruption into the film seems at first sight to be no more than a characteristic piece of Fellinian bravura), which is not proved subsequently to be necessary to trick Cabiria into making an act of ill-placed faith; for if such men do exist, then every miracle is possible and we, too, will be without mistrust when Perier appears.

I do not intend to repeat what has been written about Fellini's message. It has, anyway, been noticeably the same since *I vitelloni*. This is not to be taken as a sign of sterility. On the contrary, while variety is the mark of a "director," it is unity of inspiration that connotes the true "author." But in the light of this new masterpiece maybe I can still attempt to throw a little more light on what in essence is Fellini's style.

A REALISM OF APPEARANCES

It is absurd, preposterous even, to deny him a place among the neorealists. Such a judgment could only be possible on ideological grounds. It is true that Fellini's realism, though social in origin, is not social in intent. This remains as individual as it is in Chekhov or Dostoyevsky. Realism, let me repeat, is to be defined not in terms of ends but of means, and neorealism by a specific kind of relationship of means to ends. What De Sica has in common with Rossellini and Fellini is obviously not the deep meaning of their films—even if, as it happens, these more or less coincide—but the pride of place they all give to the representation of reality at the expense of dramatic structures.

To put if more precisely, the Italian cinema has replaced a "realism" deriving in point of content from the naturalism of novels and structurally from theater with what, for brevity's sake, we shall call "phenomenological" realism that never "adjusts" reality to meet the needs imposed by psychology or drama. The relation between meaning and appearance having been in a sense inverted, appearance is always presented as a unique discovery, an almost documentary revelation that retains its full force of vividness and detail. Whence the director's art lies in the skill with which he compels the event to reveal its meaning or at least the meaning he lends it—without removing any of its ambiguity.

Thus defined, neorealism is not the exclusive property of any one ideology nor even of any one ideal, no more than it excludes any other ideal—no more, in point of fact, than reality excludes anything. I even tend to view Fellini as the director who goes the farthest of any to date in this neorealist aesthetic, who goes even so far that he goes all the way through it and finds himself on the other side.

Let us consider how free Fellini's direction is from the encumbrances of psychological after-effects. His characters are never defined by their "character" but exclusively by their appearance. I deliberately avoid the word "behavior" because its meaning has become too restricted; the way people behave is only one element in the knowledge we have of them. We know them by many other signs, not only their faces, of course, but by the way they move, by everything that makes the body the outer shell of the inner man—even more, perhaps, by things still more external than these, things on the frontier between the individual and the world, things such as haircut, mustache, clothing, eye-glasses (the one prop that Fellini has used to a point where it has become a gimmick). Then, beyond that again, setting, too, has a role to play—not, of course, in an expressionistic sense but rather as establishing a harmony or a disharmony between setting and character. I am thinking in particular of the extraordinary relationship established between Cabiria and the unaccustomed settings into which Nazzari inveigles her, the nightclub and the luxurious apartment.

ON THE OTHER SIDE OF THINGS

But it is here that we reach the boundaries of realism; here, too, that Fellini, who drives on further still, takes us beyond them. It is a little as if, having been led to this degree of interest in appearances, we were now to see the characters no longer among the objects but, as if these had become transparent, through them. I mean by this that without our noticing the world has moved from meaning to analogy, then from analogy to identification with the supernatural. I apologize for this equivocal word; the reader may replace it with whatever he will—"poetry" or "surrealism" or "magic"—whatever the term that expresses the hidden accord that things maintain with an invisible counterpart of which they are, so to speak, merely the adumbration.

Let us take one example from among many others of this process of "supernaturalization," which is to be found in the metaphor of the angel. From his first films, Fellini has been haunted by the angelizing of his characters, as if the angelic state were the ultimate referent in his universe, the final measure of being. One can trace this tendency in its explicit development at least from *I vitelloni* on: Sordi dresses up for the carnival as a guardian angel; a little later on what Fabrizi steals, as if by chance, is the carved wooden statue of an angel. But these allusions are direct and concrete. Subtler still, and all the more interesting because it seems unconscious, is the shot in which the monk who has come down from working in a tree loads a long string of little branches on his back. This detail is nothing more than a nice "realistic" touch for us, perhaps even for Fellini himself, until at the end of *Il bidone* we see Antonio dying at the side of the road: in the white light of dawn he sees a procession of children and women bearing bundles of sticks on their backs: angels pass! I must note, too, how in the same film Picasso races down a street and the tails of his raincoat spread out behind him like little wings. It is that same Richard Basehart again who appears before Gelsomina as if he were weightless, a dazzling sight on his high wire under the spotlights.

There is no end to Fellini's symbolism. Certainly, it would be possible to study the whole body of his work from this one angle. What needed to be done was simply to place it within the context of the logic of neorealism, for it is evident that these associations of objects and characters which constitute Fellini's universe derive their value and their importance from realism alone—or, to put it a better way, perhaps, from the objectivity with which they are recorded. It is not in order to look like an angel that the friar carries his bundles of sticks on his back, but it is enough to see the wing in the twigs for the old monk to be transformed into one. One might say that Fellini is not opposed to realism, any more than he is to neorealism, but rather that he achieves it surpassingly in a poetic reordering of the world.

A REVOLUTION IN NARRATIVE

Fellini creates a similar revolution at the narrative level. From this point of view, to be sure, neorealism is also a revolution in form that comes to bear on content. For example, the priority which they accord incident over plot has led De Sica and Zavattini to replace plot as such with a microaction based on an infinitely divisible attention to the complexities in even the most ordinary of events. This in itself rules out the slightest hierarchy, whether psychological, dramatic, or ideological, among the incidents that are portrayed. This does not mean, of course, that the director is obliged to renounce all choice over what he is to show us, but it does mean that he no longer makes the choice in reference to some pre-existing dramatic organization. In this new perspective, the important sequence can just as well be the long scene that "serves no purpose" by traditional screenplay standards. (This is true of the Saint-Vincent-de-Paul sequence that has been deleted from the film.)

Nonetheless—this is true even of *Umberto D.* (1952), which perhaps represents the limits of experimentation in this new dramaturgy—the evolution of film follows an invisible thread. Fellini, I think, brings the neorealist revolution to its point of perfection when he introduces a new kind of script, with the scenario lacking any dramatic linking, based as it is, to the exclusion of all else, on the phenomenological description of the characters. In the films of Fellini, the scenes that establish the logical relations, the significant changes of fortune, the major points of dramatic articulation, only provide the continuity links, while the long descriptive sequences, seeming to exercise no effect on the unfolding of the "action" proper, constitute the truly important and revealing scenes. In *I vitelloni*, these are the nocturnal walks, the senseless strolls on the beach; in *La strada*, the visit to the convent; in *Il bidone*, the evening at the nightclub or the New Year's celebration. It is not when they are doing something specific that Fellini's characters best reveal themselves to the viewer but by their endless milling around.

If there are, still, tensions and climaxes in the films of Fellini that leave nothing to be desired as regards drama or tragedy, it is because, in the absence of traditional dramatic causality, the incidents in his films develop effects of analogy and echo. Fellini's hero never reaches the final crisis (which destroys him and saves him) by a progressive dramatic linking but because the circumstances somehow or other affect him, build up inside him like the vibrant energy in a resonating body. He does not develop; he is transformed, overturning finally like an iceberg whose center of buoyancy has shifted unseen.

EYE TO EYE

By way of conclusion, and to compress the disturbing perfection of *Le notti di Cabiria* into a single phrase, I would like to analyze the final shot of the film, which strikes me, when everything else is taken into account, as the boldest and the most powerful shot in the whole of Fellini's work. Cabiria, stripped of everything—her money, her love, her faith—emptied now of herself, stands on a road without hope. A group of boys and girls swarm into the scene singing and dancing as they go, and from the depths of her nothingness Cabiria slowly returns to life; she starts to smile again; soon she is dancing, too. It is easy to imagine how artificial and symbolic this ending would have been, casting aside as it does all the objections of verisimilitude, if Fellini had not succeeded in projecting his film onto a higher plane by a single detail of direction, a stroke of real genius that forces us suddenly to identify with his heroine.

Chaplin's name is often mentioned in connection with *La strada*, but I have never thought the comparison between Gelsomina and Charlie (which I find hard to take in itself) very convincing. The first shot that is not only up to Chaplin's level but the true equal of his best inventions is the final shot of

Le notti di Cabiria, when Giulietta Masina turns toward the camera and her glance crosses ours. As far as I know, Chaplin is the only man in the history of film who made successful systematic use of this gesture, which the books about filmmaking are unanimous in condemning. Nor would it be in place if when she looked us in the eye Cabiria seemed to come bearing some ultimate truth. But the finishing touch to this stroke of directorial genius is this, that Cabiria's glance falls several times on the camera without ever quite coming to rest there. The lights go up on this marvel of ambiguity.

Cabiria is doubtless still the heroine of the adventures which she has been living out before us, somewhere behind that screen, but here she is now inviting us, too, with her glance to follow her on the road to which she is about to return. The invitation is chaste, discreet, and indefinite enough that we can pretend to think that she means to be looking at somebody else. At the same time, though, it is also definite and direct enough to remove us quite finally from our role of spectator.

Chronology and Credits of the Films of Italian Neorealism (including precursors and successors)

ABBREVIATIONS:

prod. = production company
dir. = director
sc. = scenario
adapt. = adaptation
cin. = cinematography
des. = design (art direction)
cos. = costumes
mus. = music
ed. = editor

Sperduti nel buio
(*Lost in the Dark*), 1914

Credits *prod.*: Morgana Films, Rome; *dir.*: Nino Martoglio; *sc.*: from the play by Roberto Bracco (1901); *adapt.*: Roberto Bracco; *mus.*: Enrico De Leva.

Cast Giovanni Grasso (The Blind Man, Nunzio), Maria Carmi (Livia Blanchard), Virginia Balistrieri (Paolina), Vittorina Moneta (Paolina's Mother), Dillo Lombardi (The Duke of Vallenza), Totò Majorana (Nunzio's Godfather), Gina Benvenuti (Nunzio's Mother), Ettore Mazzanti.

Note: This film disappeared in 1943 during the evacuation of the Centro Sperimentale. *Sperduti nel buio* was remade in 1947.

Assunta Spina
1915
Credits prod.: Caesar Films, Rome; dir.: Gustavo Serena; sc.: from the play by Salvatore Di Giacomo (1909); cin.: Alberto G. Carta.
Cast Francesca Bertini (Assunta Spina), Gustavo Serena (Michele), Carlo Benetti (Federico Funelli), Alberto Albertini (Raffaele), Antonia Crucchi (Assunta's Father), Amelia Cipriani (Peppina), Alberto Collo.
Note: *Assunta spina* was remade in 1948. It was produced by Ora-Titanus and directed by Mario Mattòli; the adaptation was by Eduardo De Filippo and Gino Capriolo, from the play by Salvatore Di Giacomo (1909); the cinematography was by Gabor Pogany; the design was by Piero Filippone; and the music was by Renzo Rossellini. Among the actors were Anna Magnani, Antonio Centa, Eduardo De Filippo, and Titina De Filippo.

Teresa Raquin
1915
Credits dir.: Nino Martoglio; sc.: from the novel by Émile Zola (1867).
Cast Maria Carmi, Dillo Lombardi, Giacinta Pezzana.

Cavalleria rusticana
(*Rustic Chivalry*), 1916
Credits dir.: Ubalda Maria Del Colle; sc.: from the story by Giovanni Verga (1880).
Cast Tilde Pini, Bianca Lorenzoni, Ugo Gracci.
Note: *Cavalleria rusticana* was remade in 1939. It was produced by Scalera (Cesare Zanetti) and directed by Amleto Palermi; the adaptation was by Tomaso Smith, Amleto Palermi, P. M. Rosso di San Secondo, and Santi Savarino, from the story by Giovanni Verga (1880); the cinematography was by Massimo Terzano; the design was by Nino Maccarones; the music was by Alessandro Cicognini; and the editor was Eraldo Da Roma. Cast: Isa Pola (Santuzza), Carlo Ninchi (Compar Alfio), Doris Duranti (Gna Lola), Leonardo Cortese (Turiddu), Bella Starace Sainati (Gna Nunzia), Luigi Almirante (Zio Brasi), Carlo Romano (Bammulu).

Cavalleria rusticana was again remade in 1953 with the alternate title *Fatal Desire*. It was produced by Excelsa/Ultra (Carlo Ponti) and directed by Carmine Gallone; the adaptation was by Mario Monicelli, Basilio Franchina, Francesco De Feo, Art Cohn, and Carmine Gallone, from the story by Giovanni Verga (1880) and the opera by Pietro Mascagni; the cinematography was by Karl Struss and Riccardo Pallottini; the design was by Gastone Medin;

the music was by Oliviero De Fabritiis; and the editor was Rolando Benedetti. Cast: Anthony Quinn (Alfio), Kerima (Lola), May Britt (Santuzza), Ettore Manni (Turiddu), Umberto Spadaro (Uncle Brasi), Grazia Spadaro (Aunt Camilla), Virginia Balestrieri (Mamma Lucia), Tito Gobbi (Voice).

Cenere
(Ashes), **1916**

Credits *prod.:* Ambrosio Film, Turin/Cines, Rome; *dir.:* Febo Mari, Arturo Ambrosio, Jr.; *sc.:* Febo Mari and Eleonora Duse, from the novel by Grazia Deledda (1904); *cin.:* Pietro Marelli.

Cast Eleonora Duse (Rosalia), Febo Mari (Anania), Ettore Casarotti, Carmen Casarotti, and Ilda Sibiglia (The Children).

Sole
(Sun), **1929**

Credits *prod.:* S. A. Augustus, Rome; *dir.:* Alessandro Blasetti; *sc.:* Alessandro Blasetti, Aldo Vergano; *adapt.:* Alessandro Blasetti, Aldo Vergano; *cin.:* Giuseppe Caracciolo, with the collaboration of Carlo Montuori, Giorgi Orsini, and Giulio De Luca; *mus.:* Mario De Risi; *ed.:* Alessandro Blasetti.

Cast Marcello Spada (The Engineer, Rinaldi), Vasco Creti (Marco), Dria Paolo (Giovanna), Vittorio Vaser (Silvestro), Lia Bosco (Barbara), Anna Vinci, Rolando Costantino, Rinaldo Rinaldi, Igino Muzio.

Note: Sole was destroyed during World War II except for surviving still photographs.

Rotaie
(Rails), **1931**

Credits *prod.:* SACIA; *dir.:* Mario Camerini; *sc.:* Corrado D'Errico; *adapt.:* Umberto Torri, Mario Camerini; *cin.:* Ubaldo Arata; *des.:* Umberto Torri, with the collaboration of Vittorio Cafiero, Angelo Canevari, and Daniele Crespi; *mus.:* Marcello Lattes.

Cast Käthe von Nagy (The Girl), Maurizio D'Ancora (The Young Man), Daniele Crespi (Passenger on the Train), Aldo Moschino (aka Giacomo Moschini) (Frequenter of the Casino), Pia Carolo Lotti (His Female Companion), Guido Celano.

Campane d'Italia
(documentary)
(*The Bells of Italy*), 1932
Credits   *dir.*: Mario Serandrei.

La tavola dei poveri
(*The Table of the Poor*), 1932
Credits   *prod.*: Cines (Carlo J. Bassoli); *dir.*: Alessandro Blasetti; *sc.*: Raffaele Viviani and Mario Soldati; *adapt.*: Raffaele Viviani, Mario Soldati, Emilio Cecchi, Alessandro De Stefani; *cin.*: Carlo Montuori and Giulio De Luca; *des.*: Gastone Medin; *mus.*: Roberto Caggiano; themes by R. Viviani.
Cast   Raffaele Viviani (Marquis Fusaro), Leda Gloria (Giorgina), Salvatore Costa (Biase), Marcello Spada (Nello Valmadonna), Mario Ferrari (The Lawyer Volterra), Vincenzo Flocco (Mezzapalla), Armida Cozzolino (Madam Lida Valmadonna), Lina Bacci (Committee Secretary), Cesare Zoppetti (The Professor), Vasco Creti (Servant to the Marquis Fusaro), Renato Navarrini.

Acciaio
(*Steel*), 1933
Credits   *prod.*: Cines; *dir.*: Walter Ruttmann; *sc.*: from Luigi Pirandello's original script *Play, Pietro!*; *adapt.*: Walter Ruttmann, Mario Soldati, Emilio Cecchi; *cin.*: Massimo Terzano, Domenico Scala; *des.*: Gastone Medin; *mus.*: Gian Francesco Malipiero; *ed.*: Walter Ruttmann, Giuseppe Fatigati.
Cast   Isa Pola (Gina), Piero Pastore (Mario), Vittorio Bellaccini (Pietro), Alfredo Polveroni (His Father), Romolo Costa, Domenico Serra.

T'amerò sempre
(*I Will Always Love You*), 1933
Credits   *prod.*: Cines (Carlo J. Bassoli); *dir.*: Mario Camerini; *sc.*: Mario Camerini; *adapt.*: Ivo Perilli and Guglielmo Alberti; *cin.*: Ubaldo Arata; *des.*: Gastone Medin; *mus.*: Ezio Carabella; *ed.*: Fernando Tropea.
Cast   Elsa De Giorgi (Adriana), Nino Besozzi (Mario Fabbrini), Mino Doro (The Count), Roberto Pizani, Pina Renzi, Nora Dani, Loris Gizzi, Giacomo Moschini, Maria Persico, Claudio Ermelli, Giancarlo Cappelli.
Note: *T'amerò sempre* was remade in 1943. It was once again produced by

Cines and directed by Mario Camerini; the scenario was by Sergio Amidei and Mario Camerini; the cinematography was by Arturo Gallea; the design was by Gastone Medin; and the music was by Ezio Carabella. Among the actors were Alida Valli (Adriana), Gino Cervi (The Boy Faustini), Antonio Centa (Diego), Jules Berry (Oscar), Tina Lattanzi, and Loris Gizzi.

Ragazzo
(*Kid*), 1933
Credits   *prod.:* Cines (Carlo J. Bassoli); *dir.:* Ivo Perilli; *sc.:* Sandro De Feo; *adapt.:* Ivo Perilli and Emilio Cecchi; *cin.:* Massimo Terzano, Domenico Scala; *des.:* Gastone Medin; *mus.:* Luigi Colacicchi.
Cast   Isa Pola, Costantino Frasca, Giovanna Scotto, Anna Vinci, Osvaldo Valenti, Marcello Martire, Aristide Garbini.

Come le foglie
(*Like the Leaves*), 1934
Credits   *prod.:* ICI (La Società Anonima Industrie Cinematografiche Italiane)/Roberto Dandi; *dir.:* Mario Camerini; *sc.:* from the comedy by Giuseppe Giacosa; *adapt.:* Ivo Perilli and Ercole Patti; *cin.:* Massimo Terzano; *des.:* Guido Fiorini; *mus.:* Ezio Carabella; *ed.:* Fernando Tropea.
Cast   Isa Miranda (Nennele), Mimì Aylmer (Giulia), Nino Besozzi (Massimo), Ernesto Sabbatini (Giovanni Rosani), Cesare Bettarini (Tommy), Achille Majeroni (A Friend of the Rosani Family).

1860
1934
Credits   *prod.:* Cines; *dir.:* Alessandro Blasetti; *sc.:* from a story by Gino Mazzucchi; *adapt.:* Alessandro Blasetti, Gino Mazzucchi; *cin.:* Anchise Brizzi, Giulio De Luca; *des.:* Vittorio Cafiero, Angelo Canevari; *cos.:* Vittorio Nino Novarese; *mus.:* Nino Medin; *ed.:* Ignazio Ferronetti, Alessandro Blasetti.
Cast   Aida Bellia (Gesuzza), Gianfranco Giachetti (Costanzo), Otello Toso, Maria Denis, Giuseppe Gulino (Carmeliddu), Laura Nucci, Mario Ferrari (Col. Carini), Totò Majorana, Cesare Zoppetti, Vasco Creti, Ugo Gracci, Umberto Sacripante, Amedeo Trilli, Arnaldo Baldaccini, Arcangelo Aversa, Aldo Frosi, Nais Lago.

Il grande appello
(*The Last Roll Call; The Great Call; A Call to Arms*), 1936
Credits prod.: Artisti Associati (Roberto Dandi); dir.: Mario Camerini; sc.: Mario Camerini; adapt.: Mario Camerini, Ercole Patti, Piero Solari, Mario Soldati; cin.: Massimo Terzano, Ferdinando Martini; des.: Gino Franzi; mus.: Annibale Bizzelli.
Cast Camillo Pilotto (Giovanni Bertani), Roberto Villa (Enrico), Lina Da Costa, Guglielmo Sinaz, Lina D'Acosta, Pietro Valdes, Enrico Poggi, Nino Marchetti, Angelo Pelliccioni.

Pianto delle zittelle
(documentary)
(*The Crying of Old Maids*), 1939
Credits dir.: Giacomo Pozzi Bellini.

Addio giovinezza!
(*Farewell, Youth!*), 1940
Credits prod.: ICI (La Società Anonima Industrie Cinematografiche Italiane)–SAFIC/Giacomo Giannuzzi; dir.: Ferdinando Maria Poggioli; sc.: from the comedy by Sandro Camasio and Nino Oxilia (1911); adapt.: Salvator Gotta and Ferdinando Maria Poggioli; cin.: Carlo Montuori; des.: Gastone Medin; cos.: Gino Sensani; mus.: Giuseppe Blanc; ed.: Ferdinando Maria Poggioli.
Cast Maria Denis (Dorina), Clara Calamai (Elena), Adriano Rimoldi (Mario), Carlo Campanini (Leone), Mario Casaleggio, Bella Starace Sainati, Bianca Della Corte (Emma), Carlo Minello, Aldo Fiorelli, Nuccia Robella, Franca Volpini, Mario Giannini, Paolo Carlini (Pino), Umberto Bonsignori, Arturo Bragaglia.
Note: *Addio giovinezza!* was first made as a silent film in 1913. It was produced by Itala Film (Turin) and directed by Nino Oxilia; the scenario was taken from the comedy by Sandro Camasio and Nino Oxilia (1911). Cast: Lidia Quaranta (Dorina), Alessandro Bernard (Leone), Amerigo Manzini, Letizia Quaranta.

Addio giovinezza! was remade as a silent film in 1918 by Augusto Genina. Genina then remade it again as a silent film, in 1927. It was produced by Films Genina (Rome) and directed by Augusto Genina; the scenario was taken from the comedy by Sandro Camasio and Nino Oxilia (1911), and the adaptation was by Augusto Genina and Luciano Doria; the cinematography was by Carlo Montuori and Antonio Martini; and the design was by Giulio Folchi. Cast: Carmen Boni (Dorina), Walter Slezak (Mario), Elena Sangro (Elena), Augusto

Bandini (Leone), Piero Cocco (Carlo), Gemma De Ferrari (Mario's Mother), A. Ricci (Mario's Father), Lya Christa.

L'assedio dell' Alcázar
(*The Siege of the Alcázar*), 1940
Credits   prod.: ICI (La Società Anonima Industrie Cinematografiche Italiane)/Carlo J. Bassoli; dir.: Augusto Genina; sc.: Alessandro De Stefani, Augusto Genina, Pietro Caporilli; adapt.: Augusto Genina, Alessandro De Stefani; cin.: Jan Stallich, Francesco Izzarelli, Vincenzo Seratrice; des.: Gastone Medin; mus.: Antonio Veretti; ed.: Fernando Tropea.
Cast   Rafael Calvo (Col. Moscardò), Maria Denis (Conchita), Carlos Muñoz, Mireille Balin (Carmen), Fosco Giachetti (Capt. Vela), Andrea Checchi (Pedro), Aldo Fiorelli (Francisco), Silvio Bagolini, Carlo Tamberlani, Guido Notari, Guglielmo Sinaz, Giovanni Dal Cortivo, Carlo Duse, Eugenio Duse, Adele Garavaglia, Oreste Fares, Carlo Bressan, Nino Crisman, Vasco Creti, Angelo Dessy, Anita Farra, Nino Marchesini, Cesare Polacco, Checco Rissone, Ugo Sasso.

Piccolo mondo antico
(*Little Old-Fashioned World; The Little World of the Past*), 1940
Credits   prod.: ATA/ICI (La Società Anonima Industrie Cinematografiche Italiane); dir.: Mario Soldati; sc.: from the novel by Antonio Fogazzaro (part of a trilogy that includes *Malombra*); adapt.: Mario Bonfantini, Emilio Cecchi, Alberto Lattuada, Mario Soldati; cin.: Carlo Montuori, Arturo Gallea; des.: Gastone Medin, Ascanio Coccè; cos.: Maria De Matteis and Gino Sensani; mus.: Enzo Masetti; ed.: Gisa Radicchi Levi.
Cast   Alida Valli (Luisa), Massimo Serato (Franco), Ada Dondini (The Marquise), Annibale Betrone (Uncle Piero), Mariù Pascoli (Ombretta), Giacinto Molteni (Gilardoni), Elvira Bonecchi (Barborin), Enzo Biliotti (Pasotti), Renato Cialente (Greisberg), Adele Garavaglia (Mamma Teresa), Carlo Tamberlani (Don Costa), Giovanni Barrella (The Curate of Puria), Nino Marchetti (Pedraglio), Giorgio Costantini (The Lawyer from Varenna), Jone Morino (Donna Eugenia), Anna Carena (Carlotta), Domenico Viglione Borghese (Dino).

Fari nella nebbia
(*Headlights in the Fog*), 1941
Credits   *prod.*: ICI (La Società Anonima Industrie Cinematografiche Italiane)–Fauno Film/Giampaolo Bigazzi; *dir.*: Gianni Franciolini; *sc.*: Rinaldo Dal Fabbro, O. Gasperini, Giuseppe Mangione, Alberto Pozzetti; *adapt.*: Corrado Alvaro, Edoardo Antòn, Giuseppe Zucca; *cin.*: Aldo Tonti; *des.*: Gastone Medin; *mus.*: Enzo Masetti; *ed.*: Mario Serandrei.
Cast   Fosco Giachetti (Cesare), Luisa Ferida (Piera), Mariella Lotti (Anna), Antonio Centa (Carlo), Mario Siletti, Lauro Gazzolo, Carlo Lombardi, Nelli Corradi, Dhia Cristiani, Lia Orlandini, Piero Pastore (A Mechanic), Arturo Bragaglia (A Cobbler).

La corona di ferro
(*The Iron Crown; Crown of Iron*), 1941
Credits   *prod.*: ENIC (Ente Nazionale Industrie Cinematografiche)/Lux Film; *dir.*: Alessandro Blasetti; *sc.*: Alessandro Blasetti, Renato Castellani; *adapt.*: Corrado Pavolini, Renato Castellani, Alessandro Blasetti, Guglielmo Zorzi, Giuseppe Zucca; *cin.*: Vaclav Vich, Mario Craveri; *des.*: Virgilio Marchi; *cos.*: Gino Sensani; *mus.*: Alessandro Cicognini; *ed.*: Marío Serandrei.
Cast   Elisa Cegani (Elsa), Luisa Ferida (Tundra), Gino Cervi, Massimo Girotti (Arminio), Osvaldo Valenti, Rina Morelli, Dina Perbellini, Paolo Stoppa, Ugo Sasso, Primo Carnera, Adele Garavaglia.

La nave bianca
(*The White Ship*), 1941
Credits   *prod.*: Scalera/Centro Cinematografico del Ministero della Marina; *dir.*: Roberto Rossellini; *sc.*: Francesco De Robertis; *adapt.*: Francesco De Robertis, Roberto Rossellini; *cin.*: Giuseppe Caracciolo; *des.*: Amleto Bonetti; *mus.*: Renzo Rossellini; *ed.*: Eraldo Da Roma.
Cast   nonprofessionals.

Un colpo di pistola
(*The Pistol Shot*), 1941
Credits   *prod.*: Lux Film; *dir.*: Renato Castellani; *sc.*: from the story by Pushkin in *The Tales of Belkin*; *adapt.*: Mario Bonfantini, Renato Castellani, Corrado Pavolini, Mario Soldati; *cin.*: Massimo Terzano; *des.*: Gastone Medin, Nicola Benois; *cos.*: Maria De Matteis; *mus.*: Vincenzo Tommasini; *ed.*: Mario Serandrei.

Cast Assia Norris (Mascia), Fosco Giachetti (Andrea), Antonio Centa (Sergio), Ruby Dalma (Mascia's Aunt), Renato Cialente, Mimì Dugini.

Uomini sul fondo
(*S.O.S. Submarine; S.O.S. 103; Men on the Bottom; Men Under the Sea*), 1941
Credits *prod.*: Scalera/Centro Cinematografico del Ministero della Marina; *dir.*: Francesco De Robertis; *sc. and adapt.*: Francesco De Robertis, with the collaboration of Ivo Perilli and Giorgio Bianchi; *cin.*: Giuseppe Caracciolo; *des.*: Amleto Bonetti; *mus.*: Edgardo Carducci-Agustini; *ed.*: Francesco De Robertis, with the collaboration of Ivo Perilli and Giorgio Bianchi.
Cast nonprofessionals.

Comacchio
(**documentary**)
1942
Credits *dir.*: Fernando Cerchio.

Giacomo L'idealista
(*Giacomo the Idealist*), 1942
Credits *prod.*: ATA; *dir.*: Alberto Lattuada; *sc.*: from the novel by Emilio De Marchi; *adapt.*: Emilio Cecchi, Aldo Buzzi, Alberto Lattuada; *cin.*: Carlo Nebiolo; *des.*: Fulvio Paoli (aka Fulvio Jacchia), Ascanio Coccé; *cos.*: Gino Sensani; *mus.*: Felice Lattuada.
Cast Massimo Serato (Giacomo), Marina Berti (Celestina), Andrea Checchi (Giacinto), Tina Lattanzi (His Mother), Armando Migliari, Giacinto Molteni (The Count), Domenico Viglione Borghese, Roldano Lupi, Giulio Tempesti, Paolo Bonecchi, Silvia Melandri, Dina Romano, Giselda Gasperini, Nelly Morgan, Piero Palermini, Elvira Bonecchi, Adele Baratelli, Felice Minotti, Attilio Dottesio, F. M. Costa.

Malombra
(*The Woman*), 1942
Credits *prod.*: Lux Film; *dir.*: Mario Soldati; *sc.*: from the novel by Antonio Fogazzaro (part of a trilogy that includes *Piccolo mondo antico*); *adapt.*: Mario Bonfanti, Renato Castellani, Ettore M. Margadonna, Tino Richelmy, Mario Soldati; *cin.*: Massimo Terzano; *des.*: Gastone

Medin; *cos.:* Maria De Matteis; *mus.:* Giuseppe Rosati; *ed.:* Gisa Radicchi Levi.
Cast Isa Miranda (Marina di Malombra), Irasema Dilian (Edith), Andrea Checchi (Corrado Silla), Gualtiero Tumiati (Count Cesare), Nino Crisman (Nepo Salvador), Enzo Biliotti (Vezza), Giacinto Molteni (Steinegge), Ada Dondini (Fosca Salvador), Nando Tamberlani (Don Innocenzo), Corrado Racca (The Friar), Luigi Pavese, Doretta Sestan (Fanny), Paolo Bonecchi, Giovanni Barrella, Giacomo Moschini.

Ossessione
(*Obsession*), 1942
Credits *prod.:* ICI (La Società Anonima Industrie Cinematografiche Italiane)–Rome/Libero Solaroli; *dir.:* Luchino Visconti; *sc.:* from the novel *The Postman Always Rings Twice* (1934), by James M. Cain (uncredited); *adapt.:* Mario Alicata, Antonio Pietrangeli, Gianni Puccini, Giuseppe De Santis, Luchino Visconti, Rosario Assunto; *cin.:* Aldo Tonti, Domenico Scala; *des.:* Gino Franzi, Ferrare and Ancône; *cos.:* Maria De Matteis; *mus.:* Giuseppe Rosati; *ed.:* Mario Serandrei.
Cast Dhia Cristiani (The Dancer, Anita), Elio Marcuzzo (The Spaniard), Vittorio Duse (The Truck Driver/Undercover Policeman), Clara Calamai (Giovanna Bragana), Massimo Girotti (Gino Costa), Juan De Landa (Giovanna's Husband, Giuseppe Bragana), Michele Sakara (The Child), Michele Riccardini (Don Remigio).

Quattro passi fra le nuvole
(*Four Steps in the Clouds; A Walk Among the Clouds*), 1942
Credits *prod.:* ENIC (Ente Nazionale Industrie Cinematografiche)–Cines/Giuseppe Amato; *dir.:* Alessandro Blasetti; *sc.:* Cesare Zavattini, Piero Tellini; *adapt.:* Cesare Zavattini, Piero Tellini, Giuseppe Amato, Aldo De Benedetti, Alessandro Blasetti; *cin.:* Vaclav Vich; *des.:* Virgilio Marchi; *mus.:* Alessandro Cicognini; *ed.:* Mario Serandrei.
Cast Gino Cervi (Paolo), Adriana Benetti (Maria), Aldo Silvani, Giacinto Molteni, Guido Celano, Giuditta Rissone (Clara), Enrico Viarisio, Carlo Romano (The Chauffeur), Lauro Gazzolo, Silvio Bagolini, Margherita Seglin, Mario Siletti, Oreste Bilancia, Gildo Bocci, Arturo Bragaglia, Anna Carena, Pina Gallini, Luciano Manara, Armando Migliari, Umberto Sacripante.

Sissignora
(*Yes, Ma'am*), 1942

Credits   *prod.*: ICI (La Società Anonima Industrie Cinematografiche Italiane)–ATA/ Clemente Fracassi and Libero Solaroli; *dir.*: Ferdinando Maria Poggioli; *sc.*: Anna Banti, Emilio Cecchi, Bruno Fallaci, Alberto Lattuada, and Ferdinando Maria Poggioli, from the novel *Sissignora*, by Flavia Steno; *adapt.*: Emilio Cecchi and Alberto Lattuada; *cin.*: Carlo Montuori; *des.*: Fulvio Paoli (aka Fulvio Jacchia); *cos.*: Maria De Matteis; *mus.*: Felice Lattuada; *ed.*: Ferdinando Maria Poggioli.

Cast   Emma Gramatica (Lucia Robbiano), Irma Gramatica (Anna Robbiano), Maria Denis (Cristina), Evi Maltagliati (Signora Valdata), Rina Morelli (Sister Valeria), Leonardo Cortese (Vittorio), Dhia Cristiani (Paolina), Jone Salinas (Enrichetta), Dora Bini, Anna Carena, Elio Marcuzzo (Emilio), Roldano Lupi, Giovanni Grasso, Silverio Pisu (The Valdata child), Guido Notari (The Doctor), Federico Collino (The Butler).

Gente del Po
(documentary)
(*People of the Po River*), 1941–47

Credits   *prod.*: Artisti Associati/I.C.E.T.–Carpi (Milan); *dir.*: Michelangelo Antonioni; *sc.*: Michelangelo Antonioni; *cin.*: Piero Portalupi; *mus.*: Mario Labroca; *ed.*: Carlo Alberto Chiesa.

Note: The final version was edited in 1947 from barely half the original footage, which was lost or destroyed during the last years of the war.

I bambini ci guardano
(*The Children Are Watching Us; The Little Martyr*), 1943

Credits   *prod.*: Scalera Film-Invicta Production; *prod. dir.*: Franco Magli; *dir.*: Vittorio De Sica; *Assistants to the director*: Paolo Moffa, Luisa Alessandri, Lidia C. Ripandelli, Vittorio Cottafavi; *sc. and adapt.*: Viola, Cesare Zavattini, Margherita Maglione, Adolfo Franci, Gherardo Gherardi, and De Sica, from Cesare Giulio Viola's novel *Pricò* (1928); *Photography:* Giuseppe Caracciolo; *des.*: Amleto Bonetti; *Set design:* Vittorio Valentini; *Editor:* Mario Bonotti; *Sound:* Tullio Parmegiani; *mus.*: Renzo Rossellini; *Released:* Italy: late 1943, 1944, 1945 (release interrupted by war); new edition: 1950; U.S.: New York, 1947, as *The Little Martyr*; *Running time:* 85 minutes; *Distributor:* Scalera Film; Filmed at Scalera Studio, Rome, and Alassio, late 1942 to early 1943.

Cast Luciano De Ambrosis (Pricò), Isa Pola (his mother, Ines), Emilio Cigoli (his father, Andrea), Adriano Rimoldi (Roberto), Giovanna Cigoli (Agnese), Ione Frigerio (the grandmother), Maria Gardena (Signora Uberti), Dina Perbellini (Zia Berelli), Nicoletta Parodi (Giuliana), Tecla Scarano (Signora Resta), Olinta Cristina (the school director), Mario Gallina (the doctor), Zaira La Fratta (Paolina), Armando Migliari, Guido Morisi, Achille Majeroni, Augusto Di Giovanni, Luigi A. Garrone, Agnese Dubbini, Aristide Garbini, Rita Livesi, Lina Marengo, Riccardo Fellini, Claudia Marti, Gino Viotti, Carlo Ranieri, Vasco Creti, Giulio Alfieri, Giovanna Ralli, Gabrielli the Magician.

Sorelle Materassi
(*The Materassi Sisters*), 1943
Credits prod.: ENIC (Ente Nazionale Industrie Cinematografiche)–Cines/Sandro Ghenzi; *dir.*: Ferdinando Maria Poggioli; *sc.*: Bernard Zimmer, from the novel by Aldo Palazzeschi; *adapt.*: Bernard Zimmer; *cin.*: Arturo Gallea; *des.*: Gastone Simonetti; *cos.*: Gino Sensani; *mus.*: Enzo Masetti; *ed.*: Ferdinando Maria Poggioli.
Cast Pietro Bigerna (The Moneylender), Paola Borboni (The Russian Woman), Margherita Bossi (The Butcher's Wife), Clara Calamai (Peggy), Loris Gizzi (The Priest), Emma Gramatica (Carolina), Irma Gramatica (Teresa), Anna Mari (Laurina), Leo Melchiorri (Otello), Dina Romano (Niobe), Massimo Serato (Remo), Olga Solbelli (Giselda).

La nostra guerra
(documentary)
(*Our War*), 1944
Credits prod.: Sezione cinematografica Stato maggiore esercito; *dir.*: Alberto Lattuada.

Aldo dice 26 X 1
(documentary)
(*Aldo's Saying*), 1945
Credits *dir.*: Fernando Cerchio.

Giorni di gloria
(documentary)
(*Days of Glory*), 1945
Credits   *prod.*: Titanus–A.N.P.I.–Psychological Warfare Branch of the United States Army/Fulvio Ricci; *dir.*: Giuseppe De Santis and Mario Serandrei, in collaboration with Marcello Pagliero (dir. of the episode in the Ardeatine Caves) and Luchino Visconti (dir. of the lynching of Carretta and the Caruso trial); *sc. and adapt.*: Mario Serandrei, with commentary written by Umberto Calosso and Umberto Barbaro, and spoken by Calosso; *cin.*: Giovanni Pucci and Massimo Terzano, with documentary footage from Della Valle, De West, Di Venanzo, Jannarelli, Lastricati, Navarro, Reed, Ventimiglia, Werdier, Vittoriano, Manlio, Caloz, and technicians of the CLN in Milan; *mus.*: Costantino Ferri; *ed.*: Mario Serandrei, Carlo Alberto Chiesa.

La vita ricomincia
(*Life Begins Again*), 1945
Credits   *prod.*: Excelsa Film; *dir.*: Mario Mattòli; *sc. and adapt.*: Aldo De Benedetti, Mario Mattoli, and Steno.
Cast   Fosco Giachetti, Alida Valli, Eduardo De Filippo.

O' sole mio
(*Oh, My Sun*), 1945
Credits   *prod.*: Rinascimento; *dir.*: Giacomo Gentilomo; *sc.*: Mario Amendola and Vincenzo Rovi; *adapt.*: Akos Tolnay, Mario Sequi, Gaspare Cataldo; *cin.*: Anchise Brizzi.
Cast   Tito Gobbi, Adriana Benetti, Vera Carmi, Carlo Ninchi, Ernesto Almirante, Vittorio Caprioli, Lilly Granado, Arnoldo Foà, Salvatore Cuffaro.

Roma, città aperta
(*Open City; Rome, Open City*), 1945
Credits   *prod.*: Excelsa Film; *dir.*: Roberto Rossellini; *sc.*: Sergio Amidei, Alberto Consiglio; *adapt.*: Sergio Amidei, Federico Fellini, Roberto Rossellini; *cin.*: Ubaldo Arata; *des.*: R. Megna; *mus.*: Renzo Rossellini; *ed.*: Eraldo Da Roma.
Cast   Anna Magnani (Pina), Aldo Fabrizi (Don Pietro Pellegrini), Marcello Pagliero (Giorgio Manfredi, alias Luigi Ferrari), Harry Feist (Major Bergmann), Maria Michi (Marina Mari), Francesco

Grandjacquet (Francesco, the Typist), Giovanna Galletti (Ingrid), Vito Annichiarico (Marcello, Pina's Son), Carla Rovere (Lauretta, Pina's Sister), Nando Bruno (Agostino), Carlo Sindici (Roman Police Chief), Joop van Hulzen (Hartmann), Akos Tolnay (The Austrian Deserter), Eduardo Passarelli (Police Officer), Amalia Pellegrini (The Landlady), Alberto Tavazzi (A Priest), C. Giudici.

Bambini in città
(documentary)
(*Children of the City*), 1946
Credits   *prod.*: Gigi Martello; *dir.*: Luigi Comencini, with narration by Mario Amerio; *cin.*: Plinio Novelli.

Davanti a Lui tremava tutta Roma
(*Before Him All Rome Trembled*), 1946
Credits   *prod.*: Excelsa Film; *dir.*: Carmine Gallone; *sc.*: Carmine Gallone; *adapt.*: Gherardo Gherardi, Carmine Gallone, Gaspare Cataldo; *cin.*: Anchise Brizzi.
Cast   Anna Magnani, Tito Gobbi, Gino Sinimberghi, Edda Albertini, Varni.

Il bandito
(*The Bandit*), 1946
Credits   *prod.*: Lux–R.D.L. (Dino De Laurentiis); *dir.*: Alberto Lattuada; *sc.*: Alberto Lattuada; *adapt.*: Oreste Biàncoli, Mino Caudana, Alberto Lattuada, Ettore M. Margadonna, Tullio Pinelli, Piero Tellini; *cin.*: Aldo Tonti; *des.*: Luigi Borzone; *mus.*: Felice Lattuada.
Cast   Amedeo Nazzari (Ernesto), Anna Magnani (Lydia), Carla del Poggio (Maria), Carlo Campanini (Carlo), Eliana Banducci (Rosetta), Mino Doro (Mirko), Folco Lulli (Andrea), Mario Perrone (The Hunchback), Gianni Appelius (Signorina), Thea Ajmaretti (The Landlady), Amato Garbini (The Landowner), Ruggero Madrigali (The Slavetrader).

Io t'ho incontrata a Napoli
(*To Meet in Naples*), 1946
Credits   *prod.*: EDI Film; *dir.*: Piero Francisci; *sc.*: John Ford and Evelina Levi; *adapt.*: Piero Francisci and Morbelli; *cin.*: Augusto Tiezzi.
Cast   Anna Nievo, Leo Dale, Peppino De Filippo, Giuseppe Porelli, Claudio Gora, Paolo Stoppa.

Montecassino
1946

Credits *prod.:* Pastor; *dir.:* Arturo Gemmiti; *sc.:* Arturo Gemmiti; *adapt.:* Arturo Gemmiti, Giovanni Paolucci, Virgilio Sabel; *cin.:* Vittorio Solito.

Cast Zora Piazza, Piero Bigerna, Pietro Germi, Fosca Freda, Ubaldo Lay, Vira Salenti.

Paisà
(*Paisan*), 1946

Credits *prod.:* Organization Films International (O.F.I.; Mario Conti and Rod E. Geiger) in collaboration with Foreign Film Productions, Inc.; *dir.:* Roberto Rossellini; *sc.:* Sergio Amidei, with the collaboration of Roberto Rossellini, Marcello Pagliero, Federico Fellini, Klaus Mann, Alfred Hayes, Vasco Pratolini, Victor Haines; *adapt.:* Sergio Amidei, Federico Fellini, Roberto Rossellini, with English dialogue by Annalena Limentani; *cin.:* Otello Martelli; *mus.:* Renzo Rossellini; *ed.:* Eraldo Da Roma.

Cast SICILY—Carmela Sazio (Carmela), Robert van Loon (Joe from Jersey), Benjamin Emmanuel, Raymond Campbell, Albert Heinz, Harold Wagner, Merlin Berth, Leonard Parrish, Mats Carlson (Soldier), Carlo Piscane (Peasant); NAPLES—Dots M. Johnson (The Negro M.P.), Alfonsino Pasca (The Little Boy); ROME—Gar Moore (Fred, the Soldier), Maria Michi (Francesca); FLORENCE—Harriet White (Harriet, the Nurse), Renzo Avanzo (Massimo); FRANCISCAN CONVENT—Bill Tubbs (Captain Bill Martin, the Catholic Chaplain) and Franciscan monks; Po DELTA—Dale Edmonds (Dale, the OSS Man), Cigolani (The Partisan), Allan Dan, Van Loel. PLUS— Marcello Pagliero, Vito Chiari, M. Hugo, Anthony La Penna, Gigi Gori, Lorena Berg.

Sciuscià
(*Shoeshine*), 1946

Credits *prod.:* Paolo William Tamburella (for Società Cooperativa Alfa Cinematografica); *prod. dir.:* Nino Ottavi; *Assistant producer:* Franco Serino; *dir.:* Vittorio De Sica; *Assistant directors:* Umberto Scarpelli, Armando W. Tamburella, Argi Rovelli, Elmo De Sica; *sc.:* Cesare Zavattini, Vittorio De Sica, Sergio Amidei, Adolfo Franci, and Cesare Giulio Viola; *Photography:* Anchise Brizzi; *Cameraman:* Elio Paccara; *des.:* Ivo Battelli, with Giulio Lombardozzi (sets);

Editor: Nicolò Lazzari; *Sound:* Tullio Parmegiani; *mus.:* Alessandro Cicognini; theme: variations on a children's song, "Girogirotondo"; *Released:* Italy: April 1946; U.S.: Fifth Avenue Playhouse, New York, 26 August 1947; *Running Time:* 93 minutes; *Distributor:* ENIC (Ente Nazionale Industrie Cinematografiche)/Lopert (UA); Filmed on location in Rome and at Scalera Film Studio, Rome, January to April 1946.

Cast Rinaldo Smordoni (Giuseppe), Franco Interlenghi (Pasquale), Aniello Mele (Raffaele), Bruno Oretensi (Arcangeli), Emilio Cigoli (Staffera), Gino Saltamerenda ("Il panza"), Anna Pedoni (Nannarella), Enrico De Silva (Giorgio), Antonio Lo Nigro (Righetto), Angelo D'Amico (the Sicilian), Antonio Carlino (The Abruzzese), Francesco De Nicola (Ciriola), Pacifico Astrologo (Vittorio), Maria Campi (the palmist), Leo Garavaglia (the inspector), Giuseppe Spadaro (the lawyer Bonavino), Irene Smordoni (Giuseppe's mother), Antonio Nicotra (Bartoli, the social worker), Claudio Ermelli (the orderly at the prison infirmary), Guido Gentili (Attilio), Mario Volpicelli (prison warden), Armando Furlai, Leonardo Bragaglia, Tony Amendola, Edmondo Costa, Gino Marturano, Edmondo Zappacarta, Achille Ponzi, Piero Carini, Mario Del Monte Jr., Mario Jafrati.

Un giorno nella vita
(*A Day in the Life; A Day of Life*), 1946

Credits *prod.:* Orbis Film; *dir.:* Alessandro Blasetti; *sc.:* Alessandro Blasetti, Cesare Zavattini; *adapt.:* Alessandro Blasetti, Cesare Zavattini, Mario Chiari, Anton Giulio Majano, Diego Fabbri; *cin.:* Mario Craveri; *des.:* Salvo D'Angelo; *mus.:* Enzo Masetti; *ed.:* Gisa Radicchi Levi.

Cast Amedeo Nazzari, Massimo Girotti, Mariella Lotti, Elisa Cegani, Dina Sassoli, Ave Ninchi, Ada Dondini, Arnoldo Foà, Dante Maggio.

Vivere in pace
(*To Live in Peace*), 1946

Credits *prod.:* Lux Film-Pao (Carlo Ponti); *dir.:* Luigi Zampa; *sc. and adapt.:* Suso Cecchi D'Amico, Aldo Fabrizi, Piero Tellini, Luigi Zampa; *cin.:* Carlo Montuori and Mario Montuori; *des.:* Ivo Battelli; *mus.:* Nino Rota.

Cast Aldo Fabrizi (Uncle Tigna), Gar Moore (Ronald), Mirella Monti (Silvia), John Kitzmiller (Joe), Heinrich Bode (Hans), Ave Ninchi

(Corinna), Ernesto Almirante (The Grandfather), Nando Bruno (The Party Secretary), Aldo Silvani (The Doctor), Gino Cavalieri (The Priest), Piero Palermini (Franco), Franco Serpilli (Citta).

Caccia tragica
(*Tragic Hunt; Pursuit*), 1947
Credits prod.: A.N.P.I. (G. Giorgi Agliani); dir.: Giuseppe De Santis; sc.: Giuseppe De Santis, Carlo Lizzani, Lamberto Rem Picci; adapt.: Umberto Barbaro, Michelangelo Antonioni, Carlo Lizzani, Giuseppe De Santis, Cesare Zavattini, Corrado Alvaro, Ennio De Concini, Gianni Puccini; cin.: Otello Martelli; des.: Carlo Egidi; mus.: Giuseppe Rosati; ed.: Mario Serandrei.
Cast Vivi Gioi (Daniela), Andrea Checchi (Alberto), Carla del Poggio (Giovanna), Vittorio Duse (Giuseppe), Massimo Girotti (Michele), Checco Rissone (Mimi), Guido Dalla Valle (The German), Folco Lulli, Piero Lulli, Michele Riccardini, Ermano Randi, Eugenia Grandi, Umberto Sacripante, Antonio Nediani.

Come persi la guerra
(*How I Lost the War*), 1947
Credits prod.: Lux Film–R.D.L.; dir.: Carlo Borghesio; sc.: Carlo Borghesio, Benvenuti, Giannini; adapt.: Mario Amendola, Steno, Monicelli, Tullio Pinelli, Carlo Borghesio; cin.: Aldo Tonti.
Cast Erminio Macario, Vera Carmi, Nando Bruno, Carlo Campanini, Folco Lulli, Piero Lulli, Nunzio Filogamo, Fritz Marlat, Aldo Tonti.

Germania, anno zero
(*Germany, Year Zero*), 1947
Credits prod.: Tevere Film (Alfredo Guarini, Roberto Rossellini)–Salvo D'Angelo Production (Rome)–Sadfi (Berlin)–UGC (Paris); dir.: Roberto Rossellini; sc.: Roberto Rossellini; adapt.: Roberto Rossellini, Max Kolpet, Carlo Lizzani; cin.: Robert Juillard; des.: Piero Filippone; mus.: Renzo Rossellini; ed.: Eraldo Da Roma.
Cast Edmund Moeschke (Edmund), Werner Pittschau (Edmund's Father), Ingetraut Hintze (Eva, Edmund's Sister), Franz Krüger (Karl-Heinz, Edmund's Brother), Erich Gühne (Edmund's Teacher), Barbara Hintz, Alexandra Manys, Babsy Reckvell, Hans Sangen, Hedi Blankner, Count Treuberg, Karl Kauger.

Gioventù perduta
(*Lost Youth*), 1947
Credits   prod.: Lux Film (Carlo Ponti); *dir.*: Pietro Germi; *sc.*: Pietro Germi; *adapt.*: Pietro Germi, Antonio Pietrangeli, Mario Monicelli, Leopoldo Trieste, Enzo Provenzale, Bruno Valeri; *cin.*: Carlo Montuori; *des.*: Gianni Mazzocca; *mus.*: Carlo Rustichelli; *ed.*: Renato May.
Cast   Jacques Sernas, Carla Del Poggio, Massimo Girotti, Franca Maresa, Diana Borghese, Nando Bruno, Leo Garavaglia, Dino Maronetto, Michele Sakara, Ugo Metrailler, Angelo Dessí.

Il sole sorge ancora
(*The Sun Rises Again*), 1947
Credits   *prod.*: C.V.L.–A.N.P.I./G. Giorgi Agliani; *dir.*: Aldo Vergano; *sc.*: Giuseppe Gorgerino (from an idea by Anton Giulio Majano); *adapt.*: Guido Aristarco, Giuseppe De Santis, Carlo Lizzani, Carlo Alberto Felice, Aldo Vergano; *cin.*: Aldo Tonti; *des.*: Fausto Galli; *mus.*: Giuseppe Rosati; *ed.*: Gabriele Varriale.
Cast   Vittorio Duse (Cesare), Elli Parvo (Matilde), Lea Padovani (Laura), Massimo Serato (Major Heinrich), Carlo Lizzani (The Priest), Marco Sevi, Checco Rissone, Marco Sarri, Riccardo Passani, Gillo Pontecorvo, Mirkan Korcinsoi, Ruggerio Giacobbi.

L'onorevole Angelina
(*The Virtuous Angelina; Angelina*), 1947
Credits   *prod.*: Ora–Lux Film/Paolo Fasca; *dir.*: Luigi Zampa; *sc. and adapt.*: Piero Tellini, Suso Cecchi D'Amico, Luigi Zampa; *cin.*: Mario Craveri; *des.*: Luigi Gervasi, Piero Filippone; *mus.*: Enzo Masetti; *ed.*: Eraldo Da Roma.
Cast   Anna Magnani (Angelina), Nando Bruno (Pasquale), Gianni Glori (Libero), Maria Grazia Francia (Annetta), Anita Angius (Adriane), Adalberto Tenaglia (Giuseppe), Ave Ninchi (Carmela), Agnese Dubbini (Cesira), Ugo Bertucci (Benedetto), Vittorio Mottini (Roberto), Armando Migliari (Callisto), Franco Zeffirelli (Filippo), Maria Donati (Signora Garrone), Ernesto Almirante (Luigi), Aristide Baghetti, Diego Calcagno.

Anni difficili
(*Difficult Years; The Little Man*), 1948
Credits   *prod.*: Briguglio Film (Folco Laudati); *dir.*: Luigi Zampa; *sc.*: from

the novel *The Old Man and His Boots (Il vecchio con gli stivali)*, by Vitaliano Brancati; *adapt.*: Sergio Amidei, Vitaliano Brancati, Franco Evangelisti, Enrico Fulchignoni, Luigi Zampa; *cin.*: Carlo Montuori; *des.*: Ivo Battelli; *mus.*: Franco Casavola; *ed.*: Eraldo Da Roma.

Cast Umberto Spadaro (Aldo Piscitello), Ave Ninchi (Rosina, His Wife), Massimo Girotti (Giovanni, Their Son), Odette Bedogni (Elena, Their Daughter), The Stefano Twins (The Twin Sons), Ernesto Almirante (The Grandfather), Enzo Biliotti (The Fascist Mayor), Carletto Sposito (The Mayor's Son), Aldo Silvani (The Chemist), Milly Vitale (Maria), Giovanni Grasso, Olunto Cristina, Agostino Salvietti, Rainero De Cenzo, Giuseppe Nicolosi (The Malcontents).

Fuga in France
(Escape to France), 1948
Credits *prod.*: Lux Film (Carlo Ponti); *dir.*: Mario Soldati; *sc.*: Mario Soldati, Carlo Musso; *adapt.*: Mario Soldati, Carlo Musso, Ennio Flaiano, Mario Bonfantini, Tino Richelmy; *cin.*: Domenico Scala; *des.*: Piero Gherardi; *mus.*: Nino Rota; *ed.*: Mario Bonotti.
Cast Folco Lulli, Rosi Mirafiore, Mario Vercellone, Enrico Olivieri, Pietro Germi, Giovanni Dufour.

La terra trema
(The Earth Trembles; The Earth Will Shake), 1948
Credits *prod.*: Universalia (Salvo D'Angelo); *dir.*: Luchino Visconti; *sc. and adapt.*: Luchino Visconti (inspired by Giovanni Verga's 1881 novel *Bad Blood [I Malavoglia]*), with commentary written by Visconti and Antonio Pietrangeli, and spoken by Mario Pisu; *cin.*: G. R. Aldo (aka Aldo Graziati), Gianni di Venanzo; *mus.*: Luchino Visconti, Willy Ferrero; *ed.*: Mario Serandrei.
Cast Workers and fishermen from Aci Trezza, Sicily (i.e., nonprofessionals): Antonio Arcidiacono ('Ntoni), Giuseppe Arcidiacono (Cola), Giovanni Greco (The Grandfather), Nelluccia Giammona (Mara), Agnese Giammona (Lucia), Nicola Castorina (Nicola), Rosario Galvagno (Don Salvatore), Lorenzo Valastro (Lorenzo), Rosa Costanzo (Nedda).

Ladri di biciclette
(The Bicycle Thief; Bicycle Thieves), 1948
Credits *prod.*: Vittorio De Sica (for PDS, Produzioni De Sica); *prod. dir.*:

Umberto Scarpelli; *Production inspector:* Nino Misiano; *Production secretary:* Roberto Moretti; *dir.:* Vittorio De Sica; *Assistant directors:* Gerardo Guerrieri, Luisa Alessandri; *sc. and adapt.:* Cesare Zavattini, Vittorio De Sica, Oreste Biàncoli, Suso Cecchi D'Amico, Adolfo Franci, Gherardo Gherardi, and Gerardo Guerrieri, from an original story by Zavattini, based on the novel *Ladri di biciclette* (1946), by Luigi Bartolini; *Photography:* Carlo Montuori; *Cameraman:* Mario Montuori; *Art director:* Antonio Traverso; *Editor:* Eraldo Da Roma; *Sound:* Bruno Brunacci; *Music:* Alessandro Cicognini; *Music director:* Willy Ferrero; *Released:* Italy: November 1948; U.S.: World Theater, New York, 13 December 1949; *Running time:* 87 minutes; *Distributor:* ENIC/Mayer-Burstyn; Filmed on location in Rome and at SAFA Studios, June to August 1948.

Cast   Lamberto Maggiorani (Antonio Ricci), Enzo Staiola (Bruno, his son), Lianella Carell (Maria Ricci), Gino Saltamerenda (Baiocco), Vittorio Antonucci (the thief), Giulio Chiari (the old man), Elena Altieri (the mission patroness), Ida Bracci Dorati (La Santona), Michele Sakara (the secretary of the charity), Fausto Guerzoni (the amateur actor), Carlo Jachino (the beggar), Massimo Randisi (the middle-class boy at the restaurant), Umberto Spadaro, Memmo Carotenuto, Nando Bruno, Peppino Spadaro (the police sergeant), Mario Meniconi (the garbage man), Checco Rissone (the watchman at Vittorio Square), Giulio Battiferri (a citizen who shields the real thief), Sergio Leone (a seminarian), Emma Druetti, Giovanni Corporale, Eolo Capritti.

Senza pietà
(*Without Pity*), 1948

Credits   *prod.:* Lux Film; *dir.:* Alberto Lattuada; *sc.:* Federico Fellini, Tullio Pinelli (from an idea by Ettore M. Margadonna); *adapt.:* Federico Fellini, Tullio Pinelli, Alberto Lattuada; *cin.:* Aldo Tonti; *des.:* Piero Gherardi; *mus.:* Nino Rota; *ed.:* Mario Bonotti.

Cast   Carl del Poggio (Angela), John Kitzmiller (Jerry), Pierre Claudé (Pier Luigi), Folco Lulli (Giacomo), Giulietta Masina (Marcella), Lando Muzio (The South American Captain), Daniel Jones (Richard), Otello Fava (The Dumb Man), Romano Villi (The Bandit), Mario Perrone (The Second Bandit), Enza Giovine (Sister Gertrude), Armando Libianchi, Max Lancia, Enza Giovine.

Sotto il sole di Roma
(*Under the Roman Sun*), 1948

Credits *prod.:* Universalcine (Sandro Ghenzi); *dir.:* Renato Castellani; *sc.:* Renato Castellani and Fausto Tozzi; *adapt.:* Renato Castellani, Fausto Tozzi, Sergio Amidei, Emilio Cecchi, Ettore M. Margadonna; *cin.:* Domenico Scala; *mus.:* Nino Rota; *ed.:* Jolanda Benvenuti.

Cast Oscar Blando, Francesco Golisano, Liliana Mancini, and nonprofessionals.

Cielo sulla palude
(*Heaven over the Marshes*), 1949

Credits *prod.:* Arx Film (Renato and Carlo Bassoli); *dir.:* Augusto Genina; *sc. and adapt.:* Augusto Genina, Suso Cecchi D'Amico, Fausto Tozzi; *cin.:* G. R. Aldo (aka Aldo Graziati); *des.:* Virgilio Marchi; *mus.:* Antonio Veretti; *ed.:* Edmondo Lozzi, Otello Colangeli.

Cast Ines Orsini (Maria Goretti), Mauro Matteucci (Alessandro Serenelli), Giovanni Martella (Luigi Goretti), Assunta Radico (Assunta Goretti), Francesco Tomalillo (Giovanni Serenelli), Rubi Dalma (The Countess), Michele Malaspina (The Count), Domenico Viglione Borghese (The Doctor).

È primavera
(*Springtime in Italy*), 1949

Credits *prod.:* Universalcine (Sandro Ghenzi); *dir.:* Renato Castellani; *sc. and adapt.:* Renato Castellani, Suso Cecchi D'Amico, Cesare Zavattini; *cin.:* Tino Santoni; *mus.:* Nino Rota; *ed.:* Jolanda Benvenuti.

Cast Mario Angelotti (Beppe), Elena Varzi (Maria Antonia), Donato Donati (Cavallucio), Ettore Janetti (The Lawyer Di Salvo), Grazia Idonea (Signora Di Salvo), Gianni Santi (Albertino Di Salvo), Irene Genna (Lucia), Adia Giannini (Portinaia).

Il mulino del Po
(*The Mill on the River; The Mill on the Po*), 1949

Credits *prod.:* Lux Film (Carlo Ponti); *dir.:* Alberto Lattuada; *sc.:* from the three-volume novel by Riccardo Bacchelli (published 1938–1945); *adapt.:* Federico Fellini, Tullio Pinelli, Riccardo Bacchelli, Alberto Lattuada, Mario Bonfantini, Carlo Musso, Sergio Romano, Luigi Comencini; *cin.:* Aldo Tonti; *des.:* Aldo Buzzi; *mus.:* Ildebrando Pizzetti; *ed.:* Mario Bonotti.

Cast Carla del Poggio (Berta), Jacques Sernas (Orbino), Leda Gloria (La Suiza), Dina Sassoli (Susanna), Guilio Calì (Smarazzacucco), Anna Carena (L'Argia), Giacomo Giuradei (Princivale), Nino Pavese (Raibolini), Domenico Viglione Borghese (Luca), Isabella Riva (Cecilia), Pina Gallini, Mario Besesti.

In nome della legge
(*In the Name of the Law; Mafia*), 1949

Credits prod.: Lux Film (Luigi Rovere); *dir.*: Pietro Germi; *sc.*: Giuseppe Mangione (from the novel *Lower District Court [Piccola pretura]*, by Giuseppe Loschiavo); *adapt.*: Aldo Bizzarri, Federico Fellini, Pietro Germi, Giuseppe Mangione, Mario Monicelli, Tullio Pinelli, Leonida Barboni; *cin.*: Leonida Barboni; *des.*: Gino Morici; *mus.*: Carlo Rustichelli; *ed.*: Rolando Benedetti.

Cast Massimo Girotti (Guido Schiavi), Jone Salinas (The Baroness), Camillo Mastrocinque (The Baron), Charles Vanel (Passalacqua, the Mafia Chief), Turi Pandolfini (Don Fifì), Peppino Spadaro (The Lawyer), Saro Urzì (The Police Sergeant), Ignazio Balsamo (Ciccio Messana), Saro Arcidiacono (The Clerk of the Court), Nanda De Santis (Lorenzina), Nadia Niver (Vastianedda), Bernardo Indelicato (Paolino).

Riso amaro
(*Bitter Rice*), 1949

Credits prod.: Lux Film (Dino De Laurentiis); *dir.*: Giuseppe De Santis; *sc.*: Giuseppe De Santis, Carlo Lizzani, Gianni Puccini; *adapt.*: Corrado Alvaro, Giuseppe De Santis, Carlo Lizzani, Carlo Musso, Ivo Perilli, Gianni Puccini, Franco Monicelli; *cin.*: Otello Martelli; *des.*: Carlo Egidi; *mus.*: Goffredo Petrassi; *ed.*: Gabriele Varriale.

Cast Raf Vallone (Marco), Silvana Mangano (Silvana), Vittorio Gassman (Walter), Doris Dowling (Francesca), Checco Rissone (Aristide), Nico Pepe (Beppe), Adriana Sivieri (Celeste), Lia Corelli (Amelia), Maria Grazia Francia (Gabriella), Dedi Ristori (Anna), Anna Maestri (Irene), Mariemma Bardi (Gianna), Attilio Dottesio.

Domenica d'agosto
(*Sunday in August*), 1950

Credits prod.: Colonna Film (Sergio Amidei); *dir.*: Luciano Emmer; *sc.*: Sergio Amidei; *adapt.*: Franco Brusati, Luciano Emmer, Giulio Macchi, Cesare Zavattini, Sergio Amidei; *cin.*: Domenico Scala,

Leonida Barboni, Ubaldo Marelli; *mus.:* Roman Vlad; *ed.:* Jolanda Benvenuti.

Cast Anna Baldini (Marcella), Franco Interlenghi (Enrico), Anna Di Leo (Yolanda), Massimo Serato (Roberto), Marcello Mastroianni (Ercole), Vera Carmi (Adriana), Elvy Lissiak (Luciana), Ave Ninchi (Fernanda Meloni), Andrea Campagnoni (Cesare Meloni), Fernando Milani (Catone), Emilio Cigoli (Mantovani), Pina Malgarini (Ines), Anna Medici, Mario Vitale.

Francesco, giullare di Dio
(*Francis, God's Jester; The Flowers of St. Francis*), 1950
Credits *prod.:* Cineriz (Angelo Rizzoli, Giuseppe Amato); *dir.:* Roberto Rossellini; *sc.:* Roberto Rossellini, from *The Little Flowers of St. Francis* and *The Life of Brother Ginepro; adapt.:* Roberto Rossellini, Federico Fellini, Brunello Rondi, Sergio Amidei, with the collaboration of Father Felix Morlion and Father Antonio Lisandrini; *cin.:* Otello Martelli; *des.:* Virgilio Marchi; *mus.:* Renzo Rossellini; for the liturgical songs, Father Enrico Buondonno; *ed.:* Jolanda Benvenuti.
Cast Aldo Fabrizi (Nicolaio, the Tyrant), Arabella Lemaître (Saint Clair), and the monks of Nocere Inferiore Monastery, including Brother Nazario Gerardi (Saint Francis).

Il cammino della speranza
(*The Road to Hope; The Path of Hope; The Way to Hope*), 1950
Credits *prod.:* Lux Film (Luigi Rovere); *dir.:* Pietro Germi; *sc.:* Pietro Germi, Federico Fellini, and Tullio Pinelli, from the novel *Hearts on the Edge (Cuori sugli abissi),* by Nino Di Maria; *adapt.:* Federico Fellini, Tullio Pinelli; *cin.:* Leonida Barboni; *des.:* Luigi Ricci; *mus.:* Carlo Rustichelli; *ed.:* Rolando Benedetti.
Cast Raf Vallone (Saro), Elena Varzi (Barbara), Saro Urzì (Ciccio), Saro Arcidiacono (The Accountant), Franco Navarra (Vanni), Liliana Lattanzi (Rosa), Mirella Ciotti (Lorenza), Carmela Trovato (Cirmena), Assunta Radico (Beatificata), Francesca Russella (The Grandmother), Francesco Tomolillo (Misciu), Angelo Grasso (Antonio), Giuseppe Priolo (Luca), Paolo Reale (Brasi), Renato Terra (Mommino), Giuseppe Cibardo (Turi), Nicolò Gibilaro (Nanno), Gino Caizzi, and the Children: Ciccio Coluzzi (Buda), Luciana Coluzzi (Luciana), Angelina Scaldaferri (Diodata).

Il Cristo proibito
(*Forbidden Christ; Strange Deception*), 1950
Credits prod.: Excelsa Film–Minerva; dir.: Curzio Malaparte; sc. and adapt.: Curzio Malaparte; cin.: Gabor Pogany; des.: Leonida Maroulis and Orfeo Tamburi; mus.: Curzio Malaparte and Ugo Giacomazzi; ed.: Giancarlo Cappelli.
Cast Raf Vallone (Bruno), Elena Varzi (Nella), Alain Cuny (Master Antonio), Rina Morelli (Bruno's Mother), Philippe Lemaire (Pinin), Anna-Maria Ferrero (Maria), Gualtiero Tumiati (Bruno's Father), Luigi Tosi (Andrea), Ernesta Rosmino (The Old Woman), Gino Cervi (The Hermit), Lianella Carell.

Nel Mezzogiorno qualcosa è cambiato
(documentary)
(*Something Has Changed in the South*), 1950
Credits dir.: Carlo Lizzani.

Non c'è pace tra gli ulivi
(*No Peace among the Olives; Bloody Easter*), 1950
Credits prod.: Lux Film (Domenico Forges Davanzati); dir.: Giuseppe De Santis; sc.: Giuseppe De Santis, Gianni Puccini; adapt.: Libero De Libero, Giuseppe De Santis, Carlo Lizzani, Gianni Puccini; cin.: Piero Portalupi; des.: Carlo Egidi; mus.: Goffredo Petrassi; ed.: Gabriele Varriale.
Cast Lucia Bosé (Laura), Raf Vallone (Francesco Dominici), Folco Lulli (Agostino Bonfiglio), Maria Grazia Francia (Maria Grazia), Dante Maggio (Salvatore Capuano), Michele Riccardini (The Police Sergeant), Vincenzo Talarico (The Lawyer).

Achtung, banditi!
(*Watch Out, Bandits!*), 1951
Credits prod.: Cooperative Spettatori Produttori Cinematografici; dir.: Carlo Lizzani; sc. and adapt.: Carlo Lizzani, Rodolfo Sonego, Giuseppe Dagnino, Ugo Pirro, Massimo Mida, Enrico Ribulsi, Mario Socrate, Gaetano De Negri, Giuliani; cin.: Gianni De Venanzo; des.: Carlo Egidi; mus.: Mario Zafred; ed.: Enzo Alfonsi.
Cast Gina Lollobrigida, Andrea Checchi, Vittorio Duse, Maria Laura Rocca, Giuliano Montaldo, Lamberto Maggiorani, G. Taffarel, F. Bologna, Pietro Tordi, Bruno Berellini, Pietro Ferro, Carla del Poggio, Elena Varzi.

Bellissima
(*The Most Beautiful*), 1951
Credits   prod.: Film Bellissima (Salvo D'Angelo); dir.: Luchino Visconti; sc.: from a story by Cesare Zavattini; adapt.: Suso Cecchi D'Amico, Francesco Rosi, Luchino Visconti; cin.: Piero Portalupi, Paul Roland; des.: Gianni Polidori; cos.: Piero Tosi; mus.: Franco Mannino, using *The Elixir of Love (L'elisir d'amore)*, by Donizetti; ed.: Mario Serandrei.
Cast   Anna Magnani (Maddalena Cecconi), Walter Chiari (Alberto Annovazzi), Tina Apicella (Maria Cecconi), Gastone Renzelli (Spartaco Cecconi), Alessandro Blasetti (Himself), Tecla Scarano (The Acting Teacher), Lola Braccini (The Photographer's Wife), Arturo Bragaglia (The Photographer), Linda Sini (Mimmetta), Amedeo Nazzari, Massimo Girotti, Titina De Filippo, Silvana Pampanini, Nora Ricci, Vittorio Glori (Himself), Iris (Herself), Geo Taparelli (Himself), Mario Chiari (Himself), Filippo Mercati (Himself), Vittorina Benvenuti, Gisella Monaldi, Amalia Pellegrini, Teresa Battaggi, Luciana Ricci, Giuseppina Arena.

Due soldi di speranza
(*Two Cents' Worth of Hope*), 1951
Credits   prod.: Universalcine (Sandro Ghenzi); dir.: Renato Castellani; sc.: Renato Castellani, Ettore M. Margadonna; adapt.: Renato Castellani, Titina De Filippo; cin.: Arturo Gallea; mus.: Alessandro Cicognini; ed.: Jolanda Benvenuti.
Cast   Maria Fiore (Carmela), Luigi Astarita (Carmela's Father), Vincenzo Musolino (Antonio), Filomena Russo (His Mother), Gina Mascetti (Signora Flora), Luigi Barone (The Priest), Carmela Cirillo (Giulia), Felicia Lettieri (Signora Artu), Alfonso Del Sorbo (Sacristan), Tommaso Balzano (Luigi Bellomo), Anna Raida (Signora Bellomo), and the inhabitants of Boscotrecase.

Miracolo a Milano
(*Miracle in Milan*), 1951
Credits   prod.: Vittorio De Sica (for PDS, Produzioni De Sica, in association with ENIC); prod. dir.: Nino Misiano; Production inspector: Elmo De Sica; Production secretary: Roberto Moretti; General organization: Umberto Scarpelli, Carmine Bologna; dir.: Vittorio De Sica; Assistant directors: Luisa Allessandri, Umberto Scarpelli; sc. and adapt.: Cesare Zavattini and Vittorio De Sica, with Suso Cecchi

D'Amico, Mario Chiari, and Adolfo Franci; story by Zavattini, from his novel *Totò il buono* [*Totò the Good*] (1943); *Photography:* G. R. Aldo [Aldo Graziati]; *Cameraman:* Gianni Di Venanzo; *Assistant cameramen:* Augusto Tinelli, Michele Cristiani; *Art director:* Guido Fiorini; *Wardrobe/Costumes:* Mario Chiari; *Special photographic effects:* Ned Mann, with Sid Howell, Dave Mature, Mattia Triznya; *Special effects camera operators:* Vaclav Vich, Enzo Barboni; *Editor:* Eraldo Da Roma; *Assistant editor:* Marcella Benvenuti; *Sound:* Bruno Brunacci; *Music, music director:* Alessandro Cicognini; *Released:* Italy: February 1951; U.S.: World Theater, New York, 17 December 1951; *Running time:* 96 minutes; *Distributor:* ENIC/Joseph Burstyn; Filmed on location in Milan, at I.C.E.T. Studios in Milan, and at Titanus and Cinecittà Studios, Rome, between March and December 1950.

Cast Emma Gramatica (Lolotta, the old woman), Francesco Golisano (Totò), Paolo Stoppa (Rappi, the villain), Guglielmo Barnabo (Mobbi, the rich man), Brunella Bovo (Edvige), Anna Carena (Matta, the proud lady), Alba Arnova (the statue), Virgilio Riento (Sgt. Riento), Arturo Bragaglia (Alfredo), Ermino Spalla (Gaetano), Ricardo Bertazzolo (the wrestler), Flora Cambi (unhappy girl in love), Angelo Prioli (first singing policeman), Francesco Rissone (second singing policeman), Jubel Schembri (the man with the bald head), Walter Scherer (Arturo), Jerome Johnson (the colored man), Egisto Olivieri (Mobbi's lawyer), Giuseppe Spalla, Giuseppe Berardi (Giuseppe), Renato Navarrini (the stutterer), Enzo Furlai (Brambi, the landowner), Leonfi Trivaldi, and the squatters of Milan.

Rome, ore undici
(***Rome, Eleven O'Clock***), **1952**
Credits prod.: Transcontinental-Titanus (Paul Graetz); *dir.:* Giuseppe De Santis; *sc. and adapt.:* Cesare Zavattini, Giuseppe De Santis, Basilio Franchina, Rodolfo Sonego, Gianni Puccini; *cin.:* Otello Martelli; *des.:* Léon Barsacq; *mus.:* Mario Nascimbene.
Cast Eva Vanicek (Gianna), Carla del Poggio (Lucinna), Massimo Girotti (Mando), Lucia Bosé (Simona), Raf Vallone (Carlo), Elena Varzi (Adriana), Lea Padovani (Caterina), Delia Scala (Angelina), Irene Galter (Clara), Paolo Stoppa (Clara's Father), Maria Grazia Francia (Cornelia), Naudio Di Claudio (Mr. Ferrari), Armando Francioli (Romolo), Paola Borboni, Loretta Paoli, Alberto Farnese, Checco Durante.

I Vinti
(*The Vanquished; The Beaten Ones; Youth and Perversion*), 1952
Credits   *prod.*: Film Constellazione, S.G.C.; *dir.*: Michelangelo Antonioni; *sc. and adapt.*: Michelangelo Antonioni, Suso Cecchi D'Amico, Diego Fabbri, Turi Vasile, Giorgio Bassini, Roger Nimier (French episode): *cin.*: Enzo Serafin; *ed.*: Eraldo Da Roma; *mus.*: Giovanni Fusco; *des.*: Gianni Polidori and Roland Berthon.
Cast   Italian episode: Franco Interlenghi (Claudio), Anna-Maria Ferrero (Marina), Evi Maltagliati (Claudio's mother), Eduardo Cianelli (Claudio's father), Umberto Spadaro, Gastone Renzelli; French episode: Jean-Pierre Mocky (Pierre), Etchika Choureau (Simone), Henri Poirier, André Jacques, Annie Noel, Guy de Meulan, Jacques Sempey; English episode: Peter Reynolds (Aubrey), Fay Compton (Mrs. Pinkerton), Patrick Barr (Ken Whatton), Eileen Moore, Raymond Lovell, Derek Tansley, Jean Stuart, Tony Kilshaw, Fred Victor, Charles Irwin.

Europa '51
(*Europe '51; The Greatest Love*), 1952
Credits   *prod.*: Dino De Laurentiis and Carlo Ponti; *dir.*: Roberto Rossellini; *sc.*: Roberto Rossellini; *adapt.*: Roberto Rossellini, Sandro De Feo, Mario Pannunzio, Ivo Perilli, Brunello Rondi; *cin.*: Aldo Tonti; *des.*: Virgilio Marchi; *mus.*: Renzo Rossellini; *ed.*: Jolanda Benvenuti.
Cast   Ingrid Bergman (Irene Girard), Alexander Knox (George Girard), Ettore Giannini (Andrea Casatti), Teresa Pellati (Ines), Giulietta Masina (Passerotto), Marcella Rovena (Mrs. Puglisi), Tina Perna (Cesira), Sandro Franchina (Michele Girard), Giancarlo Vigorelli (Judge), Maria Zanoli (Mrs. Galli), William Tubbs (Professor Alessandrini), Alberto Plebani (Mr. Puglisi), Alfred Brown (Hospital Priest), Gianna Segale (Nurse), Antonio Pietrangeli (Psychiatrist)

Umberto D.
1952
Credits   *prod.*: Giuseppe Amato (for Rizzoli-De Sica-Amato); *prod. dir.*: Nino Misiano; *Production secretary*: Pasquale Misiano; *dir.*: Vittorio De Sica; *Assistant directors*: Luisa Alessandri, Franco Montemurro; *Script*: Cesare Zavattini; *Photography*: G. R. Aldo [Aldo Graziati]; *Cameraman*: Giuseppe Rotunno; *Assistant cameramen*: Augusto Tinelli, Michele Cristiani; *Art director*: Virgilio Marchi; *Editor*: Eraldo Da Roma; *Assistant editor*: Marcella Benvenuti; *Sound*:

Ernio Sensi; *Music:* Alessandro Cicognini; *Musical recording:* Bixio-S.A.M., Milan Orchestra: "Organizzazione Rizzi"; *Released:* Italy: 20 January 1952; U.S.: Guild Theater, New York, 7 November 1955; *Running time:* 89 minutes; *Distributor:* Dear Film/Harrison Pictures; Filmed on location in Rome and at Cinecittà Studios, mid–1951.

Cast Carlo Battisti (Umberto D., or Umberto Domenico Ferrari), Maria Pia Casilio (Maria), Lina Gennari (Antonia, the landlady), Alberto Albani Barbieri (Paolo, the landlady's fiancé), Ilena Simova (the lady in the park), Elena Rea (the nun at the hospital), Memmo Carotenuto (patient at the hospital), and other nonprofessional actors.

I vitelloni
(*The Young and the Passionate*), 1953

Credits *prod.:* Jacques Bar, Mario De Vecchi, Lorenzo Pegoraro; *dir.:* Federico Fellini; *sc.:* Federico Fellinii; *adapt.:* Federico Fellini, Ennio Flaiano, Tullio Pinelli; *cin.:* Carlo Carlini, Otello Martelli, Luciano Trasatti; *des.:* Mario Chiari; *mus.:* Nino Rota; *ed.:* Rolando Benedetti.

Cast Franco Interlenghi (Moraldo Rubini), Alberto Sordi (Alberto), Franco Fabrizi (Fausto Moretti), Leopoldo Trieste (Leopoldo Vannucci), Riccardo Fellini (Riccardo), Leonora Ruffo (Sandra Rubini), Jean Brochard (Francesco Moretti), Claude Farell (Olga), Carlo Romano (Michele Curti), Enrico Viarisio (Signor Rubini), Paola Borboni (Signora Rubini), Lída Baarová (Giulia Curti), Vira Silenti (Gisella), Maja Nipora (Caterina), Achille Majeroni (Sergio Natali), Guido Martufi (Guido), Silvio Bagolini (Giudizio)

L'amore in città
(an anthology film)
(*Love in the City; Love in the Town*), 1953

Credits *prod.:* Faro Film (Cesare Zavattini, Riccardo Ghione, Marco Ferreri); *dir.:* Dino Risi (*Heaven for Four Hours [Paradiso per quattro ore]*); Michelangelo Antonioni (*Attempted Suicide [Tentato suicidio]*); Federico Fellini (*A Matrimonial Agency [Una agenzia matrimoniale]*); Francesco Maselli (*Catherine's Story [Stòria di Caterina]*); Alberto Lattuada (*The Italians Turn Their Heads [Gli Italiani si voltano]*); Carlo Lizzani (*Love That Pays [L'amore che si paga]*); *sc. and adapt.:* Cesare Zavattini, Aldo Buzzi, Luigi Chiarini, Luigi Malerba, Tullio Pinelli, Vittorio Veltroni, Francesco Maselli; *cin.:*

Gianni Di Venanzo; *des.:* Gianni Polidori; *mus.:* Mario Nascimbene; *ed.:* Eraldo Da Roma.

Cast nonprofessionals re-creating their own roles: Maresa Gallo, Angela Pierro, Rita Andreana, Lia Natali, Cristina Drago, Ilario Malaschini, Sue Ellen Blake, Silvio Lillo, Antonio Cifariello, Livia Venturini, Mara Berni, Ugo Tognazzi, Raimondo Vianello, Edda Evangelisti, Liana Poggiali, Maria Pia Trepaoli, Giovanna Ralli, Valeria Moriconi, Caterina Rigoglioso.

La strada
(*The Road*), 1954

Credits *prod.:* Dino De Laurentiis, Carlo Ponti; *dir.:* Federico Fellini; *sc.:* Federico Fellini; *adapt.:* Federico Fellini, Tullio Pinelli, Ennio Flaiano; *cin.:* Otello Martelli; *des.:* Mario Ravasco; *mus.:* Nino Rota; *ed.:* Leo Cattozzo.

Cast Anthony Quinn (Zampanò), Giulietta Masina (Gelsomina), Richard Basehart (The Fool), Aldo Silvani (Mr. Giraffe), Marcella Rovere (The Widow), Livia Venturini (The Sister).

Senso
(*The Wanton Contessa*), 1954

Credits *prod.:* Lux Film; *dir.:* Luchino Viscontii; *sc.:* Luchino Visconti; *adapt.:* Luchino Visconti, Suso Cecchi D'Amico, Camillo Boito, Carlo Alianello, Giorgio Bassani, Giorgio Prosperi, Tennessee Williams, Paul Bowles; *cin.:* G. R. Aldo, Robert Krasker; *des.:* Ottavio Scotti; *mus.:* Renzo Rossellini; *ed.:* Mario Serandrei.

Cast Alida Valli (La contessa Livia Serpieri), Farley Granger (Il tenente Franz Mahler), Heinz Moog (Il conte Serpieri), Rina Morelli (Laura, la governante), Christian Marquand (Un ufficiale boemo), Sergio Fantoni (Luca), Tino Bianchi (Il capitano Meucci), Ernst Nadherny (Il comandante della piazza di Verona), Tonio Selwart (Il colonello Kleist), Marcella Mariani (Clara, la prostituta), Massimo Girotti (Il marchese Roberto Ussoni).

L'oro di Napoli
(*Gold of Naples*), 1954

Credits *prod.:* Dino De Laurentiis, Carlo Ponti (for Ponti-De Laurentiis); *prod. dir.:* Nino Misiano; *Production secretary:* Elmo De Sica; *General organization:* Marcello Girosi; *dir.:* Vittorio De Sica; *Assistant directors:* Luisa Alessandri, Sandro Montemurro, Elmo De Sica;

	sc. and adapt.: Cesare Zavattini, Giuseppe Marotta, and Vittorio De Sica, as adapted by Zavattini from Marotta's collection of short stories in *L'oro di Napoli* (1947); *Photography:* Otello Martelli, Carlo Montuori; *Assistant cameraman:* Goffredo Bellisario; *Art directors:* Virgilio Marchi, Gastone Medin; *Set decoration:* Ferdinando Ruffo; *Costumes:* Marcello Marchesi; *Make-up:* R. De Martino; *Editor:* Eraldo Da Roma; *Sound:* Bruno Brunacci; *mus.:* Alessandro Cicognini; *Released:* Italy: 23 December 1954; U.S.: Paris Theater, New York, 11 February 1957; *Running time:* Original Italian edition: 118 minutes (five episodes); general release edition: 107 minutes (four episodes); *Distributor:* Paramount/Distributor's Corp. of America; Filmed on location in Naples, 1953.
Cast	"Il guappo" (The Racketeer), based on Marotta's story "Trent'anni diconsi trenta": Totò (Don Saverio), Lianella Carell (his wife, Carolina), Pasquale Cennamo (Don Carmine), Agostino Salvietti, Nino Vingelli; "Pizza a credito" (Pizza on Credit), based on Marotta's stories "Gente nel vicolo" and "La morte a Napoli": Sophia Loren (Sofia), Giacomo Furia (Rosario, her husband), Alberto Farnese (Alfredo, her lover), Paolo Stoppa (Don Peppino), Tecla Scarano, Pasquale Tartaro; "I giacotori" (The Gamblers), based on Marotta's story of the same name: Vittorio De Sica (Count Prospero B), Pierino Bilancioni (the doorman's son), Mario Passante (the valet), Irene Montalto (the countess), L. Borgostrom (the doorman); "Teresa," based on Marotta's story "Personaggi in busta chiusa": Silvana Mangano (Teresa), Erno Crisa (Nicola, her husband), Ubaldo Maestri (the go-between); "Il professore" (The Professor), based on Marotta's story of the same name: Eduardo De Filippo (Don Ersilio De Miccio, the "professor"), Tina Pica (one of his clientele), Nino Imparato, Gianni Crosio.

Il bidone
(*The Swindle*), 1955

Credits	*prod.:* Mario Derecchi; *dir.:* Federico Fellini; *sc.:* Federico Fellini; *adapt.:* Federico Fellini, Ennio Flaiano, Tullio Pinelli; *cin.:* Otello Martelli; *des.:* Dario Cecchi; *mus.:* Nino Rota; *ed.:* Mario Serandrei, Giuseppe Vari.
Cast	Broderick Crawford (Augusto), Giulietta Masina (Iris), Richard Basehart (Picasso), Franco Fabrizi (Roberto), Sue Ellen Blake (Anna), Irene Cefaro (Marisa), Alberto De Amicis (Rinaldo), Lorella De Luca (Patrizia), Giacomo Gabrielli (Il Baron Vargas),

Riccardo Garrone (Riccardo), Xenia Valderi (Luciana), Mara Werlen (Maggie), Maria Zanoli (Stella Florina), Ettore Bevilacqua (Swindled Man).

Il ferroviere
(*The Railroad Man*), 1956
Credits   prod.: ENIC (Ente Nazionale Industrie Cinematografiche)/Carlo Ponti; dir.: Pietro Germi; sc. and adapt.: Alfredo Giannetti, Luciano Vincenzoni, Pietro Germi; cin.: Leonida Barboni; mus.: Carlo Rustichelli.
Cast   Pietro Germi, Luisa Della Noce, Sylva Koscina, Saro Urzì, Giulia, Edoardo Nevola, Carlo Giuffrè.

Il tetto
(*The Roof*), 1956
Credits   prod.: Vittorio De Sica, Marcello Girosi (for De Sica Produzione); Goffredo Lombardo (for Titanus); prod. dir.: Nino Misiano; *Production secretaries:* Pasquale Misiano, Elmo De Sica; *Production inspector:* Roberto Moretti; dir.: Vittorio De Sica; *Assistant directors:* Luisa Alessandri, Franco Montemurro, Elmo De Sica; *Script:* Cesare Zavattini; *Photography:* Carlo Montuori; *Cameraman:* Goffredo Bellisario; *Assistant cameraman:* Dario Regis; *Art director:* Gastone Medin; *Set decorator:* Ferdinando Ruffo; *Costumes:* Fabrizio Carafa; *Make-up:* Michele Trimarchi; *Hair stylist:* Lina Cassini; *Editor:* Eraldo Da Roma; *Assistant editor:* Marcella Benvenuti; *Sound:* Kurt Doubrawsky, Emilio de Rosa; *Music:* Alessandro Cicognini; *Music director:* Franco Ferrara; *Music recording:* Nazionalmusic, Milan; *Released:* Italy: 6 October 1956; U.S.: Trans-Lux Theater, New York, 12 May 1959; *Running time:* 91 minutes; original Italian version: 120 minutes; *Distributor:* Titanus/Trans-Lux Distribution; Filmed on location in Rome, on the beach at Terracina, and at Titanus Studio, Rome, October 1955 through April 1956.
Cast   Gabriella Pallotta (Luisa), Giorgio Listuzzi (Natale, her husband), Gastone Renzelli (Cesare, the brother-in-law), Maria Di Fiori (Giovanna, his wife), Maria Di Rollo (Gina), Maria Sittoro (Natale's mother), Angelo Visentin (Natale's father), Emilia Martini (Luisa's mother), Giuseppe Martini (Luisa's father), Aldo Boi (the boy), Luisa Alessandri (Signora Baj), Angelo Bigioni, Luciano Pigozzi, Carolina Ferri, Ferdinando Gerra (and other nonprofessionals).

Le notti di Cabiria
(*The Nights of Cabiria*), 1957

Credits   prod.: Dino De Laurentiis; *dir.*: Federico Fellini; *sc.*: Federico Fellini; *adapt.*: Federico Fellini, Ennio Flaiano, Tullio Pinelli, Pier Paolo Pasolini, Maria Molinari; *cin.*: Aldo Tonti; *des.*: Piero Gherardi; *mus.*: Nino Rota; *ed.*: Leo Cattozzo.

Cast   Giulietta Masina (Maria 'Cabiria' Ceccarelli), François Périer (Oscar D'Onofrio), Franca Marzi (Wanda), Dorian Gray (Jessy), Aldo Silvani (The wizard), Ennio Girolami (Amleto, "il magnaccia"), Mario Passante (Uncle of Amleto), Amedeo Nazzari (Alberto Lazzari).

Il Generale della Rovere
(*General della Rovere*), 1959

Credits   *dir.*: Roberto Rossellini; *Assistant dir.*: Renzo Rossellini; *Treatment*: from a story by Indro Montanelli, based on an actual incident; *Screenplay*: Sergio Amidei, Diego Fabbri, Indro Montanelli; *Photography*: Carlo Carlini; *Art director*: Piero Zuffi; *Sets*: Elio Costanzi; *Editor*: Cesare Cavagna; *Music*: Renzo Rossellini; *Sound*: Ovidio Del Grande; *Producer*: Paola Frascà; *Production*: Moris Ergas for Zebra Film, Rome/SNE Gaumont, Paris; *Country of origin*: Italy-France; *Italian distributor*: Cineriz

Cast   Vittorio De Sica (Giovanni Bardone), Hannes Messemer (Colonel Müller), Sandra Milo (Olga), Giovanna Ralli (Valeria), Anne Vernon (Fassio, a widow), Vittorio Caprioli (Banchelli), Lucia Modugno (a resistance fighter), Giuseppe Rossetti (Fabrizio), Luciano Picozzi (a street cleaner), Nando Angelini, Herbert Fischer, Kurt Polter, Giuseppe Rossetto, Kurt Selge, Franco Interlenghi, Linda Veras.

Rocco e i suoi fratelli
(*Rocco and His Brothers*), 1960

Credits   prod.: Goffredo Lombardo; *dir.*: Luchino Visconti; *sc.*: Luchino Visconti; *adapt.*: Luchino Visconti, Suso Cecchi D'Amico, Vasco Pratolini, Pasquale Festa Campanile, Massimo Franciosa, Enrico Medioli, Giovanni Testori (inspired by an episode from his novel *Il ponte della Ghisolfa*); *cin.*: Giuseppe Rotunno; *des.*: Mario Garbuglia; *mus.*: Nino Rota; *ed.*: Mario Serandrei.

Cast   Alain Delon (Rocco Parondi), Renato Salvatori (Simone Parondi), Annie Girardot (Nadia), Katina Paxinou (Rosaria Parondi), Alessandra Panaro (Ciro's Fiancée), Spiros Focás (Vincenzo

Parondi), Max Cartier (Ciro Parondi), Corrado Pani (Ivo), Rocco Vidolazzi (Luca Parondi), Claudia Mori (Laundrey Worker), Adriana Asti (Laundrey Worker), Enzo Fiermonte (Boxer), Nino Castelnuovo (Nino Rossi), Rosario Borelli (Un biscazziere), Renato Terra (Alfredo, Ginetta's brother), Roger Hanin (Morini), Paolo Stoppa (Cecchi), Suzy Delair (Luisa), Claudia Cardinale (Ginetta).

Rocco and His Brothers, dir. Luchino Visconti, 1960.

Select Bibliography of Italian Neorealism

Almendros, Nestor. "Neorealist Cinematography." *Film Culture*, 20 (1959): 39–43.
Anonymous. "Italy after the Liberation: Reality and Neorealism." [London] *Times Literary Supplement*, No. 3111 (13 October 1961): 710–711.
Aristarco, Guido. "Italian Cinema." *Film Culture*, 1.2 (March–April 1955): 29–33.
— *Neorealism and National Environment*. Rimini: Grimaldi, 1976.
Armes, Roy. *Patterns of Realism*. South Brunswick, New Jersey: A. S. Barnes, 1971—"Italy." In *A Concise History of the Cinema: Since 1940*. Peter Cowie (ed.). New York: A. S. Barnes, 1971, 120–128.
— "Rossellini and Neorealism." In Armes's *Film and Reality*. Harmondsworth, U.K.: Penguin, 1974, 64–69.
Baranski, Zygmunt G., and Robert Lumley, (eds.). *Culture and Conflict in Postwar Italy: Essays on Mass and Popular Culture*. New York: St. Martin's Press, 1990.
Bennett, Joseph. "Italian Film: Failure and Emergence." *Kenyon Review*, 26.4 (Autumn 1964): 738–747.
Bertellini, Giorgio. *The Cinema of Italy*. London: Wallflower, 2004.
Bettetini, Gianfranco. "On Neorealism." *Framework*, 2 (1975): 9–10.
Bondanella, Peter E. "Neorealist Aesthetics and the Fantastic: *The Machine to Kill Bad People* and *Miracle in Milan*." *Film Criticism*, 3.2 (Winter 1979): 24–29.
— "America and the Post-War Italian Cinema." *Rivista di Studi Italiani*, 2, No. 1 (June 1984): 106–125.
— "The Masters of Neoralism: Rossellini, De Sica, and Visconti." In Bondanella's *Italian Cinema: From Neorealism to the Present*. 3rd ed. New York: Continuum, 2001, 31–73.
Brunetta, Gian Piero. *The History of Italian Cinema: A Guide to Italian Film from Its Origins to the Twenty-First Century*. Trans. Jeremy Parzen. Princeton, New Jersey: Princeton University Press, 2009.

Brunette, Peter. "Rossellini and Cinematic Realism." *Cinema Journal*, 1 (Autumn 1985): 34–49.
Burke, Frank M. "*Variety Lights, The White Sheik,* and Italian Neorealism." *Film Criticism*, 3.2 (Winter 1979): 53–66.
— "Neorealism, Fellini's *Una agenzia matrimoniale,* and the Limitations of Objectivity." *Proceedings of the Fifth Annual Purdue Conference on Film* (1981), 165–170.
Buss, Robin. *Italian Films*. New York: Holmes & Meier, 1989.
Cannella, Mario. "Ideology and Aesthetic Hypotheses in the Criticism of Neorealism." *Screen*, 14.4 (1973–74): 5–60.
Cardullo, Bert. *What Is Neorealism?: A Critical English-Language Bibliography of Italian Cinematic Neorealism*. Lanham: University Press of America, 1991.
Carsaniga, C. M. "Realism in Italy." In *Age of Realism*. F. W. J. Hemmings (ed.). Baltimore: Penguin, 1974.
Celli, Carlo. *A New Guide to Italian Cinema*. New York: Palgrave Macmillan, 2007.
Chiaromonte, Nicola. "Rome Letter: Itaian Movies." *Partisan Review*, 16.6 (June 1949): 621–630.
Clair, René. "Nothing Is more Artificial than Neorealism." *Films and Filming*, 3.9 (June 1957): 7+.
Clark, F. M. "In Italy Today." In *Impact on Books*, No. 1: *This Film Business*. London, 1948.
— "Freedom and the Italian Cinema." In *Impact on Books*, No. 2: *Sense and Censorship*. London, 1949.
Dalle Vacche, Angela. *The Body in the Mirror: Shapes of History in Italian Cinema*. Princeton, New Jersey: Princeton University Press, 1992.
Dombroski, Robert S. (ed.). *Italy: Fiction, Theater, Poetry, and Film since 1950*. Smyrna, Delaware: Griffon House, 2000.
Eisner, Lotte H. "Notes on Some Recent Italian Films." *Sequence*, 8 (Summer 1949): 52–58.
Emmer, Luciano, and Enrico Gras. "The Film Renaissance in Italy." *Hollywood Quarterly*, 2.4 (July 1947): 353–358.
Film Criticism, 3.2 (Winter 1979): special issue on Italian neorealism.
Forgacs, David. *Italian Culture in the Industrial Era, 1880–1980: Cultural Industries, Politics, and the Public*. Manchester, U.K.: Manchester University Press, 1990.
French, Brandon. "The Continuity of the Italian Cinema." *Yale Italian Studies*, 2 (Winter 1978): 59–69.
Frongia, Eugene. "The Literary Roots of Cinematic Neorealism." *Forum Italicum*, 17.2 (Fall 1983): 176–195.
Gallagher, T. "Roberto Rossellini and Historical Neorealism." *Artforum*, 10 (Summer 1975): 40–49.
Gieri, Manuela. *Contemporary Italian Filmmaking: Strategies of Subversion;*

Pirandello, Fellini, Scola, and the Directors of the New Generation. Toronto: University of Toronto Press, 1995.

Gough-Yates, Kevin. "The Destruction of Neorealism." *Films and Filming,* 16.12 (September 1970): 14–22.

Gunsberg, Maggie. *Italian Cinema: Gender and Genre.* New York: Palgrave Macmillan, 2005.

Harcourt, Peter. "Towards a New Neorealism?" *London Magazine,* NS 2.3 (June 1962): 70–74; NS 2.4 (July 1962): 45–48.

Hay, James. *Popular Film Culture in Fascist Italy.* Bloomington: Indiana University Press, 1987.

Hewitt, Nicholas. *The Culture of Reconstruction: European Literature, Thought, and Film, 1945–1950.* Basingstoke, U.K.: Macmillan, 1989.

Hine, A. "Italian Movies." *Holiday,* 15 (February 1954): 11+.

Houston, Penelope. "The Italian Experience." In Houston's *The Contemporary Cinema,* Baltimore: Penguin, 1963, 19–34.

Huaco, George A. "Italian Neorealism." In Huaco's *The Sociology of Film Art.* New York. Basic Books, 1965, 155–209.

Issari, M. Ali, and Doris A. Paul. "Neorealism." In their *What Is Cinéma Vérité?* Metuchen, New Jersey. Scarecrow, 1979, 41–45.

Jarrett, Vernon. "The Italians." *Sight and Sound,* 17.65 (Spring 1948): 25–28; 17.66 (Summer 1948): 71–74.

— *The Italian Cinema.* London: Falcon Press, 1951.

Kass, Robert. "The Italian Film Renaissance." *Films in Review,* 4.7 (August–September 1953): 336–348.

Knight, Arthur. "The Course of Italian Neorealism." In Knight's *The Liveliest Art.* Rev. ed. New York: Mentor, 1979, 238–250.

Kumlien, Gunnar D. "The Artless Art of Italian Films." *Commonweal,* 58.7 (22 May 1953): 177–179.

Lambert, Gavin. "Notes on a Renaissance." *Sight and Sound,* NS 19.10 (February 1951): 399–409.

— "Further Notes on a Renaissance." *Sight and Sound,* NS 22.2 (October–December 1952): 61–65.

— "Italian Notes. The Signs of a Predicament." *Sight and Sound,* NS 24.3 (January-March 1955): 147–166.

Landy, Marcia. *Fascism in Film: The Italian Commercial Cinema, 1931–1943.* Princeton, New Jersey: Princeton University Press, 1986.

— *The Folklore of Consensus: Theatricality in the Italian Cinema, 1930–1943.* Albany: State University of New York Press, 1998.

— *Italian Film.* New York: Cambridge University Press, 2000.

Lane, John Francis. "De Santis and Italian Neorealism." *Sight and Sound,* NS 19.6 (August 1950): 245–247.

Lattuada, Alberto. "We Took the Actors into the Streets." *Films and Filming,* 5.7 (April 1959): 8+.

Lawson, John Howard. "Neorealism." In Lawson's *Film: The Creative Process*. New York: Hill and Wang, 1964, 146–153.

Lawton, Ben. *Literary and Socio-Political Trends in Italian Cinema*. Los Angeles: Center for Italian Studies, University of California at Los Angeles, 1975.

— "Italian Neorealism: A Mirror Construction of Reality." *Film Criticism*, 3.2 (Winter 1979): 8–23.

Leprohon, Pierre. "The Period of Neorealism (1943–1950)." In Leprohon's *The Italian Cinema*. Trans. Roger Greaves and Oliver Stallybrass. New York: Praeger, 1972, 85–124.

Liehm, Mira. *Passion and Defiance: Film in Italy from 1942 to the Present*. Berkeley: University of California Press, 1984.

Lorch, M. de Panizza. "Reflections on Roberto Rossellini and Italian Neorealism." *Barnard Alumnae*, Autumn 1971.

Luce, Candida. "Incoherence in Italian Films." *Films in Review*, 1.7 (October 1950): 15–18.

Makins, William Cooper. "The Film in Italy." *Sight and Sound*, 15.60 (Winter 1946–47): 126–129.

Manvell, Roger. *Films and the Second World War*. New York: Dell, 1974.

Marcus, Millicent. *Italian Film in the Light of Neorealism*. Princeton, New Jersey: Princeton University Press, 1986.

— *Filmmaking by the Book: Italian Cinema and Literary Adaptation*. Baltimore: Johns Hopkins University Press, 1993.

— *After Fellini: National Cinema in the Postmodern Age*. Baltimore: Johns Hopkins University Press, 2002.

Marinucci, Vincent. "Fact, Fiction, and History Were In at the Beginning." *Films and Filming*, 7.4 (January 1961): 15–16+.

— "History—Before and After Mussolini." *Films and Filming*, 7.5 (February 1961): 37–38+.

Michalczyk, John J. *The Italian Political Filmmakers*. Rutherford, New Jersey: Fairleigh Dickinson University Press, 1986.

Monaco, Paul. "Realism, Italian Style." In Monaco's *Ribbons in Time: Movies and Society since 1945*. Bloomington: Indiana University Press, 1987, 1–32.

Nowell-Smith, Geoffrey, with James Hay and Gianni Volpi. *The Companion to Italian Cinema*. London: Cassell/British Film Institute, 1996.

Overbey, David (trans. and ed.). *Springtime in Italy: A Reader on Neorealism*. Hamden, Connecticut: Archon Books, 1978.

Pacifici, Sergio J. "Notes toward a Definition of Neorealism." *Yale French Studies*, 17 (Summer 1956): 44–53.

Perry, Ted. "The Road to Neorealism." *Film Comment*, 14.6 (November–December 1978): 7–13.

— "Roots of Neorealism." *Film Criticism*, 3.2 (Winter 1979): 3–7.

Procaccini, Alfonso. "Neorealism: Description/Prescription." *Yale Italian Studies*, 2 (Winter 1978): 39–57.

Reich, Jacqueline, and Garofalo, Piero (eds.). *Re-viewing Fascism: Italian Cinema, 1922-1943*. Bloomington: Indiana University Press, 2002.
Reid, A. "The Short Film in Italy." *Sight and Sound*, 17.68 (Winter 1948-49): 166+.
Restivo, Angelo. *The Cinema of Economic Miracles: Visuality and Modernization in the Italian Art Film*. Durham, North Carolina: Duke University Press, 2002.
Rhode, Eric. "Why Neorealism Failed." *Sight and Sound*, 30.1 (Winter 1960-61): 25-32.
— "Neorealism and the Cold War." In Rhode's *A History of the Cinema: From Its Origins to 1970*. New York: Hill and Wang, 1976, 428-479.
Ricci, Steven. *Cinema and Fascism: Italian Film and Society, 1922-1943*. Berkeley: University of California Press, 2008.
Ricciardi, Alessia. "The Italian Redemption of Cinema: Neorealism from Bazin to Godard." *The Romanic Review*, 97 (May-November 2006): 483-500.
Rimanelli, Giose, (ed.). *Patterns of Italian Cinema*. Albany: Dept. of Hispanic and Italian Studies at the State University of New York, 1980.
Rocchio, Vincent F. *Cinema of Anxiety: A Psychoanalysis of Italian Neorealism*. Austin: University of Texas Press, 1999.
Rohdie, Sam. "Italian Neorealism, 1941-1943." *Australian Journal of Screen Theory*, Nos. 15-16 (1983): 133-162.
— "Capital and Realism in the Italian Cinema: An Examination of Film in the Fascist Period." *Screen*, 24.4-5 (1983): 37-46.
Rondi, Gian Luigi. *The Italian Cinema Today, 1952-1965*. New York, Hill and Wang, 1966.
Ruberto, Laura E., and Kristi M. Wilson (eds). *Italian Neorealism and Global Cinema*. Detroit: Wayne State University Press, 2007.
Sargeant, Winthrop. "Profiles: Bread, Love, and Neorealism." *The New Yorker*, 33.19 (29 June 1957): 35-58; 33.20 (6 July 1957): 35-53.
Scherk, Alfred. "The Italian Film Industry in Transition." *Penguin Film Review*, 1 (August 1946): 80-83.
Shiel, Mark. *Italian Neorealism: Rebuilding the Cinematic City*. London: Wallflower Press, 2006.
Sitney, P. Adams. *Vital Crises in Italian Cinema: Iconography, Stylistics, Politics*. Austin: University of Texas Press, 1995.
Sorlin, Pierre. "The Italian Resistance in the Second World War." In Sorlin's *The Film in History. Restaging the Past*. Totowa, New Jersey: Barnes and Noble, 1980, 189-206.
— *Italian National Cinema, 1896-1996*. London: Routledge, 1996.
Spiegel, Robert. "Verga and the Realist Cinema." *Carte Italiane: A Journal of Italian Studies*, 2 (1980-81): 43-55.
Stewart, John. *Italian Film: A Who's Who*. Jefferson, North Carolina: McFarland, 1994.

Strand, Paul. "Realism: A Personal View." *Sight and Sound*, 19 (January 1950): 23–26.
Testa, Carlo. *Italian Cinema and Modern European Literatures, 1945–2000*. Westport, Connecticut: Praeger, 2002.
— *Masters of Two Arts: Re-creation of European Literatures in Italian Cinema*. Toronto: University of Toronto Press, 2002.
Venturi, Lauro. "Notes on Five Italian Films." *Hollywood Quarterly*, 5.4 (Summer 1951): 389–400.
Verdone, Mario. "The Italian Cinema from Its Beginnings to Today." *Hollywood Quarterly*, 5.3 (Spring 1951): 270–281.
— "A Discussion of Neorealism: Rossellini Interviewed." *Screen*, 14.4 (1973–74): 69–77.
Vermilye, Jerry. *Great Italian Films: From the Thirties to the Present*. New York: Citadel, 1994.
Vessolo, Arthur. "The Italian Cinema Before the Liberation." *Sight and Sound*, 16.61 (Spring 1947): 6–7.
Vighi, Fabio. *Traumatic Encounters in Italian Film: Locating the Cinematic Unconscious*. Bristol, U.K.: Intellect, 2006.
Vitti, Antonio. *Giuseppe De Santis and Postwar Italian Cinema*. Toronto: University of Toronto Press, 1996.
Wagstaff, Christopher. "The Italian Cinema Industry During the Fascist Regime." *The Italianist*, 4 (1984): 160–174.
— *Italian Neorealist Cinema: An Aesthetic Approach*. Toronto: University of Toronto Press, 2007.
Wead, George, and George Lellis. "Italian Neorealism." In their *Film: Form and Function*. New York: Houghton Mifflin, 1981, 346–351.
Wilson, John S. "Italian Film Story: Renaissance Revisited." *Theatre Arts*, 39 (May 1955): 69–69+.
Witcombe, R. T. *The New Italian Cinema: Studies in Dance and Despair*. New York: Oxford University Press, 1982.
Wlaschin, Ken. *Italian Cinema Since the War*. Cranbury, New Jersey: A. S. Barnes, 1971.
Wollenberg, H. H. "New Developments in the Italian Cinema." *Film and Theatre Today*, No. 1 (1949).
Wood, Mary P. *Italian Cinema*. New York: Berg, 2005.
Zavattini, Cesare. "Some Ideas on the Cinema." *Sight and Sound*, NS 23.2 (October–December 1953): 64–69.

A Bazin Bibliography

BOOKS BY ANDRÉ BAZIN IN FRENCH

Bazin, André. *Qu'est-ce que le cinéma?* In four volumes: I. Ontologie et langage (1958); II. Le Cinéma et les autres arts (1959); III. Cinéma et sociologie (1961); IV. Une Esthetique de la réalité: le néoréalisme (1962). Paris: Éditions du Cerf, 1958–62.

— *Jean Renoir.* Paris: Editions Champ Libre, 1971.
— *Orson Welles.* Paris: Éditions du Cerf, 1972.
— *Le Cinéma de la cruauté.* Paris: Flammarion, 1975.
— *Le Cinéma de l'occupation et la résistance.* Paris: UnionGénérale d'éditions, 1975.
— and Eric Rohmer. *Charlie Chaplin.* Paris: Éditions du Cerf, 1972.

ARTICLES AND REVIEWS BY BAZIN IN FRENCH

1,375 items in total:
In *Le Parisien libéré:* 625 items from issue #117 in 1944 to issue #4405 the day before Bazin died in November 1958.
In *Esprit:* 52 items.
In *L'Observateur* (France-Observateur) : 275 items.
In *Cahiers du cinéma:* 111 items.
In *Télérama* (Radio-Cinéma-Télévision) : 96 items.
In *L'Education Nationale:* 33 items.
In *Arts:* 9 items.
In *Peuple et Culture* (*DOC Education Populaire*) : 7 items.
In *L'Ecran Français:* 111 items.
Also: 56 miscellaneous items (including pieces from his student period) in magazines such as *Les Temps Modernes, Ciné-Club,* etc.; and in books such as the collective work titled *Sept ans de cinéma français* (1945–1952)

[one chapter by Bazin; published by Éditions du Cerf], J. L. Rieupeyrout's *Le Westem ou le cinéma américain par excellence* [preface by Bazin; published by Éditions du Cerf], *Cinéma 53 à travers le monde* [Italian chapter by Bazin; published by Éditions du Cerf], and Pierre Leprohon's edited work *Contemporary Presences* [chapter on Welles by Bazin; published by Debressie].

BOOKS BY BAZIN IN ENGLISH

What Is Cinema? Selected and translated by Hugh Gray from the first two volumes of *Qu'est-ce que le cinéma?* Berkeley: University of Califomia Press, 1967.

What is Cinema? Volume II. Selected and translated by Hugh Gray from the last two volumes of *Qu'est-ce que le cinéma?* Berkeley: University of California Press, 1971.

Jean Renoir. Translated by W. W. Halsey II and William H. Simon. New York: Simon and Schuster, 1973.

Orson Welles. Translated by Jonathan Rosenbaum. New York: Harper and Row, 1978.

French Cinema of the Occupation and Resistance: "The Birth of a Critical Esthetic." Translated by Stanley Hochman. Preface by François Truffaut. New York: Frederick Ungar, 1981.

The Cinema of Cruelty. Translated by Sabine d'Estrée. New York: Seaver Books, 1982.

Essays on Chaplin. Translated by Jean Bodon. New Haven, Connecticut: University of New Haven Press, 1985.

Bazin at Work: Major Essays and Reviews From the Forties and Fifties. Translated by Bert Cardullo and Alain Piette. New York: Routledge, 1997.

WORKS ON BAZIN IN ENGLISH

Andrew, Dudley. "André Bazin." In Andrew's *The Major Film Theories*. New York. Oxford University Press, 1976, 134–178.

—. *André Bazin*. New York: Oxford University Press, 1978; Columbia University Press, 1990.

—. *What Cinema Is!* Malden, Massachusetts: Wilcy-Blackwell, 2010.

Andrew, Dudley, ed. *Opening Bazin: Postwar Film Theory and Its Afterlife*. New York: Oxford University Press, 2011.

Carroll, Noël. "Cinematic Representation and Realism: André Bazin and the Aesthetics of Sound Film." In Carroll's *Philosophical Problems of Classical Film Theory*. Princeton, New Jersey. Princeton University Press, 1988, 93–171.

Film International, No. 30 (November 2007). Special issue devoted to Bazin.

Henderson, Brian. "The Structure of Bazin's Thought." In *A Critique of Film Theory*. New York: E. P. Dutton, 1980, 32–47.
Morgan, Daniel. "Rethinking Bazin. Ontology and Realist Aesthetics." *Critical Inquiry*, 32.3 (2006): 443–481.
Offscreen.com, 13, No. 2 (February 2009). Special issue devoted to Bazin.
Rosen, Philip. "Subject, Ontology, and Historicity in Bazin." In *'Change Mummified': Cinema, Historicity, Theory*. Minneapolis: University of Minnesota Press, 2001, 3–41.
Velvet Light Trap, 21 (Summer 1985). Special issue devoted to Bazin.
Wide Angle, 9, No. 4 (1987). Special issue devoted to Bazin.
Williams, Christopher. "Bazin on Neorealism." *Screen*, 14.4 (Winter 1973–1974): 61–68.

Index

1860 146, 208
Abadanis, The 27
Abouna 27
Accattone 28
Adorable Creatures see Adorables créatures
Adorables créatures 114, 156
Adventure of Salvator Rosa see Un'Avventura di Salvator Rosa
Agenzia matrimoniale, Una see A Matrimonial Agency
Agostino 125
Aldo, G. R. see Alto Tonti
Alexander Nevsky 102
Althusser, Louis 15
Altri Tempi 136–7
Amelio, Gianni 28
Amore che si paga, L' see Love That Pays
Amore in città, L' see Love in the City
Anderson, Lindsay 164
Andreotti, Giulio 26–7
Antonioni, Michelangelo 16, 21, 28, 78, 97, 123–5, 128, 190
Apple, The 27
Apu trilogy (Ray) 28
Aristarco, Guido 150, 163–4, 171
Arnheim, Rudolf 1
Astruc, Alexandre 14
Attempted Suicide see Love in the City
Avventura di Salvator Rosa, Un' 32
Ayari, Kianoush 27
Ayfre, Amédée 152, 174

Babenco, Hector 27
Bachelor Party, The 192
Bambini ci guardano, I see The Children Are Watching Us

Banditi a Orgosolo see The Bandits of Orgosolo
Bandit of Tacca del Lupo, The 130–1
Bandito, Il 31, 33, 43, 217
Bandits of Orgosolo 28
Basehart, Richard 201
Battle of Stalingrad, The 11
Battleship Potemkin, The 29, 37, 52, 55, 102
Bazin, André 1–17
Bazin, Florent 3
Bazin, Janine 3
Bazin at Work 16
Beaumarchais, Pierre-Augustin Caron de 34
Becker, Jacques 106, 164
Bellocchio, Marco 28
Bergman, Ingrid 122, 146, 184
Bergson, Henri 13, 197
Berthomieu, André 96
Bianco e Nero 21
Bicycle Thieves 8, 19, 25, 61–75, 79–82, 85, 89, 96, 104, 107, 111–12, 115, 117–18, 120, 152, 155, 172, 184, 187, 194, 222–3
Bidone, Il 180–3, 194–8, 201–2, 233–4
Bitter Rice 131–4, 225
Blasetti, Alessandro 23–4, 32, 136–7, 146
Blood of a Poet, The 95–6
Body and Soul 28
Boileau, Nicolas 188, 190
Boomerang! 28
Bosé, Lucia 124, 131, 134–6
Bread, Love, and Dreams 164
Bread, Love, and Jealousy 155
Bresson, Robert 9, 12, 14, 124, 146, 160
Brief Encounter 62
Brigante di Tacca del Lupo, Il 104

Cabinet of Dr. Caligari, The 7
Cabiria 31, 97, 141
Caccia tragica 35, 54–5, 131–2, 220
Cahiers du cinéma 3, 13–15, 128, 164
Cain, James M. 24, 64
Calvino, Italo 20
Camerini, Mario 32, 84
Cammino della speranza, Il see The Road to Hope
Camus, Albert 42
Cannes Film Festival 63, 94, 107, 127, 138, 141, 144, 155–6, 158, 196
Capote, Truman 128
Carné, Marcel 33, 76, 106
Carré, Léon 92
Casque d'or 164
Castellani, Renato 104, 106–10, 117, 143, 146
Catherine's Story see Love in the City
Catholicism 4–6, 15, 65–6, 72, 92, 151–2
Cavalcanti, Alberto 62
Cayatte, André 143
Centro Sperimentale (film school) 21, 30
Cézanne, Paul 43
Chabrol, Claude 8, 14
Chaplin, Charles 9, 11, 13, 67, 70, 83–5, 96, 148, 162, 192, 202
Chardin, Pierre Teilhard de 6
Chayevsky, Paddy 192
Chekhov, Anton 199
Chiarini, Luigi 21, 62, 150, 152
Children Are Watching Us, The 23–5, 74, 214
Children of Heaven, The 27
Chirico, Giorgio de 97
Christianity 4, 9, 55, 91, 170, 182
Christian-Jaque 44, 114, 156, 179

246

Index

Chronicle of Poor Lovers 144–5
Cielo sulla palude see Heaven over the Marshes
Cinecittà (film studio) 20–1
Cinema Nuovo 128, 150, 152, 163–4
Cinema Paradiso 28
"Cinematic Realism and the Italian School of the Liberation" 53
Citizen Kane 10, 39–41, 49, 53, 95–6
Clair, René 31, 96
classicism 122
Clément, René 27
Clift, Montgomery 128
Clouzot, Henri-Georges 13, 127
Cocteau, Jean 12, 95–6
Colpa del sole see It Is the Sun's Fault
comedy 16, 22, 32, 40, 125, 136, 138, 141, 170
Comencini, Luigi 155, 164
Commedia dell'arte 40, 42, 50, 69
Communism 21, 34, 42, 51, 55, 65, 82, 120, 150–2, 170, 173
Consul, The 102
Coogan, Jackie 69
Cops and Robbers 138, 155
Corona di ferro, La 31–2, 211
Courteline, Georges 136
Cristo proibito, Il see Forbidden Christ
Critique 3
Cronaca di un amore 78, 97, 123–4, 189
Cronache di poveri amanti see Chronicle of Poor Lovers
Crossfire 28

Daquin, Louis 27
Dassin, Jules 28, 158
Day in the Life, A see Un giorno nella vita
Del Poggio, Carla 136
De Paul, Saint Vincent 92, 173, 196, 201
Dernière chance, La 35, 143
De Santis, Giuseppe 21, 43, 79, 131–6
Descartes, René 188
De Seta, Vittorio 28
De Sica, Vittorio 8–9, 19, 21–8, 32, 61–88, 96–7, 104, 106–7, 111–20, 122, 127–8, 136, 138, 146, 155–62, 166, 172–5, 184–6, 199, 201
Diary of a Country Priest 12, 146
documentary 4, 6, 22, 24, 27, 33, 36, 40, 43–4, 51, 53, 56, 61–2, 97, 105–7, 134, 139, 167, 169–70, 179, 199
Domenica d'agosto see Sunday in August

Don Camillo 83, 151
Doniol-Valcroze, Jacques 3
Dos Passos, John 42, 49
Dostoyevsky, Fyodor 121, 160, 183, 199
Dovzhenko, Alexander 29
Drago, Eleonora Rossi 134
Dreyer, Carl 9
Duca, Lo 3
Due soldi di speranza see Two Cents' Worth of Hope
Du Gard, Martin 70
Duvivier, Julien 27, 164, 179
Dymytryk, Edward 28

Earth Trembles, The 19, 51–6, 69, 72, 89–90, 97, 170, 178–9, 222
Écran français, L' 3
Education Nationale, L' 3
Églises romanes de Saintonge, Les 4
Eisenstein, Sergei 7, 29, 35, 37, 52, 55, 70, 102
Ekk, Nikolai 35
Emmer, Luciano 138–9
End of St. Petersburg, The 55
Espoir, L' 35–6
Esprit 3, 10–11, 53
Étranger, L' 42
Europe '51 13, 120–2, 146, 152, 166, 170, 173, 175, 230
"Evolution of the Language of Cinema, The" 7, 10
existentialism 6, 9
expressionism, German 7, 29, 38, 77–9, 200

Fabrizi, Aldo 35–6, 138
Fabrizi, Franco 200
farce 136, 138, 156
Fari nella nebbia see Headlights in the Fog
Farrebique 36–7, 39–40, 51, 53, 69, 90
Fascism 21, 30–1, 46, 101
Faulkner, William 42, 45
Fear see La Paura
Fellini, Federico 12, 28, 140–1, 148–54, 180–4, 190, 192–203
Fernandel 138, 159
Feuillade, Louis 49
Feyder, Jacques 76
Fille des Marais, La see Heaven over the Marshes
Film Technique 7
Fist in His Pocket 28
Flaherty, Robert 83
Flaubert, Gustav 178
Flowers of St. Francis, The 152, 166, 170, 174, 226
Fontaine, Jean de La 143

Forbidden Christ 16, 79, 94–102, 227
Forbidden Fruit see Le fruit défendu
Forbidden Games 27
For Whom the Bell Tolls 49
Four Hundred Blows, The 27
Four Steps in the Clouds 23, 31, 62, 64, 213
Fracassi, Clemente 134
France-Observateur 3
Francesco, giullare di Dio see The Flowers of St. Francis
Franciolini, Gianni 23–4
Fruit défendu, Le 114

Gabin, Jean 64
Gallone, Carmine 31, 62
Garibaldian in the Convent, A 23
Genina, Augusto 69, 89–93, 96–7, 136–7
Germania, anno zero see Germany, Year Zero
Germany, Year Zero 57–60, 67, 75, 121, 166, 170, 173, 220
Germi, Pietro 16, 21, 62, 103–5, 129–31
Gide, André 70
Giorno nella vita, Un 32, 219
Giovanna d'Arco al rogo 166
Girotti, Massimo 136
Giulietta e Romeo see Romeo and Juliet
Gli Italiani si voltano see The Italians Turn Their Heads
Gli uomini, che mascalzoni! 32
Godard, Jean-Luc 8
Gogol, Nikolai 141
Golden Helmet see Casque d'or
Gold of Naples 128, 138, 155–62, 170, 184, 232–3
Gold Rush, The 87
Gramatica, Emma 86
Grande illusion, La 31, 143
Grandson of the Three Musketeers, The 141
Grant, Cary 69–70
Greatest Love, The see Europe '51
Grede, Kjell 27
Greed 29
Grierson, John 62
Griffith, D. W. 7, 39
Guardie e ladri see Cops and Robbers
Guareschi, Giovannino 151
Guazzoni, Enrico 31

Haroun, Mahamat-Saleh 27
Hawks, Howard 8, 158
Headlights in the Fog 23, 211

248 INDEX

Heaven for Four Hours see Love in the City
Heaven over the Marshes 69, 72, 89–93, 96–7, 136, 224
Hegel, G. W. F. 16
Hemingway, Ernest 42, 45
Hitchcock, Alfred 8, 111, 158
Hollywood 7, 9, 19, 25, 29, 37, 43, 49, 96, 141, 155
Hugo and Joesphine 27
humanism 15, 33–4

Icicle Thief, The 28
Idiot, The 121
Indiscretion of an American Wife see Stazione Termini
Ingres, Jean-Auguste-Dominique 95
In nome della legge 62, 104, 130, 225
Institut des hautes études cinématographiques (I.D.H.E.C.) 2, 11, 30
In the Name of the Law see In nome della legge
Iron Crown, The see La corona di ferro
Italian, The 27
Italians Turn Their Heads, The 189, 191
It Happened in Europe 57
It Is the Sun's Fault 125
Ivan the Terrible 102

Jancsó, Miklós 8
Joan of Arc at the Stake see Giovanna d'Arco al rogo
Job, The see Il posto
Jones, Jennifer 128

Kafka, Franz 85
Kazan, Elia 28
Kiarostami, Abbas 27
Koker trilogy (Kiarostami) 27
Kore-eda, Hirokazu 27
Kracauer, Siegfried 1, 11
Kravchuk, Andrei 27
Khrushchev, Nikita 12

Lacan, Jacques 15
Ladies of the Bois de Boulogne, The 160
Ladri di biciclette see Bicycle Thieves
Ladri di saponette see The Icicle Thief
Ladro di bambini see Stolen Children
Lady without Camelias, The 124
Lang, Fritz 29, 79
Last Chance, The see La dernière chance
Lattuada, Alberto 31–2, 43, 79, 97, 106, 141, 166, 189, 191

Lawless, The 28
Lean, David 62
Leenhardt, Roger 71
Lévy, Jean Benoît 27
Libertas 26–7
Limelight 148
Lindtberg, Leopold 36, 130, 143
Little Foxes, The 9
Little Old-Fashioned World see Piccolo mondo antico
Lizzani, Carlo 144–6, 188
Lollabrigida, Gina 125, 136
Losey, Joseph 28
Love in the City 16, 187–91, 231–2
Lovers of Verona 143
Love That Pays see Love in the City
Lumière, Auguste 35, 97
Lumière, Louis 35, 97

Maddalena, Zero for Conduct 23
Magnani, Anna 35–6
Majidi, Majid 27
Makhmalbaf, Samira 27
Malaparte, Curzio 79, 94–102
Malraux, André 35, 42, 49, 95–6
Mangano, Silvana 134, 159, 161
"Manifesto of Italian Cinema" 27
Man in the Gray Flannel Suit, The 11
Mann, Delbert 192
Man's Hope 95–6
Marivaux, Pierre Carlet de Chamblain de 110
Marker, Chris 14
Marx, Groucho 125
Marxism 6, 15, 42, 150–2, 177–8
Maselli, Franceso 189
Masina, Giulietta 203
Mass Is Ended, The 28
Maternelle, La 27
Matisse, Henri 43, 171
Matrimonial Agency, A see Love in the City
Mauriac, François 125
Méliès, Georges 97
melodrama 10, 31–2, 34, 42, 62, 74, 78, 81, 115, 118, 120, 130, 134, 136, 141, 179, 195, 197–8
Menotti, Gian Carlo 102
Messa è finita, La see The Mass Is Ended
Michelangelo (di Lodovico Buonarroti Simoni) 134
Michi, Maria 35
Mill on the Po, The 97, 224–5
Miracle, The 173
Miracle in Milan 28, 74–5, 79, 81–7, 97, 115, 117, 141, 155, 186, 228–9
Miracolo, Il see The Miracle
Miracolo a Milano see Miracle in Milan
Monicelli, Mario 138, 155

Monsieur Verdoux 85
Monsieur Vincent 92
Moravia, Alberto 20, 125
Moretti, Nanni 28
Mother 70
Muddy River 27
Mulino del Po, Il see The Mill on the Po
Murnau, F. W. 8, 29, 36, 70
Mussolini, Benito 21, 24, 31
"Myth of Stalin, The" 11–12
"Myth of Total Cinema, The" 6

Nair, Mira 27
Naked City, The 28
naturalism 7, 167, 178, 199
Nave bianca, La 31, 211
Nazism 2, 21–2, 31, 48
Nazzari, Amedeo 200
Nenni, Pietro 21
neoclassicism 95, 97
neorealism, Italian 4–5, 8, 10, 13, 16–17, 18–50, 54, 61–4, 67, 70, 77–81, 89, 96–7, 99, 102, 104–7, 109, 111–12, 115–18, 120, 122, 128–9, 130, 136, 138–9, 141–4, 146–7, 150–2, 156–7, 162–7, 168–9, 170–5, 184, 187–90, 194–95, 199, 201
New Wave, French see nouvelle vague
Nibelungen, Die 29
Nichetti, Maurizio 28
The Night see La notte
Nights of Cabiria, The 194, 195–203, 235
Nobody Knows 27
Non c'è pace tra gli ulivi see No Peace among the Olives
No Peace among the Olives 131, 133–5, 227
Nosferatu 29
Notte, La 28
Notti di Cabiria, Le see The Nights of Cabiria
nouvelle vague 8, 27

Obsession see Ossessione
Occupation, Allied 33, 50
Occupation, German 2, 22, 177
Oguri, Kobei 27
O.K. Nero 125
Olmi, Ermanno 28
"Ontology of the Photographic Image, The" 4–5
Oro di Napoli, L' see Gold of Naples
Ossessione 19–20, 23–4, 89, 178, 213
Overcoat, The 141

Pact with the Devil see Il patto col diavolo

Index

Padovani, Léa 136
Padre Padrone 28
Pagliero, Marcello 35
Pagnol, Marcel 136, 160–1, 164
Paisà see *Paisan*
Paisan 19, 29, 33–5, 39, 41, 44–50, 53–4, 61, 64, 67, 69–70, 75, 104, 142–3, 146, 152, 166–7, 173, 218
Palotta, Gabrielle 186
Panahi, Jafar 27
Pane, Amore e Fantasia see *Bread, Love, and Dreams*
Pane, Amore e Gelosia see *Bread, Love, and Jealousy*
Paquis, Jean-Herold 101
Paradiso per quattro ore see *Heaven for Four Hours*
Parents terribles, Les 12
Parigi è sempre Parigi see *Paris Is Always Paris*
Parisien libéré, Le 2
Paris Is Always Paris 139
Pascal, Blaise 147
Pasolini, Pier Paolo 28
Passionate Friends, The 63
Pastrone, Giovanni 31, 97
Pather Panchali 28
Patto col diavolo, Il 62
Paura, La 166
Pavese, Cesare 20
Perier, François 197, 199
Phaedra 96
phenomenology 65, 68, 77, 92, 152, 154, 194, 199, 202
Picasso Mystery, The 13
Piccolo mondo antico 32, 210
Pieds Nickelés, Les 125
Pietrangeli, Antonio 19
Piscator, Erwin 56
Pixote 27
Pizza on Credit see *Gold of Naples*
Poil de carotte 27
Politique des auteurs 8–9
Portrait of Innocence 27
Positif 27
Postman Always Rings Twice, The 24
Posto, Il 28
Potemkin see *The Battleship Potemkin*
Pratolini, Vasco 20, 144
Prévert, Jacques 64, 76
propaganda 8, 16, 21, 56, 65, 94, 99–102
Proust, Marcel 71, 113–14, 174
Provinciale, La see *The Provincial Woman*
Provincial Woman, The 125–7
Pudovkin, Vsevolod 7, 29, 55, 70
Pugni in tasca, I see *Fist in His Pocket*

Quattro passi fra le nuvole see *Four Steps in the Clouds*
Qu'est-ce que le cinéma? 11
Quo Vadis? 31, 141

Racine, Jean 96
The Racketeer see *Gold of Naples*
Radio-Cinéma-Télévision 3
Radványi, Géza 57
Raimu 138
Ray, Nicholas 28
Ray, Satyajit 28
realism 32, 35–41, 48–54, 60, 62–4, 71, 77, 79, 89–90, 92, 95, 106–7, 111, 115–7, 120, 122, 125, 134, 136, 138, 142–3, 146–7, 151, 153, 162, 166–70, 172, 178–9, 183, 185, 188, 190, 199–201
Red Roses 23
Règle du jeu, La 49
Renoir, Jean 1, 4, 8–9, 11, 13–14, 31, 49, 60, 83–4, 106, 124, 142
Resistance (French and Italian) 21, 28, 32–5, 44, 67, 152, 167, 176–7
Resnais, Alain 14
Revolt of the Fishermen, The 56
Revue du cinéma, La 3
Rififi 158
Risi, Dino 188, 190
Riso amaro see *Bitter Rice*
Risorgimento, Italian 176
Rivette, Jacques 8
Road, The see *La strada*
Road to Hope, The 103–5, 129–30, 226
Road to Life, The 35
Rohmer, Eric 4, 8, 13
Roma, città aperta see *Rome, Open City*
Romanticism 131, 141
Rome, Eleven O'Clock 135–6, 229
Romeo and Juliet 109–10, 143
Rome, Open City 18–19, 21–2, 29–30, 32, 34–5, 61, 75, 104, 152, 166, 216–17
Rome, ore undici see *Rome, Eleven O'Clock*
Roof, The 16, 184–6, 234
Rooney, Mickey 57
Rope 111
Rosi, Francesco 28
Rossellini, Roberto 8–9, 16, 18–19, 21–2, 29, 30–3, 35, 41, 43–6, 49, 57–61, 70, 75–6, 78, 106, 120–2, 125, 128, 142, 146, 151–2, 163–75, 184, 188, 199
Rossen, Robert 28
Rotha, Paul 62
Rouch, Jean 14
Rouquier, Georges 36, 40–1, 51, 54, 69, 90

Rousseau, Henri 88
Rules of the Game, The see *La Règle du jeu*

Sadoul, Georges 29
Salaam Bombay! 27
Salvatore Giuliano 28
Saroyan, William 45, 50
Sartre, Jean-Paul 2–3, 6, 197
Sceicco bianco, Lo see *The White Sheik*
Scipio Africanus 31, 62
Sciuscià see *Shoeshine*
Screen 15
Selznick, David O. 128
Senso 16, 152, 176–9, 232
Sensualità 134
sentimentalism 28, 58, 60, 83–4, 103, 128, 162, 175,181
Shakespeare, William 110, 146, 153
Shoeshine 19, 25–7, 29, 32, 35, 44, 61, 64, 74–5, 87, 104, 117–18, 218–19
Sight and Sound 164
Signora senza camelie, La see *The Lady without Camelias*
Sirk, Douglas 8
socialism 21, 151–2
socialist realism 151
Soldati, Mario 32, 125–6
Sole sorge ancora, Il 33, 35, 221
"Some Ideas on the Cinema" 22
Sordi, Alberto 200
Sortilège 44
S.O.S. 103 31, 212
Spaak, Charles 160–1
Stazione Termini 127–9, 146, 155–6, 166
Stendhal 44
Steno 138
Stolen Children 28
Stòria di Caterina see *Catherine's Story*
Story of a Love Affair see *Cronaca di un amore*
Strada, La 148–54, 165, 180–1, 192, 194–8, 202, 232
Stroheim, Erich von 12, 29, 49
Stromboli 166, 173
Suarès, André 84
Sucksdorff, Arne 53
Sunday in August 138–9, 225–6
Sun Rises Again, The see *Il sole sorge ancora*
surrealism 200
Swindle, The see *Il Bidone*

Tabu 36–7, 70
Taviani, Paolo 28
Taviani, Vittorio 28

"Technique of *Citizen Kane*, The," 10
Temple, Shirley 57
Temps modernes, Les 3
Tentato suicidio see *Attempted Suicide*
Teresa of Avila, Saint 92
Teresa Venerdì 23
Terminal Station see *Stazione Termini*
Terra Trema, La see *The Earth Trembles*
Tetto, Il see *The Roof*
Theory of Film 11
Thérèse of Lisieux, Saint 90, 92
They Live by Night 28
Three Forbidden Tales 136–7
Threepenny Opera, The 192
Thunder over Mexico 70
Times Gone By see *Altri Tempi*
Tisse, Eduard 37
Toland, Gregg 95
Toni 13
Tonti, Aldo 89–90
Tornatore, Giuseppe 28
Totò 138
tragedy 33, 61, 64, 66–7, 72, 79–80, 85, 97, 99, 101, 107, 118, 136, 146, 172, 197, 202
Tragic Hunt see *Caccia tragica*
Travail et Culture 2
Tre storie proibite see *Three Forbidden Tales*
Trial, The 85
Trovatore, Il 176

Truffaut, François 4, 8, 14, 27
Two Adolescents see *Agostino*
Two Cents' Worth of Hope 104, 106–10, 117, 228

Ubu the King (Jarry) 141
Umberto D. 8, 16, 26, 28, 85, 111–17, 138, 155–6, 158, 166, 172, 174, 184, 186, 194, 201, 230–1

Vadim, Roger 14
Vallone, Raf 130, 136
Van Gogh, Vincent 43
Vanquished, The see *I Vinti*
Vanzino, Stefano *see* Steno
Varzi, Elena 103, 130, 136
Venice Film Festival 31, 54, 124, 130, 141, 180
Verde, Giuseppe 176
Verga, Giovanni 20, 107
Vergano, Aldo 43
verism 32, 90, 107, 167
Verneuil, Henri 114
Vertov, Dziga 77
Viaggio in Italia see *Voyage in Italy*
Vigo, Jean 27, 57, 83–4
Vinti, I 124–5, 230
Visconti, Luchino 14, 16, 19–20, 23–4, 51–6, 79, 89–90, 97, 106, 152, 170, 176–9
Vitelloni, I 12, 141, 180, 192–4, 196, 198–200, 202, 231
Vittorini, Elio 20, 50
Vivere in pace 33, 62, 64, 219–20

Voyage in Italy 164–166, 168, 170, 174–5

Wages of Fear, The 127
Wanton Contessa, The see *Senso*
Wayward Wife, The see *The Provincial Woman*
Weil, Simone 121
Welles, Orson 8, 11, 13, 39–40, 49, 53, 95, 149
What Is Cinema? 1
What Rascals Men Are! see *Gli uomini, che mascalzoni!*
Where Is the Friend's House? 27
White Balloon, The 27
White Sheik, The 140–1, 196
White Ship, The see *La nave bianca*
Wiene, Robert 7
Wilson, Sloan 12
Wood, Sam 49
Wyler, William 6, 9

Young and the Passionate, The see *I vitelloni*
Youth and Perversion see *I Vinti*

Zampa, Luigi 21
Zanuck, Darryl F. 12
Zavattini, Cesare 22, 27, 72, 76, 79, 80, 83, 88, 106–7, 111–12, 114, 116–20, 127–8, 142, 150, 152, 157, 160–2, 172–5, 186–91, 201
Zero for Conduct 27, 57
Zola, Emile 101, 107, 168